ATLAS
OF WORLD
HISTORY

LUCEM LIBRIS DISSEMINAMUS

© 1997 Geddes & Grosset Ltd, David Dale House,
New Lanark, Scotland.

Pages 8–64
Co-authors: Liz Wise and Caroline Lucas.
Design and illustration: Ralph Orme.
Maps: Malcolm Porter assisted by Andrea Fairbrass.

ISBN 1 85534 343 6

Printed and bound in the UK

2 4 6 8 10 9 7 5 3 1

Contents

Timelines

EUROPE	AMERICAS	ASIA	AFRICA
BC	**BC**	**BC**	**BC**
c. 20,000 Paintings showing hunting scenes in caves in southern France and Spain			
		c. 8000 First farming in the Middle East	
c. 6500 Agriculture in Greece			*c.* 5000 Agricultural settlements in Egypt
		c. 4000 Beginning of Bronze Age in the Near East	
		c. 3100 First writing on clay tablets	
	c. 3000 First ceramics in Mexico	*c.* 3000 First cities in Sumer	*c.* 3200 King Menes unites Egypt
		c. 2750 Growth of civilizations in Indus Valley	*c.* 2658 Beginning of 'Old Kingdom' in Egypt
	c. 2000 First metal working in Peru		*c.* 2650 First pyramid built for King Zoser of Egypt
c. 2200 Beginnings of Bronze Age Minoan civilization in Crete		*c.* 1750 Collapse of Indus Valley civilization	
		c. 1500 Rise of Shang dynasty in China	*c.* 1552 Beginning of 'New Kingdom' in Egypt
c. 1600 Mycenaean civilization in Greece			
c. 1450 Destruction of Minoan Crete			1361–52 Rule of Tutankhamun in Egypt
c. 1200 Collapse of Mycenaean Empire		*c.* 1050 Chou dynasty supplants Shang in China	
c. 1100 Phoenicians develop first alphabet			
			c. 800 Carthage founded by Phoenicians
c. 800 Rise of city-states in Greece		*c.* 720 Height of Assyrian power	
753 Foundation of Rome		*c.* 650 First iron used in China	
		586 Babylonian captivity of Jews	
510 Foundation of Roman Republic		486 Death of Siddhartha Gautama, founder of Buddhism	
431–404 Peloponnesian War between Athens and Sparta		483–221 'Warring States' period in China	
356–327 Alexander the Great of Macedonia conquers Persia		*c.* 320 Mauryan Empire in India	
290 Roman conquest of central Italy			
264–146 Punic Wars between Rome and Carthage		221 Ch'in dynasty	
146 Greece becomes part of Roman Empire		202 China under control of Han dynasty	

9

EUROPE		AMERICAS		ASIA		AFRICA	
AD		**AD**		**AD**		**AD**	
43	Roman invasion of Britain			*c.* 0	Buddhism spreads from India to Southeast Asia and China		
116	Roman empire at greatest extent			25	Han dynasty restored in China	30	Egypt becomes Roman province
283	Raids on Roman empire by Goths			132	Jewish revolt against Rome		
285	Roman empire divided into eastern and western parts			220	End of Han dynasty: China splits into three states		
		c. 300	Mayan civilization in Central America	214	Great Wall of China built		
370	Huns from Asia invade Europe	*c.* 400	Rise of Inca civilization in western South America	330	Constantinople becomes capital of Roman Empire		
410	Visigoths sack Rome			350	Huns invade Persia and India		
449	Angles, Saxons and Jutes invade Britain			407–553	First Mongol Empire	429–535	Vandal kingdom in northern Africa
486	Frankish kingdom founded by Clovis			552	Buddhism introduced to Japan	533–552	Justinian restores Roman power in North Africa
497	Franks converted to Christianity			*c.* 570–632	Mohammed: founder of Islamic religion		
597	St Augustine's Christian mission to England	*c.* 600	Height of Mayan civilization	618	China re-united under Tang dynasty	641	Conquest of Egypt by Arabs
711	Muslim conquest of Spain			635–674	Muslim conquests of Syria and Persia	*c.* 700	Rise of Empire of Ghana
793	Viking raids begin			730	First printing in China		
800	Charlemagne crowned Holy Roman Emperor			821	Conquest of Tibet by Chinese		
843	Treaty of Verdun divides Carolingian Empire into three parts						
874	First Viking settlers in Iceland						
886	Danelaw established in England					920–1050	Height of Ghana Empire
911	Vikings granted Duchy of Normandy by Frankish king			907	Last Tang Emperor deposed in China	969	Fatamids conquer Egypt and found Cairo
				939	Civil wars in Japan	*c.* 1000	First Iron Age settlement at Zimbabwe
				960	Sung dynasty re-unites China		
c. 1000	Vikings discover North America	*c.* 990	Expansion of Inca Empire				
1016	King Cnut rules England, Denmark and Norway						

EUROPE	AMERICAS	ASIA	AFRICA
1066 Defeat of Anglo-Saxons by William the Conqueror			
1071 Normans conquer Byzantine Italy		**1071** Asia Minor conquered by Seljuk Turks	
1096–99 First Crusade	**1100** Toltecs build capital city at Tula in Mexico	*c.* **1100** Polynesian Islands colonized	*c.* **1150** Beginnings of Yoruba city-states (Nigeria)
1147–49 Second Crusade		**1156–89** Civil wars in Japan	**1174** Saladin conquers Egypt
1189–93 Third Crusade	**1151** End of Toltec Empire in Mexico	**1174–87** Ottoman Turks under Saladin conquer Syria and Levant	*c.* **1200** Rise of Empire of Mali in West Africa
1202–04 Fourth Crusade and capture of Constantinople		**1190** Mongol Empire founded under Genghis Khan	*c.* **1200** Emergence of Hausa city-states (Nigeria)
1217–22 Fifth Crusade			
1228–29 Sixth Crusade		**1234** Mongols invade and destroy Chinese Empire	**1240** Collapse of Empire of Ghana
1236 Mongols invade Russia			
1241 Mongols invade Poland, Hungary, Bohemia, then withdraw			
1248–54 Seventh Crusade			
1250 Collapse of imperial power in Germany and Italy on death of Frederick II		**1261** Greek Empire restored at Constantinople	
1270–72 Eighth Crusade			*c.* **1300** Emergence of Ife Kingdom (West Africa)
1305 Papacy moves from Rome to Avignon	**1325** Rise of Aztecs in Mexico Founding of city of Tenochtitlán	**1336** Revolution in Japan	
1337– 1453 Hundred Years' war between France and England		*c.* **1341** Black Death begins	
1378– 1417 Great Schism: (break between Rome and Avignon), rival popes elected	**1370** Expansion of Chimu kingdom in South America	**1363** Tamerlane begins conquest of Asia	
	c. **1375** Beginning of Aztec expansion	**1368** Ming dynasty founded in China	
1381 Peasants' Revolt in England			
1385 Portugal gains independence from Spain		**1398– 1402** Tamerlane conquers Kingdom of Delhi and Ottoman Empire	**1415** Portuguese colonies established in Africa
1415 Henry V of England defeats French at Battle of Agincourt	**1438** Inca Empire established in Peru		**1450** Height of Songhai Empire in West Africa
1453 England loses all French possessions except Calais	**1440–69** Montezuma rules Aztecs	**1453** Ottoman Turks capture Constantinople	**1482** Portuguese settle Gold Coast (now Ghana)
	1450 Incas conquer Chimu kingdom		
1455–85 Wars of the Roses in England	**1493** First New World settlement by Spanish	**1498** Explorer Vasco da Gama reaches India around Cape of Good Hope	**1492** Spain begins conquest of North African coast
1492 Last Muslims in Spain conquered by Christians	**1502–20** Aztec conquests under Montezuma		

EUROPE	AMERICAS	ASIA	AFRICA
			1505 Portuguese establish trading posts in East Africa
1517 Martin Luther nails 95 'theses' to church door at Wittenberg	c. 1510 First African slaves taken to America	1516 Ottomans conquer Syria, Egypt and Arabia	
1519 Zwingli leads Protestant Reformation in Switzerland	1521 Cortes conquers Aztec capital, Tenochtitlán		
1522 First circumnavigation of world by Portuguese navigator, Magellan			
1525 Potato introduced to Europe from New World		1526 Foundation of Mughal Empire	
1529 Reformation Parliament begins in England			
1532 Calvin starts Protestant movement in France	1533 Pizarro conquers Peru	1533 Ivan the Terrible succeeds to Russian throne	
	1535 Spaniards explore Chile		
1545 Council of Trent marks start of Counter-Reformation		1556 Ivan the Terrible conquers Volga basin	1546 Destruction of Mali Empire by Songhai
1558 England loses Calais to French			
1562–98 Wars of Religion in France			
1571 Battle of Lepanto: end of Turkish sea power			1570 Bornu Empire in the Sudan flourishes
1572 Dutch revolt against Spain			1571 Portuguese establish colony in Angola (Southern Africa)
1588 Spanish Armada defeated by English			
			1591 Moroccans destroy Songhai Empire
1600 Foundation of English East India Company	1607 First English settlement in America (Jamestown, Virginia)		
1609 Dutch win freedom from Spain	1608 First colonists found Quebec		
1618–48 Thirty Years' War in Europe	1620 Puritans (Pilgrim Fathers) land in New England		
	1624 Dutch settle New Amsterdam	1630s Japan isolates itself from the rest of the world	
1649 Execution of Charles I in London	1644 New Amsterdam seized by British and re-named New York	1644 Ch'ing dynasty founded in China by Manchus	1652 Foundation of Cape Colony by Dutch

EUROPE	AMERICAS	ASIA	AFRICA
	1654 Portuguese take Brazil from Dutch		1686 French annex Madagascar
1688 England's 'Glorious Revolution'	1693 Gold discovered in Brazil	1690 Foundation of Calcutta by British	
1701–14 War of Spanish Succession			1700 Rise of Assantu power (Gold Coast)
1704 Battle of Blenheim		1707 Break-up of Mughal Empire	1705 Turks over-thrown in Tunis
1707 Union of England and Scotland		1724 Hyderabad in India gains freedom from Mughals	
1740–48 War of Austrian Succession			
1756–63 Seven Years' War			
	1759 British capture Quebec from French	1757 British rule in India established by Battle of Plassey	
1765 Invention of James Watts' steam engine. Beginning of Industrial Revolution in Britain	1775–83 American War of Independence	1768 Captain James Cook begins exploration of the Pacific	
	1776 Declaration of American Independence	1775 Peasant revolts in Russia	
		1783 India Act gives Britain control of India	1787 British acquire Sierra Leone
1789 French Revolution	1789 Washington becomes first US President	1788 British penal colony founded at Botony Bay, Australia	
	1791 Slave revolt in Haiti	1799 Napoleon invades Syria	1798 Napoleon attacks Egypt
1804 Napoleon pro-claimed Emperor	1803 Louisiana Purchase doubles size of USA	1804–15 Serbs revolt against Turkey	1811 Muhammad Ali takes control in Egypt
1812 Napoleon's Russian cam-paign	1808–28 Independence movements in South America		1814 British take control of South Africa from Boers
1815 Napoleon defeat-ed at Waterloo		1819 British found Singapore	1818 Zulu Empire founded in south-ern Africa
1821–29 Greek War of Independence			1822 Liberia founded for free slaves
1825 First steam rail-way			1830 French begin con-quest of Algeria
1830 Revolutions in France, Germany, Poland and Italy		1830–54 Russia conquers Kazakhstan	1835–37 Great Trek of Boers in South Africa
	1840 Union of Upper and Lower Canada	1840 Britain annexes New Zealand	
1845–46 Irish potato famine	1845 Texas annexed by USA	1842 Hong Kong ceded to Britain by China	
1848 Year of Revolutions	1846–48 War between USA and Mexico		
1854–56 Crimean war	1848 Californian Gold Rush begins	1854 Trade treaty between Japan and USA	
	1861–65 American Civil War		1860 French expansion in West Africa

EUROPE	AMERICAS	ASIA	AFRICA
		1857 Indian troops mutiny against British Army	
1861 Kingdom of Italy established	1865 Assassination of US President, Abraham Lincoln		1869 Opening of Suez Canal
	1867 Dominion of Canada formed		
1870–71 Franco-Prussian War			1879 Zulu War
1871 Proclamation of German Empire			1882 British occupy Egypt
1872– Triple Alliance 1914 between Germany, Austria and Italy		1885 Indian National Congress formed	1884 Germany acquires African colonies
		1886 British annex Burma	1885 Belgium acquires Congo
		1894–95 Sino-Japanese War	1886 Germany and Britain divide East Africa
	1898 Spanish-American War		1889– Anglo-Boer 1902 War
		1901 Unification of Australia	
1904 Anglo-French Entente		1902–03 Russo-Japanese War	
1905 First revolution in Russia		1906 Revolt in Persia	1910 Union of South Africa formed
		1910 Japan annexes Korea	1911 Italians conquer Libya
1912–13 Balkan Wars	1911 Revolution in Mexico	1911–49 Chinese Revolution	
1914–18 World War I	1914 Panama Canal opens		1914 British Protectorate in Egypt
1917 Russian Revolution	1917 USA enters World War I		1919 Nationalist revolt in Egypt
1919 Treaty of Versailles			
1920 League of Nations established			
1922 Irish Free State created Mussolini takes power in Italy		1922 Republic proclaimed in Turkey	1922 Egyptian independence
1926 General strike in Britain		1926 Chiang Kai-shek unites China	
	1929 Wall Street crash heralds world depression	1931 Japanese occupy Manchuria	
1933 Hitler becomes German Chancellor	1933 Roosevelt introduces New Deal in USA	1934–35 Mao Zedong's (Mao Tse Tung) Long March	1935 Italy annexes Ethiopia (Abyssinia)
1936–39 Civil War in Spain		1937 Japanese capture Peking	
1939–45 World War II		1940 Japan allies with Germany	
1945 United Nations established		1941 Japanese attack US fleet at Pearl Harbor	
	1941 USA enters World War II	1942 Japanese fleet defeated by US at Battle of Midway	

14

EUROPE	AMERICAS	ASIA	AFRICA
		1945 First nuclear bombs dropped on Japan	
1948 Communist takeover in Hungary and Czechoslovakia		1946–49 Civil War in China	
		1947 India and Pakistan independent	
		1948 Jewish state founded in Palestine	1949 Apartheid established in South Africa
		1948–49 First Arab-Israeli War	
		1950–53 Korean War	
		1954–75 Vietnam War	
1956 Hungarian revolt crushed by Russians		1956 Second Arab-Israeli War	1956 Suez crisis
1958 European Economic Community (EEC) set up	1959 Cuban revolution	1957 Malaysia independent	1957 Ghana becomes independent, followed by other African states
	1962 Cuban missile crisis	1962 Sino-Indian War	
1961 Berlin Wall built; beginnings of Cold War in Europe	1963 President Kennedy assassinated		1960 Civil war follows independence in the Congo
1968 USSR invades Czechoslovakia	1964–73 US involvement in Vietnam War	1967 Third Arab-Israeli War	1967–70 Nigerian civil war
	1969 Neil Armstrong becomes first man on the moon		
	1970–73 Chilean Revolution		
		1971 East Pakistan becomes Bangladesh	
1973 Britain, Eire and Denmark join EEC		1973 Fourth Arab-Israeli War	
	1974 Resignation of President Nixon	1974 Portuguese African colonies independent	
1975 Restoration of monarchy in Spain		1975 Civil war in Lebanon	
		1978 Fifth Arab-Israeli War	
		1979 Soviet invasion of Afghanistan	1979 General Amin flees from Uganda
		1979 Shah of Iran deposed. An Islamic republic is declared	
1980 Polish Solidarity trade union, led by Lech Walesa, confronts Communist government		1980 Iran-Iraq war	1980 Zimbabwe, last British colony in Africa, becomes independent
1981 Greece becomes 10th member of the EEC	1981 US hostages in Iran freed		1981 President Sadat of Egypt assassinated
	1982 Argentines invade Falkland Islands	1982 Israel invades Lebanon	

EUROPE	AMERICAS	ASIA	AFRICA
	1983 US troops invade Grenada		
1985 Mikhail Gorbachev elected new Soviet leader		1984 Indira Gandhi, Indian prime minister, assassinated	1985 Renewed unrest in South Africa
1986 Prime Minister Palme of Sweden assassinated	1986 US raid on Libya Nuclear arms talks resume between USA and USSR	1986 Overthrow of Marcos regime in Philippines	1986 Ethiopia has worst famine in more than 10 years
	1987 Falling dollar and Wall Street crash	1987 Ongoing civil war in Lebanon	
1989 Berlin Wall dismantled	1989 US troops invade Panama		
1991 Break-up of Soviet Union West and East Germany are reunited		1990 Gulf War begins; Iran invades Kuwait, USA and Allies send troops to Gulf region	1990 Political prisoner, Nelson Mandela, is freed in South Africa; process of dismantling apartheid begins
1992 Bloody civil war in Yugoslavia European Commission recognizes independence of Croatia and Slovenia	1992 Bill Clinton is elected US president		
1993 Czechoslovakia is split into Slovakia and the Czech Republic			
1994 Russia invades breakaway Caucasian state of Chechenia	1994 US troops invade Haiti to oust military government	1994 Israel and PLO sign pact ending Israeli occupation of Gaza Strip and Jericho	1994 ANC (African National Congress) wins first multi-racial election in Africa Massacre of Tutsis by Hutus in Rwanda leaves estimated 500,000 dead and 1.5 million homeless
1995 President Clinton visits Northern Ireland, the first US president to do so Dayton peace agreement signed to end civil war in former Yugoslavia		1995 Israeli Prime Minister Yitzakh Rabin assassinated	
1997 Labour Party wins British general election with largest majority in postwar years		1997 Hong Kong returned to Chinese rule	1997 End of civil war in Zaire and country is renamed as the Democratic Republic of Congo

The First Humans

Our closest relations in the animal world are chimpanzees and gorillas. By about 4 million years ago, the earliest human ancestors had evolved in Africa. They were called *Australopithecus* (which means 'southern ape'), but unlike apes they had the ability to walk upright. The first *Homo* (man) fossils which have been found date to 2 million years ago, but it was not until about 100,000 years ago that the first fully modern humans evolved in Africa. Over these millions of years of human evolution, the most noticeable development was in the size of the skull and the brain. As our ancestors' brains became larger, they developed other skills: the ability to make tools, to use language, to work together as a group, to create the first art.

During the cold phases of the last Ice Age, which lasted from about 2 million to 10,000 years ago, temperatures were, on average, 10–15°C lower than the present day. Humans were therefore forced to adapt to a hostile world. In cold climates, they learned to use fire, find or build shelters and make warm clothes. They became skilled at making tools and weapons, and were lethal hunters. By about 10,000 years ago modern humans had spread from Africa to the most remote corners of the globe. During cold periods, a great deal of water was locked up in the large ice sheets (glaciers) that covered much of the northern hemisphere. This caused sea levels to fall, revealing land 'bridges' that linked the continents, enabling our ancestors to cross from Asia into North America and from Southeast Asia into Australia.

When the ice finally retreated, large game, such as woolly mammoths, was increasingly scarce. Humans had to find new sources of food and began to experiment with the domestication of certain plants and animals – the agricultural revolution had begun.

Homo habilis ('handy man') was so called because of his ability to make tools. Feet and hand fossils show some similarities to modern humans'. They indicate that he would have had a strong grip and would be able to manipulate tools effectively. He was probably a meat-eater – tools were needed to separate the flesh from the carcass.

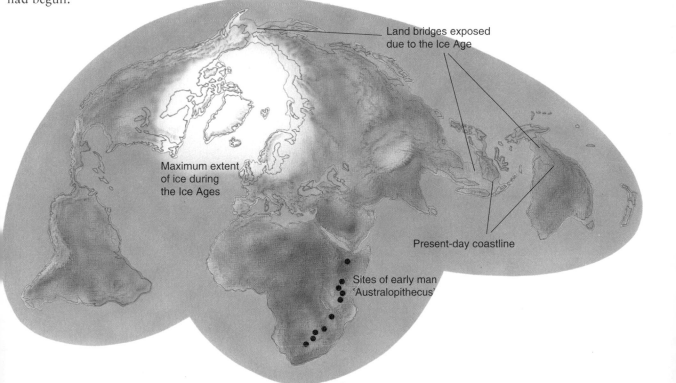

Land bridges exposed due to the Ice Age

Maximum extent of ice during the Ice Ages

Present-day coastline

Sites of early man 'Australopithecus'

The First Civilizations 3500–1000 BC

The cultivation of plants, such as wheat and barley, and the domestication of animals, such as sheep, goats and cattle, began in the Near East in about 8500 BC. As people turned to farming, they began to live in fixed settlements, which became small towns. In about 5000 BC, farmers moved down into the fertile river valleys of Mesopotamia, and built dykes and ditches to irrigate the arid land. Their labours bore fruit; surplus food freed some of the population from farming. These people became merchants, craftsmen and priests. As the settlements grew into cities, they became more organized; laws were made, writing evolved, and religious and public buildings were built.

Between 3500 and 1800 years ago, three great civilizations evolved in Mesopotamia, Egypt and the Indus valley of northern India. All three civilizations were located in the fertile valleys of great rivers. Each civilization was based on substantial cities, inhabited by several thousand people and containing imposing public buildings, such as temples and palaces. Each civilization had evolved a form of writing. All three civilizations show evidence of a strong, centralized administration or all-powerful rulers – in Mesopotamia, for example, rulers were buried with their sacrificed servants as well as a vast array of their worldly possessions.

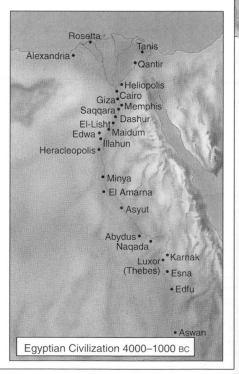

Egypt
The cities, tombs and temples of Ancient Egypt lined the banks of the River Nile. Every year the river flooded, depositing fertile mud along its banks – when the waters receded, these lands could be cultivated. During the Nile flood (August to October), the vast majority of the Egyptian population, who lived by farming, could work for the pharaoh, building temples, tombs and pyramids. During the Old Kingdom (c. 2685–2185 BC), when all of Egypt was under the rule of one pharaoh, the important centres were in the north, around Giza and Memphis. In the New Kingdom (c. 1552–1071), the main royal city was Thebes, in Middle Egypt.

Egyptian Civilization 4000–1000 BC

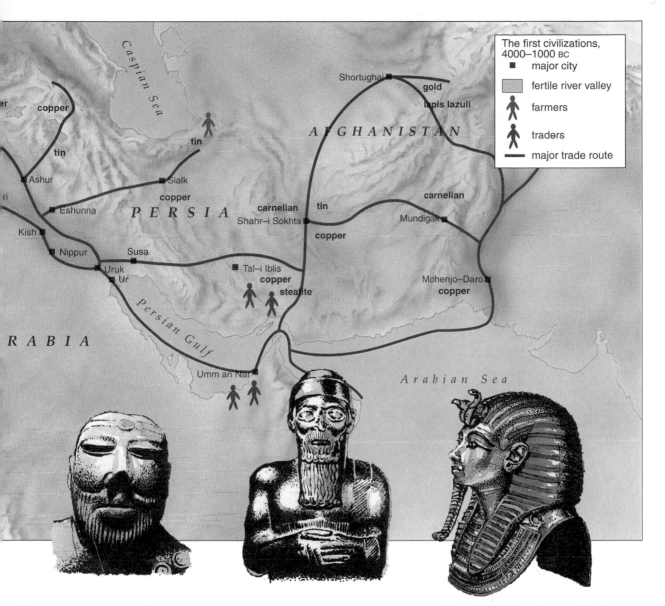

The first civilizations,
4000–1000 BC
- ■ major city
- ▨ fertile river valley
- 🧍 farmers
- 🧍 traders
- ▬ major trade route

This head from the Indus valley city Mohenjo-Daro c. 2100 BC may represent a priest-king.

Ishtup-Ilum, c. 2100 BC the ruler of Mari, a city-state in northern Mesopotamia.

The solid gold funeral mask of the Egyptian pharaoh, Tutankhamun, c. 1340 BC.

The Temple of Ur

The temple at the Mesopotamian city of Ur was a ziggurat, comprising an ascending series of terraces, made from mud-bricks, and decorated with mosaics. Each terrace would have been planted with a 'hanging garden' of trees. The temple was dedicated to the worship of the city's patron deity, the moon-god, Nanna. Surrounding the temple stood the houses of the lower town, which contained 20,000 people at its peak.

Greece 750–150 BC

Europe's earliest advanced civilization flourished on the island of Crete from 2200 to 1400 BC. Minoan civilization, centred on palace-cities, prospered by trading goods such as olive oil and pottery within the Mediterranean. Meanwhile, on the Peloponnese, another Bronze Age civilization was emerging, based on fortified palace-cities such as Mycenae. This more warlike civilization collapsed in about 1200 BC. A period known as the 'dark ages' followed in Greece but, in about 800 BC, populations began to expand, and small city-states, consisting of a city surrounded by towns, villages and agricultural land, began to evolve. By about 500 BC, Athens had become the richest and most important city-state in Classical Greece, as well as the cultural and intellectual centre of the Greek world. Democracy was born in Athens: Athenian citizens (free men) had the right to vote on all matters of government, and any citizen could serve for a year as a city magistrate, paid by the state. But, in 404 BC, Athens was crushed by Sparta, a rival city-state, where a small elite ruled over their subject peoples with the help of a well-trained army. In the 4th century BC the Greeks were united under the Macedonian leader, Alexander, who conquered the mighty empire of Persia. Wherever he went, he founded cities, spreading Greek culture and language throughout the Middle East.

Alexander the Great, son of King Philip of Macedonia, conquered a vast area, stretching from Greece to the borders of India from 334–323 BC. He died when he was just 33.

Athens

Most Greek cities clustered around a rocky outcrop, or acropolis, which could be defended in times of crisis. The Athenian acropolis is crowned by the famous Parthenon, dedicated to Athena, the city's patron deity. Below the acropolis, lay the market place, or *agora*, and the law courts and government offices. The Greeks were dedicated to the health of both mind and body, so large public gymnasiums and amphitheatres were found in most Greek cities.

Map legend:
- • main cities
- ▲ theatres
- ■ temples
- → route of Alexander
- ✕ battles

Adria

ITALY

Tyrrhenian Sea

- • Neapolis (Naples)
- • Elea
- ■ M
- • Syba
- • Terina
- ■ Hipponiu
- • Locri
- ■ Segesta
- Selinus • ■
- Akragas • ■
- Gela

R. Danube

R. Granicus 334 BC ✕

Ilium

Ancyra

GREECE

• Athens
Corinth ○
Sparta •

Knossos

Mediterranean Sea

Cyrene •

Alexandria (Rhacotis) •

Memphis

Sanctuary of Amon

EGYPT

R. Nile

• Sy

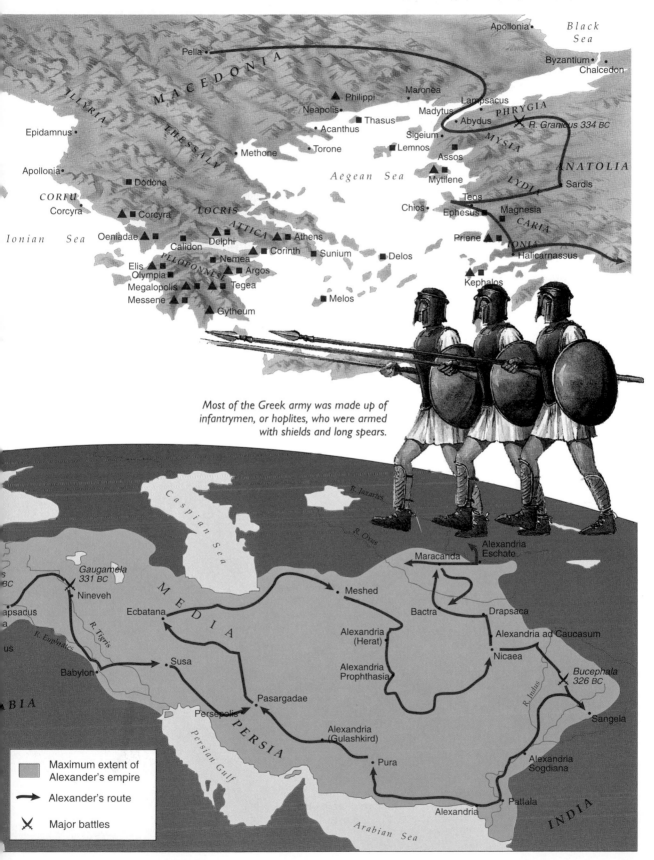

Most of the Greek army was made up of infantrymen, or hoplites, who were armed with shields and long spears.

Black Sea

Apollonia•

Byzantium•
Chalcedon•

Pella•

MACEDONIA

Maronea•

Lampsacus•

PHRYGIA

Philippi▲

Madytus•

Neapolis•

Abydus•

Thasus■

R. Granicus 334 BC ✕

Acanthus•

Sigeium•

MYSIA

Epidamnus•

ILLYRIA

THESSALY

•Methone

•Torone

Lemnos■

ANATOLIA

Apollonia•

Sardis•

Dodona■

Mytilene▲

Assos■

LYDIA

CORFU

Teos■

Corcyra

LOCRIS

Chios•

Ephesus■

Magnesia■

CARIA

Ionian Sea

Oeniadae▲■

ATTICA

Delphi▲

Athens▲■

Priene■▲

IONIA

Calidon

Corinth■

Nemea■

Sunium■

Delos•

Halicarnassus•

Elis▲

Olympia

Argos■

Messene▲

Megalopolis▲■

Tegea■

Kephalos▲

PELOPONNESE

Gytheum▲

Melos•

Aegean Sea

Caspian Sea

R. Jaxartes

R. Oxus

Maracanda

Alexandria Eschate

Gaugamela 331 BC ✕

Nineveh•

MEDIA

Meshed•

Bactra

Drapsaca•

apsacus

Ecbatana•

Alexandria ad Caucasum

R. Tigris

Alexandria (Herat)

Nicaea•

R. Euphrates

Susa•

Bucephala 326 BC ✕

Babylon•

Alexandria Prophthasia•

R. Indus

Pasargadae•

Persepolis•

PERSIA

Sangela•

ABIA

Alexandria (Gulashkird)•

Alexandria Sogdiana•

Persian Gulf

Pura•

Pattala•

Alexandria•

INDIA

Arabian Sea

	Maximum extent of Alexander's empire
→	Alexander's route
✕	Major battles

Rome 500 BC–AD 500

In 1000 BC Rome was no more than a collection of farming villages clustered around seven hills. Yet by 203 BC the Romans controlled the Italian peninsula, the whole of the Mediterranean Sea, Spain and Greece. The Romans had evolved a form of republican government: two rulers, or consuls, presided over the Senate, drawn from the Roman aristocracy and rich landowners. But as the gulf between rich and poor within Rome grew wider, the ordinary people felt that they held none of the power. This discontent led to a series of bitter civil wars between powerful generals. In 27 BC, the Roman republic became an empire under the rule of Augustus, the adopted son of the general and conqueror, Julius Caesar.

Under the rule of the Emperor Augustus more territories were conquered, the army was reorganized into an efficient and loyal fighting force, magnificent buildings and sculptures adorned all the empire's major cities. During this period a Roman citizen could travel from Mesopotamia or North Africa to the northern borders of England along straight, paved roads. Latin was spoken throughout the empire, the currency was universal. Even cities in distant provinces were built on the Roman model, with a forum (market place), basilica (assembly hall), temples, theatres, palaces, libraries and stadia, where huge crowds gathered to watch chariot racing and gladiatorial combat. As new provinces were conquered they brought wealth to the empire. But when the empire stopped growing, its vast size became a problem; the expenses of an army of over 300,000 men had to be met by increased taxes, which led to discontent, weakening the empire from within.

The Roman Army

The basic unit of the Roman army was the century, which consisted of 100 foot soldiers. Soldiers were professionals; they signed up for 16 to 20 years service and were rewarded with money or land.

The Roman Empire

As new provinces were added to the Roman empire, the conquerors set about 'Romanizing' them. Towns and capital cities were built to follow the layout and design of Rome. Straight, paved roads and aqueducts linked these new settlements. In the countryside, land was cleared and irrigated so that it was ready for cultivation. A provincial governor was appointed to run the province and ensure that there were no revolts against Roman rule. Legions of the Roman army were sent to the provinces to help keep the peace and were often stationed in fortresses along the borders of the empire.

North Sea

Eburacum
Deva
Isca
Londinium
Dubris
Noviomag
Vete
Duocortorum
Mogontiacu
Argentoratum
Lutetia

GAUL

Limonum
Lugdunum
Burdigala
Tolosa
Narbo
Massilia
Cen
Tarraco

IBERIA

Legio
Emerita Augusta
Cordoba
Carthago Nova
Caesarea
Gades
Tingis

NORTH AFRIC

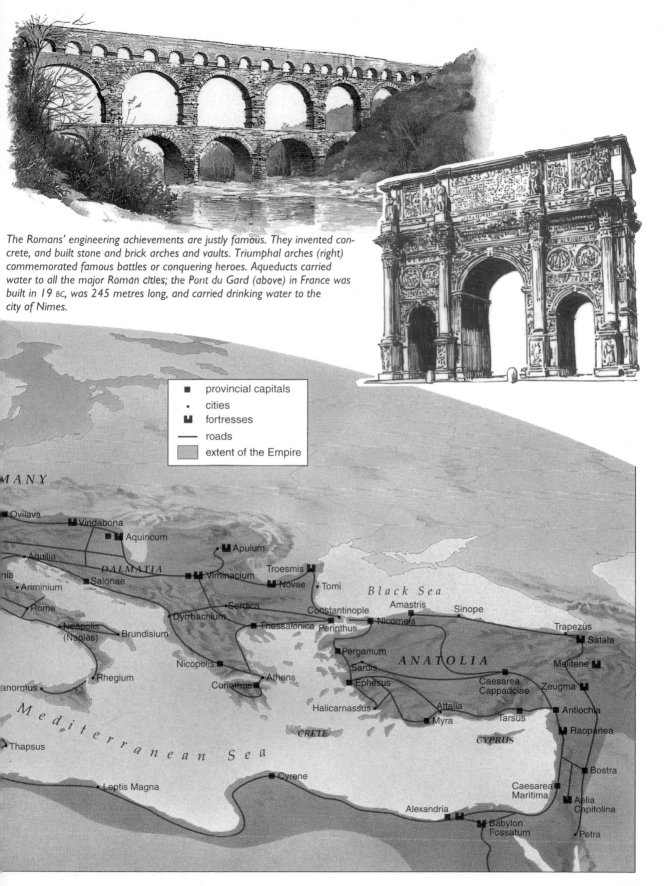

The Romans' engineering achievements are justly famous. They invented concrete, and built stone and brick arches and vaults. Triumphal arches (right) commemorated famous battles or conquering heroes. Aqueducts carried water to all the major Roman cities; the Pont du Gard (above) in France was built in 19 BC, was 245 metres long, and carried drinking water to the city of Nimes.

■ provincial capitals
· cities
▉ fortresses
— roads
▭ extent of the Empire

GERMANY

Ovilava

Vindabona

Aquincum

Aquilia

Apulum

DALMATIA

Ariminium

Salonae

Viminacium

Troesmis

Novae

Tomi

Black Sea

Amastris

Sinope

Rome

Serdica

Constantinople

Nicomedia

Neapolis (Naples)

Dyrrhachium

Thessalonica

Perinthus

Brundisium

Trapezus

Satala

Pergamum

ANATOLIA

Melitene

Nicopolis

Sardis

Rhegium

Athens

Ephesus

Caesarea Cappadciae

Zeugma

Corinthus

anormus

Halicarnassus

Attalia

Tarsus

Antiochia

Myra

Raopanea

Mediterranean Sea

CRETE

CYPRUS

Thapsus

Cyrene

Bostra

Caesarea Maritima

Leptis Magna

Alexandria

Aelia Capitolina

Babylon Fossatum

Petra

Europe Attacked AD 600–1100

The success of the Roman empire led to its downfall, its sheer size making administration increasingly difficult. In the 3rd century the empire split into the Byzantine empire and the Western empire. Throughout the 3rd century AD, nomadic tribes from central Asia, such as the Visigoths and Franks, had been pressing on Rome's northern frontiers. With the weakening of the empire, they broke through, sweeping south in search of new lands. These tribes were pastoralists; accompanied by their animal herds they travelled long distances, living in tented camps. With the collapse of the Western Roman empire in the 5th century AD, one of the nomadic tribes, the Franks, became Europe's most powerful rulers. Under their great king, Charlemagne, the Frankish kingdom became known as the Holy Roman Empire and extended from France to Italy.

Charlemagne
A gold bust of Charlemagne (742–814), king of the Franks.

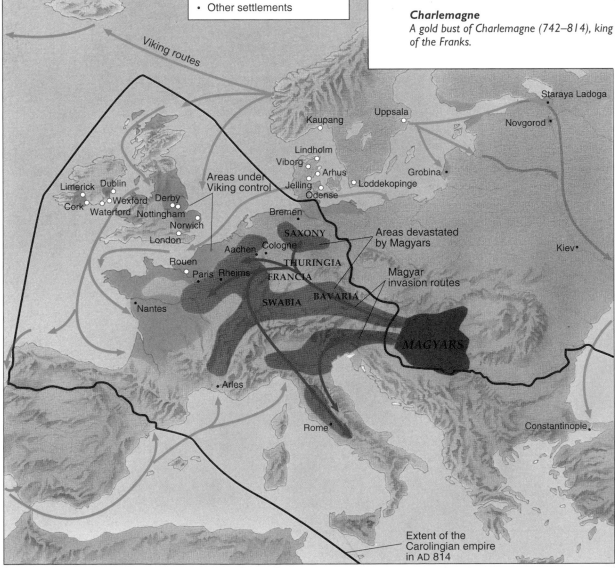

The Vikings

In the 8th century a seafaring people called the Vikings sailed in their long-boats from Norway, Denmark and Sweden to find new lands to colonize. They raided coastal settlements, murdering and terrorizing the native populations and plundering their monasteries, returning to their homelands laden with treasure. In the mid-9th century, instead of returning home, Viking raiders began to make permanent settlements. They were good farmers, adapting themselves to the culture of the peoples they conquered. Accomplished traders, they established settlements and trade routes throughout northwestern Europe. Some reached America. By crossing the Baltic Sea, Vikings entered the great river systems of European Russia, and in *c.* 862 formed the first Russian state in Novgorod. Using the south-flowing rivers, they penetrated the forests and frozen wastes of Russia, establishing trading stations as far as the Black Sea and the Mediterranean. They even reached Constantinople, capital of the Byzantine empire. Though fearless warriors, the Vikings were also fine craftsmen, producing fine swords and beautiful woodcarvings.

The Viking warrior was a formidable enemy.

GREENLAND

ICELAND
870

984

982

FAEROE ISLANDS
825

NORTH
AMERICA

ATLANTIC

OCEAN

VINLAND
(Newfoundland, CANADA)
1000

Viking Settlement

The Vikings established a trading centre at Hedeby in Denmark where several major trade routes intersected. Over the years, Hedeby became a major trading centre. To protect the town from hostile German tribes, an earth embankment topped with a timber palisade was built around it. The houses were constructed of wood and earth. The entire family slept, ate, worked and played together in one small room. The house of a more prosperous Viking might have two or three rooms. Their food came from fishing, hunting and from local farms.

Asian Empires 100 BC–AD 1300

The Han dynasty (202 BC–AD 220) ruled a united China for over four centuries. During this period, China grew prosperous, with an efficient administration, extensive road and canal network, and a growing number of large towns. Paper was invented. Chang'an (or Xi'an), the Han capital, stood at the beginning of the Silk Road, the great trade route across central Asia. Merchants travelled the road, their camels laden with silk. After a long period of decline, the Han empire collapsed and for 400 years China was fragmented. Its unification, begun during the Sui dynasty, was consolidated by the T'ang (618–907), one of the greatest periods in Chinese history. Chang'an became one of the world's largest cities. The T'ang were famed for their arts, literature and poetry. With the decline of the T'ang, a new dynasty, the Sung (AD 960–1279), began. The Sung built a centrally controlled bureaucracy and army. Ocean-going junks laden with tea, silk and porcelain sailed for India and Africa. Urban centres grew and flourished. Printing was invented, developing later into movable type, 400 years before it reached the West. Among the Sung's finest products were its superb pottery and porcelain. The refinement of the Sung period lasted for 300 years until it was shattered by the Mongol invasion. In Japan, imperial rule was established in about the 5th century AD. In the 9th century it was dominated by military overlords, called shoguns.

Model Army
In 221 BC Shi Huang Ti founded the Ch'in dynasty. On his death he was buried with thousands of life-size pottery figures and horses.

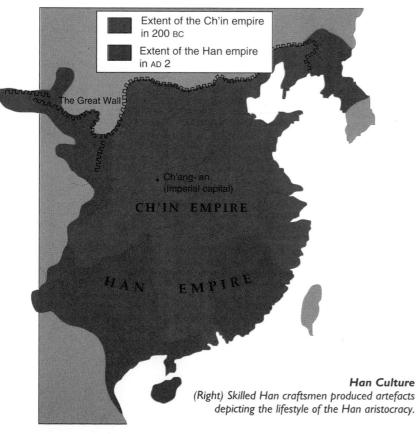

Extent of the Ch'in empire in 200 BC

Extent of the Han empire in AD 2

The Great Wall

Ch'ang-an (Imperial capital)

CH'IN EMPIRE

HAN EMPIRE

Han Culture
(Right) Skilled Han craftsmen produced artefacts depicting the lifestyle of the Han aristocracy.

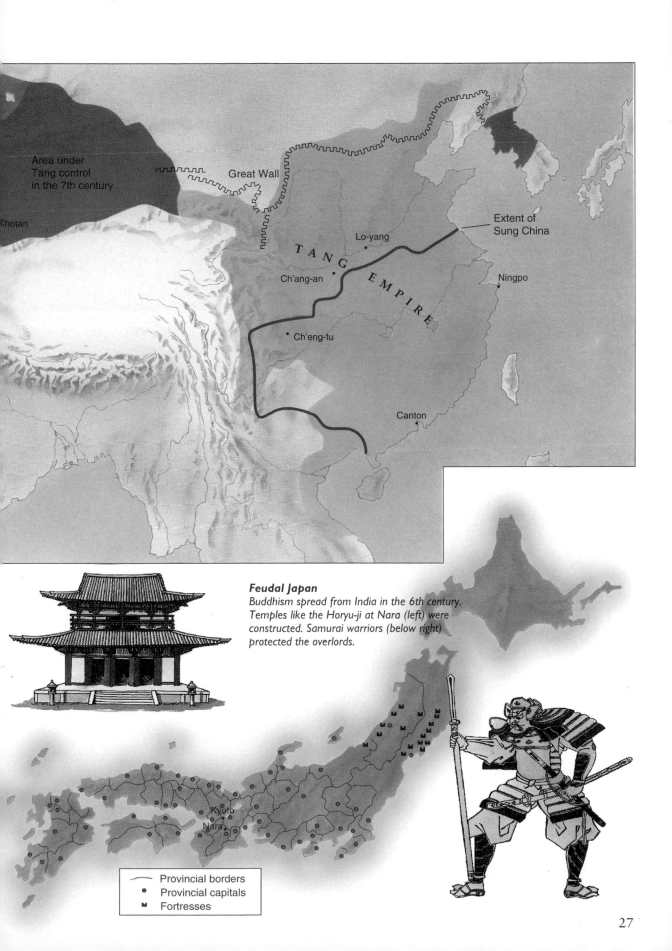

Area under
Tang control
in the 7th century

Great Wall

Khotan

Lo-yang

Extent of
Sung China

Ch'ang-an

T A N G   E M P I R E

Ningpo

Ch'eng-tu

Canton

Feudal Japan
Buddhism spread from India in the 6th century.
Temples like the Horyu-ji at Nara (left) were
constructed. Samurai warriors (below right)
protected the overlords.

Kyoto
Nara

——— Provincial borders
• Provincial capitals
⚑ Fortresses

The Rise of Islam AD 632

In the 7th century AD the prophet Mohammed founded the Islamic religion. Based on the simple message that there is no God but the one God, Allah, the religion united the warring nomadic tribes of the Arabian peninsular. Arab armies advanced east and west, engulfing the ancient world. By the time of the prophet's death in AD 632 the tide of conquest had spread from West Africa to the Far East. Today there are over 400 million Muslims in the world, about one-seventh of the world's population. While western Europe struggled through the Dark Ages (5th–10th century AD), the Arab world pushed forward the frontiers of learning in science, medicine, astronomy and mathematics. Arab merchants travelled the trade routes, carrying with them not only goods but a new and sophisticated culture. A prosperous Arab bathed in a 'Turkish' bath, strolled among the geometrically laid-out paths and water courses of his garden, or went shopping in the great covered markets – or souks – where everything was for sale under one roof. He could even send his son to university, whereas it was to be three hundred years before such centres of learning existed in Europe. Islamic architects designed exquisite buildings that contained intricate mosaics, brilliantly coloured glazed tiles and splashing fountains.

The Minaret
The tall slender minaret of the Ahmad ibn Tulun mosque towers above the rooftops of Cairo, capital of Egypt.

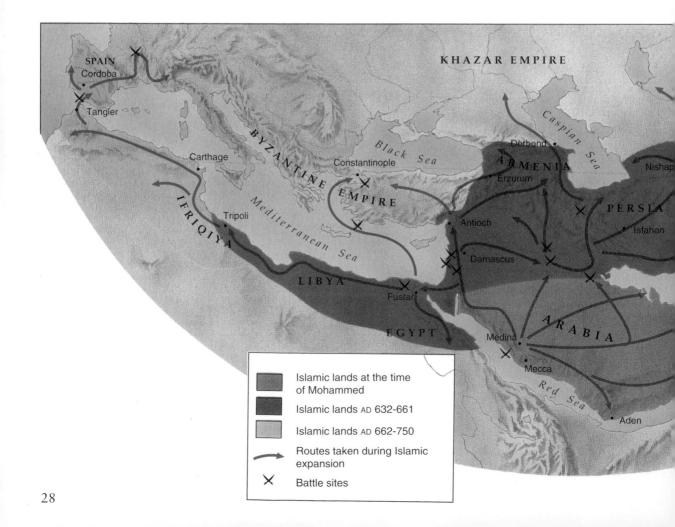

SPAIN
Cordoba

KHAZAR EMPIRE

Tangier

Caspian Sea

Derbend

Nishap

Carthage

Black Sea

BYZANTINE

Constantinople

ARMENIA

Erzurum

PERSIA

EMPIRE

Antioch

Isfahan

IFRIQIYA

Tripoli

Mediterranean Sea

Damascus

LIBYA

Fustat

ARABIA

EGYPT

Medina

Mecca

Red Sea

Aden

■	Islamic lands at the time of Mohammed
■	Islamic lands AD 632-661
■	Islamic lands AD 662-750
→	Routes taken during Islamic expansion
×	Battle sites

Islamic Religion

The Islamic religion is based on a series of revelations that Muslims (followers of Islam) believe were received directly from God by the Prophet Mohammed (*c.* 570–632). These revelations are contained in the Koran, the Holy Book of Islam. Islam means submission to the will of God, known as Allah to Muslims. The Koran lays down strict rules for every aspect of a Muslim's life. A devout Muslim should pray to Allah five times a day, either in a mosque or wherever he happens to be so long as he kneels facing towards Mecca, the birthplace of Mohammed and the holiest city of Islam. The Koran also decrees that once in a lifetime every Muslim should make a pilgrimage to Mecca to worship at the Ka'aba, the holy shrine of Islam. It is also a Muslim's duty to fast during the daylight hours of the holy month of Ramadan.

Dome of the Rock
The magnificent Dome of the Rock in Jerusalem (right) is one of the holiest places of Islam.

Arab Trade
With the coming of Islam to North Africa in the 11th century, Arab merchants opened up trade routes across the Sahara Desert, their camel caravans carrying salt, ivory, negro slaves and gold from West Africa to the Mediterranean lands. Dates and grain were stored in pottery jars, like this one from Syria. From the Arab markets, merchants traded spices along the trade routes of Asia, returning with silk from China.

Europe in the Middle Ages 1100–1300

By the mid-10th century, the invasions of the northern tribes, like the Vikings, had been halted. Western Europe was divided into kingdoms, ruled by kings or lords. Society was organized under a system called the feudal system whereby the king or lord gave land to nobles who in return swore an oath of loyalty and provided soldiers, or knights, for his protection. Throughout Europe these rulers built castles in strategic positions as defences against their potential enemies. Peasants were owned by the lord; they farmed his land for nothing but in return were given strips of land of their own and protected by his soldiers. Trade expanded during the Middle Ages, and towns developed into cities. As Christianity spread, the Church played an increasingly important part in people's lives. Religious communities called monasteries were founded, where monks devoted their lives to prayer. As centres of pilgrimage, learning and medical care, they became an integral part of medieval life. The most powerful ruler in western Europe was the pope, head of the Roman Catholic Church. The Church owned vast amounts of land and grew rich on the payment of taxes.

Christianity
The Christian religion is based on the teachings of Jesus Christ whom Christians believe was the son of God. It began in Palestine, and after its adoption by the Romans in the 4th century AD, spread throughout Europe. Churches and cathedrals, like Santiago de Compostela in Spain (below), were built for worship and to glorify God.

Daily Life
(Right) Most people lived as farmers, cultivating crops such as wheat, barley and beans, and grazing livestock. The wool trade flourished in the Middle Ages, especially in England.

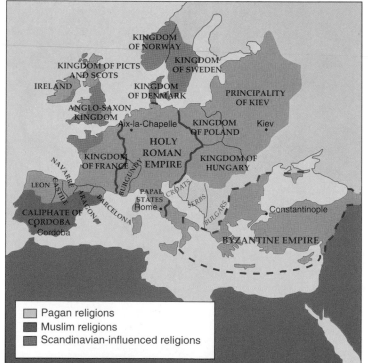

KINGDOM OF NORWAY
KINGDOM OF PICTS AND SCOTS
KINGDOM OF SWEDEN
IRELAND
KINGDOM OF DENMARK
PRINCIPALITY OF KIEV
ANGLO-SAXON KINGDOM
Aix-la-Chapelle
KINGDOM OF POLAND
Kiev
HOLY ROMAN EMPIRE
KINGDOM OF FRANCE
BURGUNDY
KINGDOM OF HUNGARY
NAVARRE
LEON
CASTILE
ARAGON
BARCELONA
PAPAL STATES
Rome
CROATS
SERBS
BULGARS
Constantinople
CALIPHATE OF CORDOBA
Cordoba
BYZANTINE EMPIRE

- ☐ Pagan religions
- ☐ Muslim religions
- ☐ Scandinavian-influenced religions

Craftsmen
(Below) Craftsmen, such as this carpenter, tended to live in towns. They were independent of the feudal system and were paid for their work.

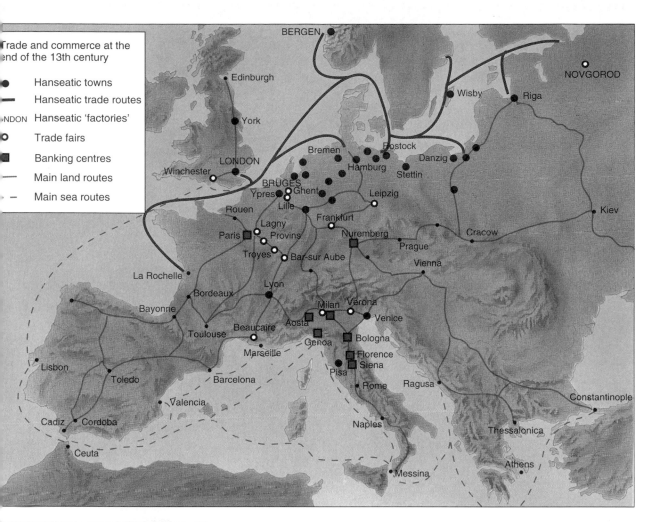

Trade and commerce at the end of the 13th century

- ● Hanseatic towns
- — Hanseatic trade routes
- ·NDON Hanseatic 'factories'
- ○ Trade fairs
- ■ Banking centres
- — Main land routes
- - - Main sea routes

BERGEN

NOVGOROD

Edinburgh

Wisby

Riga

York

Bremen · Rostock · Danzig

LONDON · Hamburg · Stettin

Winchester

BRUGES

Ypres · Ghent · Leipzig

Rouen · Lille

Lagny · Frankfurt

Paris · Provins · Nuremberg

Troyes · Bar-sur Aube

La Rochelle

Bordeaux · Lyon

Bayonne

Milan · Verona

Aosta · Venice

Beaucaire

Toulouse · Genoa · Bologna

Marseille · Florence

Pisa · Siena

Lisbon

Toledo · Barcelona · Rome

Valencia

Cadiz · Cordoba

Ceuta

Naples

Kiev

Cracow

Prague

Vienna

Ragusa

Constantinople

Thessalonica

Athens

Messina

The Crusades

With the spread of Christianity, pilgrims journeyed to Palestine (or the Holy Land) to worship at the Christian holy places. When Seljuk Turks conquered Palestine in 1071, these pilgrimages were forbidden. This sparked off the Crusades, a series of military campaigns fought by Christians against Muslims for control of the holy places. The crusaders built magnificent castles, like Krak des Chevaliers in Syria (below), to protect the pilgrim routes.

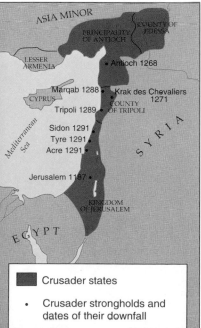

ASIA MINOR

PRINCIPALITY OF ANTIOCH

COUNTY OF EDESSA

LESSER ARMENIA

Antioch 1268

Marqab 1288

CYPRUS

Krak des Chevaliers 1271

Tripoli 1289

COUNTY OF TRIPOLI

Sidon 1291

Tyre 1291

Acre 1291

Jerusalem 1187

Mediterranean Sea

S Y R I A

KINGDOM OF JERUSALEM

E G Y P T

- ■ Crusader states
- · Crusader strongholds and dates of their downfall

The Mongol Empire 1200–1405

Covering a vast area of northern Asia are the steppes, wind-swept grasslands inhabited by tribes of pastoral nomads grazing their sheep and horses. In the early 13th century the Mongol tribes were united under Genghis Khan (c. 1162–1227) who welded them into a formidable fighting force. The Mongol's first target was China: despite the Great Wall, built by the Chinese in the 3rd century BC to repel northern barbarians, the Mongol hordes invaded China, occupying it until driven out by the Ming dynasty in 1367. In 1219 Genghis Khan's armies swept westwards, overrunning central Asia, Russia, entering Hungary and Poland and continuing their conquests until they reached the Black Sea. The Mongols then withdrew into central Asia, but within a few years a fresh onslaught began. Total domination of Europe and Muslim Asia was probably prevented only by the defeat of a Mongol army near Baghdad and by disputes between Genghis Khan's successors. Attempts to invade Java and Japan were also unsuccessful. In the late 14th century one of Genghis Khan's greatest successors, Tamerlane, led campaigns south of the Caspian Sea and as far as northern India. At its height, the Mongol empire was the largest the world had ever seen. Though the hordes left a trail of death and destruction in their wake, once the empire was established it was followed by a period of peace and consolidation.

Yurt
The Mongols lived in tents, or yurts, which were perfectly adapted to their nomadic way of life. Greased animal skins or textiles were stretched over a wooden frame, then covered with hand-woven rugs which helped to keep out the bitter winter cold. Inside the floor was covered with felt, skin or rugs. The yurt could be quickly dismantled and loaded on to a pony.

EUROPE

Liegnitz

Cr

Gr

1242

Ragusa

Constantinop

AFRICA

Ain Jal

Mongol Horsemen
Superb horsemen, the Mongols rode ponies that could travel immense distances without tiring. Armed with two bows, the Mongols could fire their arrows from the saddle at full gallop. Their manoeuvrability was aided by stirrups, such as those above, which were reputedly made for Genghis Khan himself. It was their speed, mobility and firepower that gave the Mongols their military superiority.

Trade

The Silk Road, which stretched for 2500 miles across the deserts and mountain ranges of central Asia, was vital to trade between China and the West. Traders, riding their Bactrian camels, travelled in large groups called caravans for protection. Because of Mongol domination in the region, trans-Asian trade was safeguarded from warring tribes. The route's importance declined in the 15th century as trade by sea increased.

Novgorod

KHANATE OF THE GOLDEN HORDE

MONGOLIA

JAPAN

Karakoram

1211

New Sarai

1236

Peking

1273

1223

1219

Beshbalik

1216

1281

Tiflis

CHAGATAI EMPIRE

Hsiliang

EMPIRE

Kashgar

Tabriz

Bukhara

OF THE

1221

GREAT KHAN

CHINA

IL - KHAN

Baghdad

1258

EMPIRE

Peshawar

Canton

1277

1257

Lahore

1285

1297

Area under
loose Mongol
control

1296

Pagan

ARABIA

to Java
1292

INDIA

	Campaigns of Genghis Khan and dates
	Campaigns of his successors and dates

Europe in Crisis 1300–1400

In the early 14th century Europe suffered from a number of disasters. A change in the climate caused harvests to fail, resulting in widespread famine. This was followed by a pandemic plague (called the Black Death) and the beginning of the Hundred Years' War between England and France. This was not one continuous conflict but a series of attempts by English kings to dominate France, which began with Edward III's claim to the French throne. The English armies won battles at Sluys, Crécy, Calais and Poitiers, but these were countered by later French victories, and by 1377 France had recovered most of its lost territories. War was renewed by Henry V of England who won a crushing victory over the French at Agincourt in 1415 and then went on to conquer much of Normandy. France's recovery was begun by Joan of Arc who led an army against the English at Orléans in 1429. By the mid-15th century Calais was the only English possession left in France. The misery caused by war, famine, plague and high taxes led to popular uprisings, like the Peasants' Revolt in England in 1381.

Knights
Medieval knights went into battle wearing plate armour over a layer of chain mail.

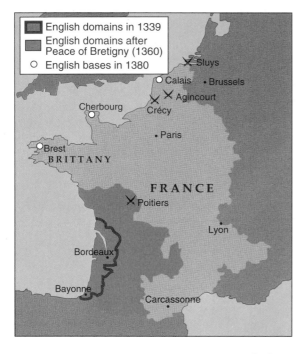

English domains in 1339
English domains after Peace of Bretigny (1360)
○ English bases in 1380

✗ Sluys
○ Calais • Brussels
✗ ✗ Agincourt
Cherbourg
Crécy
○
• Paris
○ Brest
BRITTANY
FRANCE
✗ Poitiers
Lyon
Bordeaux
Bayonne
Carcassonne

Lisbon
PORTUGAL

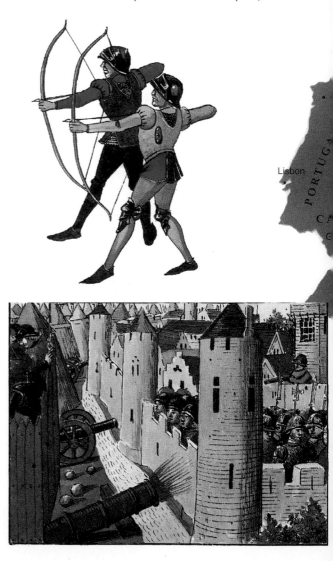

Archers
*(Above right) English archers at the Battle of Crécy.
A skilled archer could fire as many as 12 arrows per minute.*

Changes in Warfare
The various conflicts during the Hundred Years' War were dominated by sieges of fortified castles and towns. An assault began with the mining of the outer walls and bombardment by cannon, as seen here in the siege of Rouen by the English in 1419.

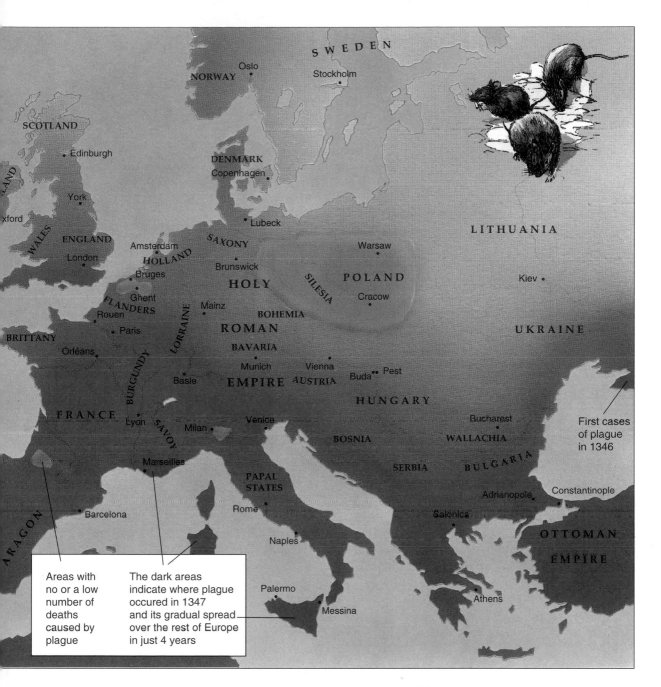

SWEDEN

NORWAY
Oslo
Stockholm

SCOTLAND
Edinburgh

DENMARK
Copenhagen

York

LITHUANIA

xford

Lubeck

WALES

ENGLAND
Amsterdam
SAXONY
Warsaw

HOLLAND
Brunswick
POLAND
Kiev

London

Bruges
SILESIA
Cracow

FLANDERS
Ghent
HOLY
Mainz
Rouen
BOHEMIA
UKRAINE

BRITTANY
Paris
ROMAN

LORRAINE
BAVARIA

Orléans
Munich
Vienna

BURGUNDY
Basle
EMPIRE
AUSTRIA
Buda
Pest

FRANCE
Venice
HUNGARY

Lyon
SAVOY
Milan
Bucharest

BOSNIA
WALLACHIA

Marseilles
SERBIA
BULGARIA

First cases
of plague
in 1346

PAPAL
STATES
Adrianople
Constantinople

ARAGON
Barcelona
Rome
Salonica

Naples
OTTOMAN

EMPIRE

Areas with
no or a low
number of
deaths
caused by
plague

The dark areas
indicate where plague
occured in 1347
and its gradual spread
over the rest of Europe
in just 4 years

Palermo
Athens

Messina

Black Death

In the 14th century western Europe was ravaged by a terrible scourge called the Black Death. Carried by infected fleas on rats, it made its first appearance in the Crimea in 1346, probably brought by ships from Asia. Victims were covered by black swellings that oozed blood and were incredibly painful. Few people who contracted the plague survived. Its effect on the populations of Europe was devastating: some towns and villages were left virtually uninhabited. The dead had to be buried in mass graves. It is estimated that some 20 million Europeans died.

The Ottoman Empire 1300–1500

Until the late 13th century the Ottoman Turks were nomadic tribesmen who patrolled the eastern borders of the Byzantine empire. United by a strong leader – Osman I – in the early 14th century, they began their conquest of eastern Europe, extending as far west as Hungary and the Balkans. In 1453, after a prolonged siege, the Ottomans captured Constantinople (now Istanbul), thus bringing to an end the Christian Byzantine empire which had lasted some six hundred years. Constantinople became the empire's cultural and administrative centre, and the residence of the sultan. In the Topkapi Palace overlooking the city, the sultan ruled his empire, surrounded by his family and protected by his personal bodyguard, the janissaries – Christians who had been captured by the Turks, converted to Islam and given a rigorous military training. No sultan could rise to power or maintain it without their support. Under Suleiman I further expansion into Europe began, but with the failure of the siege of Vienna in 1529, westward expansion by land halted. In their shipyards in Constantinople the Ottomans built a magnificent fleet of galleys with which they ravaged the coasts of Spain, Italy and Greece. But in 1571 they were defeated in a great sea battle at Lepanto, off the coast of Greece. This defeat meant further expansion was only posible to the east. Expansion continued until 1680 when the empire's slow decline began.

The Turkish janissaries (above) served the sultan, both as soldiers and administrators, with unquestioning obedience.

Hagia Sophia
Influenced by both Muslim and Byzantine architecture, the Ottomans developed a style of their own. Magnificent mosques, surmounted by several domes and often with as many as six minarets, pierced the city skylines. St Sophia in Constantinople began life as a Christian church but was converted into an Islamic mosque when the city fell to the Turks in 1453.

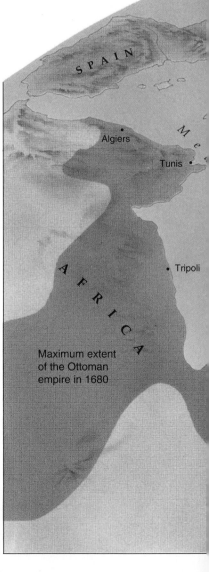

SPAIN

Algiers

Tunis

Tripoli

AFRICA

Maximum extent
of the Ottoman
empire in 1680

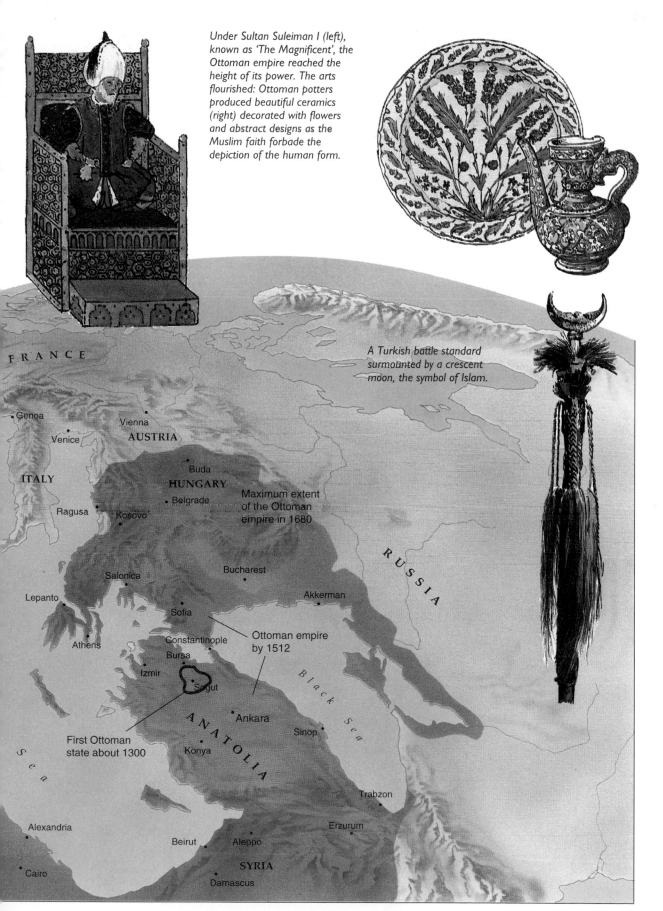

Under Sultan Suleiman I (left), known as 'The Magnificent', the Ottoman empire reached the height of its power. The arts flourished: Ottoman potters produced beautiful ceramics (right) decorated with flowers and abstract designs as the Muslim faith forbade the depiction of the human form.

A Turkish battle standard surmounted by a crescent moon, the symbol of Islam.

FRANCE

Genoa

Venice

AUSTRIA
Vienna

ITALY

Buda
HUNGARY
Belgrade

Maximum extent
of the Ottoman
empire in 1680

Ragusa

Kosovo

RUSSIA

Salonica

Bucharest

Lepanto

Akkerman

Athens

Sofia

Constantinople

Ottoman empire
by 1512

Bursa

Izmir

Black Sea

Sogut

ANATOLIA

First Ottoman
state about 1300

Ankara

Sinop

Konya

Sea

Trabzon

Alexandria

Erzurum

Beirut

Aleppo

Cairo

SYRIA

Damascus

The Americas from the Eve of Conquest to 1519

Sometime between 40,000 and 25,000 years ago hunters from Asia migrated to North America by crossing the Bering Strait. Living as hunter-gatherers, they gradually spread throughout the continent. Their descendants moved southwards, reaching Mexico in *c.* 20,000 BC. There they settled and became farmers, cultivating crops of maize and beans. Two warrior societies rose to power, first the Olmecs and then the Toltecs. The Olmecs are known for their huge helmeted stone heads and small jade axes, while the Toltecs erected temples and monumental stone warriors in their city at Tula. In the 13th century the Toltecs were succeeded by the warlike Aztecs, who established a powerful empire centred on their capital, Tenochtitlán, built on an island in Lake Texcoco – the site of Mexico City today. Believing that their gods required to be fed on human blood, the Aztecs waged continuous war on their neighbours, sacrificing their prisoners to the gods. Further south, in the tropical rain forests of Guatemala and Belize, a sophisticated civilization called the Maya had been in existence since AD 300. Great builders, their huge temple complexes and spectacular pyramids can still be seen in the jungles of Yucatán. In Peru another great civilization, the Inca, had established its empire in the Cuzco valley in the 12th century. The Inca and the Aztec were conquered by the Spanish conquistadors in the early 16th century.

Totem Pole
Tribes who settled along the Pacific coast erected painted wooden totem poles on which were carved symbolic animals and spirits.

Murder of Atahualpa
At its height, the Inca empire stretched for 2000 miles along the Andes. In 1532 Spaniards, led by Pizarro, invaded Peru, murdered the Inca leader (far left) and brought the empire to an end.

Machu Picchu
In 1911, some four centuries after it was built, archaeologists discovered a remarkable Inca town high in the Andes. Extensive buildings and great terraces clung to the bare hillsides, evidence of a thriving community. Although only 70 km from the Inca capital at Cuzco, Machu Picchu was never discovered by the Spanish conquistadors.

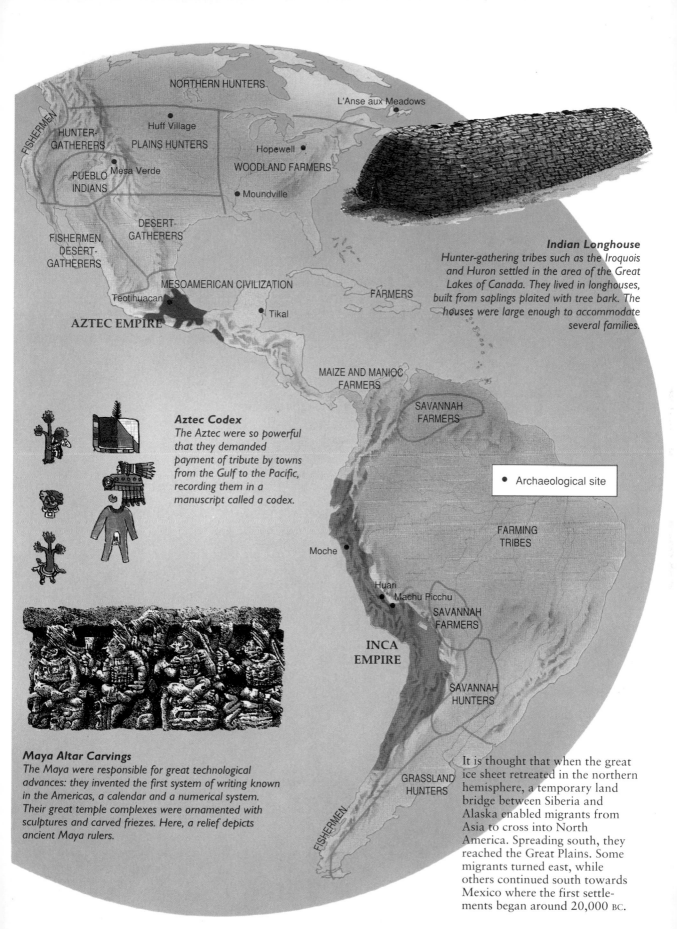

NORTHERN HUNTERS

L'Anse aux Meadows

FISHERMEN

HUNTER-GATHERERS

Huff Village

PLAINS HUNTERS

Hopewell

WOODLAND FARMERS

PUEBLO INDIANS

Mesa Verde

Moundville

DESERT-GATHERERS

FISHERMEN, DESERT-GATHERERS

MESOAMERICAN CIVILIZATION

FARMERS

Teotihuacan

Tikal

AZTEC EMPIRE

MAIZE AND MANIOC FARMERS

SAVANNAH FARMERS

Indian Longhouse
Hunter-gathering tribes such as the Iroquois and Huron settled in the area of the Great Lakes of Canada. They lived in longhouses, built from saplings plaited with tree bark. The houses were large enough to accommodate several families.

Aztec Codex
The Aztec were so powerful that they demanded payment of tribute by towns from the Gulf to the Pacific, recording them in a manuscript called a codex.

• Archaeological site

FARMING TRIBES

Moche

Huari

Machu Picchu

SAVANNAH FARMERS

INCA EMPIRE

SAVANNAH HUNTERS

Maya Altar Carvings
The Maya were responsible for great technological advances: they invented the first system of writing known in the Americas, a calendar and a numerical system. Their great temple complexes were ornamented with sculptures and carved friezes. Here, a relief depicts ancient Maya rulers.

GRASSLAND HUNTERS

FISHERMEN

It is thought that when the great ice sheet retreated in the northern hemisphere, a temporary land bridge between Siberia and Alaska enabled migrants from Asia to cross into North America. Spreading south, they reached the Great Plains. Some migrants turned east, while others continued south towards Mexico where the first settlements began around 20,000 BC.

Europe: the Expansion of Knowledge 1400–1600

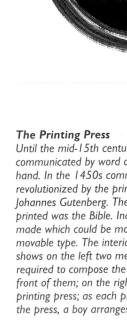

In the 15th century the great age of discovery began. Europeans sailed the seven seas in search of knowledge, goods to trade and new lands to conquer. Vasco da Gama's ships buffeted their way around the Cape of Good Hope, continuing east until they reached India. Christopher Columbus stumbled upon the Americas. Amerigo Vespucci gave his name to the American continent after his journeys along the coasts of what are now Brazil and Guiana. Ferdinand Magellan achieved the first circumnavigation of the world; the Spanish invaded Mexico and Peru; and the Portuguese explored Africa's west coast. The world began to take shape and maps began to look as they do today. These great voyagers returned with knowledge of other cultures and with their ships loaded with cargoes of gold, silver and tobacco from the Americas, ivory and slaves from Africa and spices from Indonesia. Trade routes formed a network across the oceans. The Dutch, Spanish, English, French and Portuguese founded colonies in foreign lands that grew into vast territorial possessions. In Italy a great flowering of the arts – known as the Renaissance, or rebirth – began. New forms of architecture, painting, music and literature evolved. Powerful families and wealthy members of the Church became patrons of the arts, commissioning work from artists like Raphael and Michelangelo and financing the construction of great cathedrals and palaces. The opening up of the world stimulated an interest in geography and cartography. Advances were made in navigation, astronomy and medicine, while the development of printing accelerated the spread of knowledge and new ideas throughout Europe and beyond.

European Christianity

From its early beginnings, European Christianity had been dominated by the Roman Catholic Church – so-called because it was ruled by the pope in Rome. In the 16th century a German priest called Martin Luther (right) led a movement of protest – later called the Reformation – against the corruption of the Catholic Church, which resulted in the establishment of the Protestant Church.

The Printing Press

Until the mid-15th century, information was communicated by word of mouth or written by hand. In the 1450s communication was revolutionized by the printing press, invented by Johannes Gutenberg. The first book to be printed was the Bible. Individual letters were made which could be moved and reused – movable type. The interior of a printing shop shows on the left two men choosing the letters required to compose the manuscript page in front of them; on the right paper is fed into the printing press; as each printed sheet comes off the press, a boy arranges it in order.

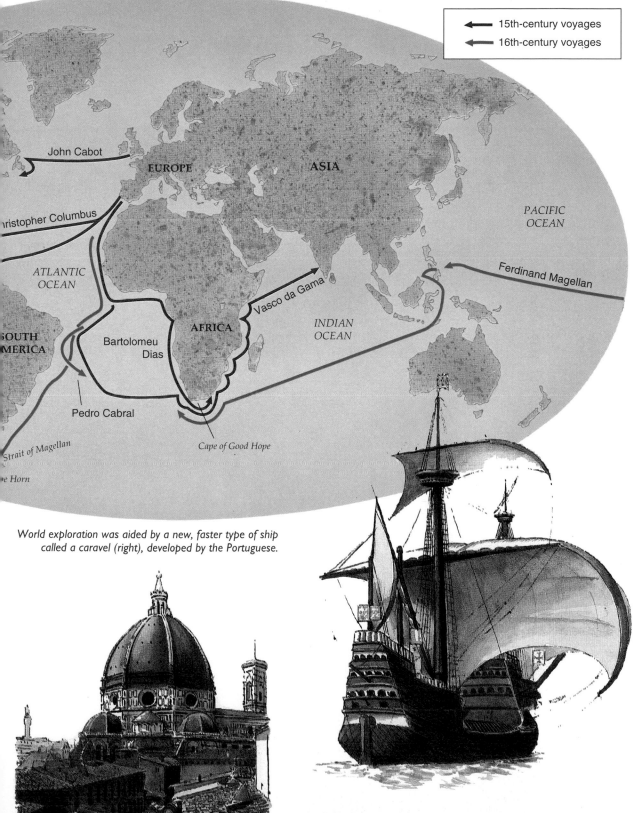

15th-century voyages

16th-century voyages

John Cabot

EUROPE

ASIA

PACIFIC
OCEAN

Christopher Columbus

ATLANTIC
OCEAN

Ferdinand Magellan

Vasco da Gama

SOUTH
AMERICA

AFRICA

INDIAN
OCEAN

Bartolomeu
Dias

Pedro Cabral

Strait of Magellan

Cape of Good Hope

e Horn

*World exploration was aided by a new, faster type of ship
called a caravel (right), developed by the Portuguese.*

*The complex construction of the dome of the cathedral in Florence (left)
was based on a study of Roman engineering. Begun in c.1300, the
cathedral took nearly 150 years to complete.*

Colonial Expansion 1500–1700

The great voyages of discovery had defined the areas of interest for the seafaring and trading nations of western Europe. In the 16th and 17th centuries they began to expand their settlements into colonies and their colonies into empires. In the Americas the Spanish consolidated their empire in Mexico, extending it throughout Central America, to the Caribbean and southwards from Peru to Chile and beyond. The Portuguese settled Brazil. The success of these overseas empires was dependent on forced labour by the native populations – as in Mexico – or by black Africans who were shipped from Africa to be sold as slaves. In North America French fur traders penetrated along the St Lawrence River deep into Canada; the Dutch settled along the Hudson Valley; in 1607 the English established a colony at Jamestown, Virginia. Trade was not the only motive for conquest and colonization; religion too played its part, some colonizers fleeing from religious persecution. In 1620 a group, later known as the 'Pilgrim Fathers', left England for America and founded a settlement at Plymouth. On the other side of the globe, the Portuguese founded a colony at Goa and set up slave-trading stations along the east African coast, while the Dutch established control of the spice trade in Indonesia. By the end of the 17th century, only Oceania remained undiscovered by the Europeans.

Between the mid-15th century and the end of the 17th century, some 10 million black Africans were crammed into the holds of slave ships and transported across the Atlantic to work the sugar, cotton and tobacco plantations of the European colonies. Here (below left) sugar cane is crushed in a Spanish sugar mill.

(Right) New York began as a Dutch trading post on Manhattan island at the mouth of the Hudson River. Its fine natural harbour attracted a flourishing trade, especially in furs. Here ships enter the Great Dock. In 1664 New York was captured by the English.

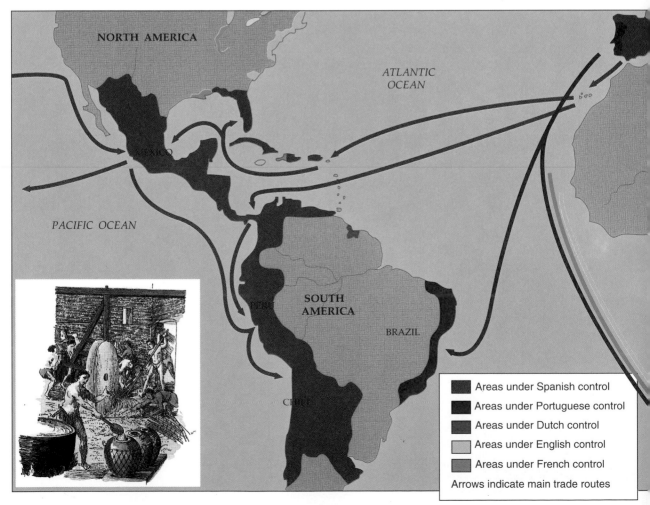

NORTH AMERICA

ATLANTIC OCEAN

MEXICO

PACIFIC OCEAN

SOUTH AMERICA

PERU

BRAZIL

CHILE

- ◼ Areas under Spanish control
- ◼ Areas under Portuguese control
- ◼ Areas under Dutch control
- ◻ Areas under English control
- ◼ Areas under French control
- Arrows indicate main trade routes

A Benin brass statue of a Portuguese soldier.

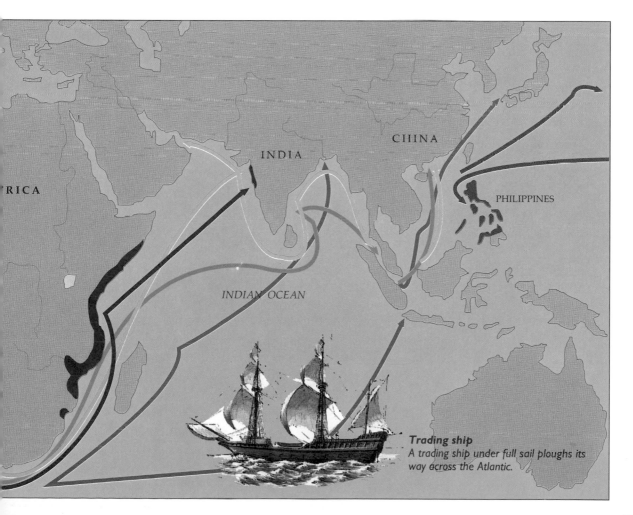

Trading ship
A trading ship under full sail ploughs its way across the Atlantic.

Asian Empires 1300–1700

Although Europeans had established trading ports in Southeast Asia, the continent remained largely unaffected by the European quest for colonization. Only the Indian subcontinent, invaded in the early 16th century by the Mughals, was radically altered by an alien culture. Of mixed Mongol and Turkish descent, the Mughals brought the Islamic religion to India. A series of remarkable rulers extended the empire and introduced the distinctive Islamic style of architecture which changed the face of Indian cities for ever. China was ruled by an equally successful dynasty, the Ming, which brought peace and stability to a population twice the size of all Europe. The arts flourished, especially the production of silk and pottery. But threatened from without by Japan and a tribe from Manchuria called the Manchus, the Ming dynasty was ended in 1644 when the Manchus seized power and founded a new imperial dynasty – the Ch'ing. During Ch'ing rule, the Chinese empire reached its greatest extent, developed a successful economy and improved cultivation, especially of rice, the staple diet. Trade with Western nations, except Russia, was not permitted. Throughout the 1400s and 1500s Japan had been torn by civil strife, but in the late 16th century a series of powerful warriors broke the power of the feudal overlords and restored peace and prosperity. In 1639 all foreigners were expelled from Japan and for the next 200 years it existed in virtual isolation from the rest of the world.

(Below left) Since time immemorial the Indian elephant which roamed the jungles of southeast Asia had been caught and tamed. Invaluable for hunting, hauling timber and riding into battle, they were also used on ceremonial occasions.

(Below) Samurai warriors were armed with superb swords. Layers of steel were hammered together to give the blade its enormous strength.

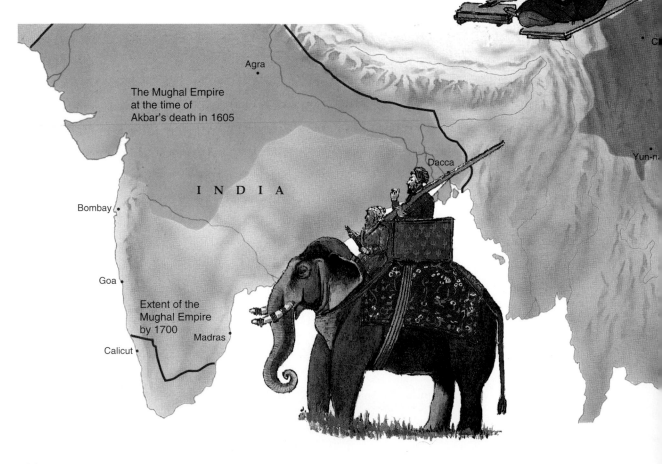

Agra

The Mughal Empire
at the time of
Akbar's death in 1605

Dacca

I N D I A

Bombay

Goa

Extent of the
Mughal Empire
by 1700

Madras

Calicut

Grea

Yun-n

JAPAN

PEKING

T'ai-yann Chi-nan

K'ai-feng Nanking

i-an

I N A Wu-ch'ang Hang-chou

Nan-ch'ang

Maximum extent
of the Ming empire
about 1450

Fu-chou

Kuei-len

Kuang-chou

The Great Wall of China
*Over the centuries, the Great Wall of China,
begun in the 3rd century BC, was extended
by successive dynasties. The wall as it stands
today was largely constructed during the
Ming dynasty. Watchtowers along its length
acted as signalling posts to warn of raiders
from Central Asia, while the gateways
enabled traffic to pass from Chinese
territory onto the wild steppe beyond. The
Great Wall is the only man-made object
visible from space.*

Europe: Nations and Conflict 1600–1715

In the 15th and 16th centuries Europe was divided into a number of small states, but in the 17th century these states were absorbed into strong nations, larger and fewer in number, and ruled by powerful kings and emperors. The nations began to compete with one another for political supremacy in Europe. A nation's strength depended on its wealth, administration, military and naval forces and on its agriculture – 90 per cent of Europe's population still derived its living from the land. Conflicts which had previously been largely religious now became territorial. To maintain a balance of power in Europe, nations formed alliances with each other.

The Thirty Years' War (1618–48)
This began as a religious war between the Catholic Habsburg emperors and their Protestant subjects in the Holy Roman Empire, but evolved into a major conflict involving the majority of the European states. The war devastated central Europe, especially large areas of Germany, which was left with its economy in ruins and its population greatly reduced. The war was ended by the Peace of Westphalia in 1648.

(Above) An illustrated drill manual of 1607 shows how soldiers in the Dutch army used their muskets.

(Right) A musketeer of the Civil War period with his flintlock musket. Over his shoulder he carries his bandolier in which he kept his cartridge pouches.

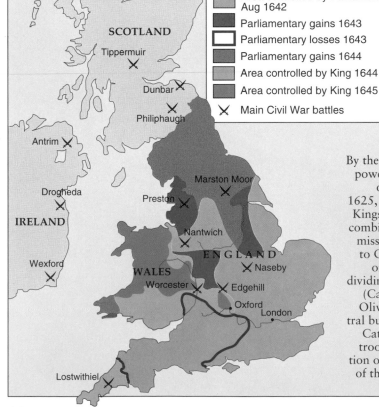

■	Area controlled by Parliament, Aug 1642
■	Parliamentary gains 1643
□	Parliamentary losses 1643
■	Parliamentary gains 1644
■	Area controlled by King 1644
■	Area controlled by King 1645
✕	Main Civil War battles

SCOTLAND
Tippermuir ✕
Dunbar ✕
Philiphaugh ✕
Antrim ✕
Drogheda ✕
IRELAND
Marston Moor ✕
Preston ✕
Nantwich
Wexford ✕
E N G L A N D
WALES
Worcester ✕ ✕ Naseby
✕ Edgehill
Oxford
London
Lostwithiel ✕

English Civil War
By the 17th century England's rulers had become so powerful that they increasingly ignored the wishes of Parliament. When Charles I became king in 1625, his belief that he ruled by the Divine Right of Kings – that he was answerable to God, not man – combined with his Catholic sympathies and his dismissive attitude towards Parliament led inevitably to Civil War. Lasting from 1642–1649 it remains one of the greatest upheavals in British history, dividing the country between supporters of the king (Cavaliers) and Parliament (Roundheads), led by Oliver Cromwell. At first Scotland remained neutral but Parliment secured Scottish support in 1644. Catholic Ireland was subjugated by Parlimentary troops in 1645. The war was ended by the execution of Charles I. For 11 years, until the restoration of the monarchy in 1660, England was a republic.

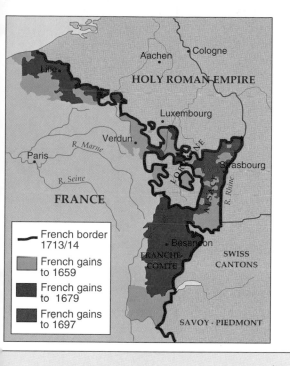

HOLY ROMAN EMPIRE

Aachen · Cologne

Lille

Luxembourg

Verdun

R. Marne

Paris

R. Seine

Strasbourg

R. Rhine

FRANCE

Besançon

FRANCHE-COMTÉ

SWISS CANTONS

SAVOY - PIEDMONT

	French border 1713/14
	French gains to 1659
	French gains to 1679
	French gains to 1697

Louis XIV's France

King of France from 1643 to 1715, Louis XIV was a prime example of an absolute monarch. Aided by a few brilliant ministers, he ruled France almost single-handed, dispensing with the French version of parliament, the Estates General. During his reign France's frontiers were extended and French culture became the envy of all Europe. But France's ascendancy was bought at a price: the country was crippled by the taxes required to finance the wars that Louis waged throughout his reign.

Louis XIV
Louis XIV's reign was the golden age of French art and literature. In his splendid palace at Versailles the 'Sun King' surrounded himself with the aristocracy.

Rise of Russia

From the 13th to 14th centuries much of European Russia was controlled by the Mongols. But in the 15th century the princes of Muscovy drove out the Mongols and created a centralized Russian state. Ivan IV (known as Ivan the Terrible), the first tsar of Russia, extended Russia's territories. During the reign of Peter the Great (1682–1725) Russia became a vast empire stretching from the Baltic to the Pacific. After travelling widely in Europe, Peter began the modernization of Russia by introducing western ideas and technology. He founded St Petersburg as the new Russian capital, modelling its architecture on European examples.

(Above) This wooden church on the island of Kizhi on Lake Onega bristles with the onion domes and many roofs so typical of Russian churches.

St Petersburg

Novgorod

Moscow

Perm

Astrakhan

Omsk

Irkutsk

	Muscovy 1462
	Land acquired by 1521
	Land acquired by 1581
	Land acquired by 1689

The Age of Revolution 1770–1815

The 18th century was an age of prosperity, elegance and new ways of thinking. It witnessed the beginning of the Industrial Revolution, the rise of the press, the novel and the publication of the first encylopedias. The population of Europe doubled, and people moved increasingly from the country to the town. It was also the age of absolute monarchy. Western Europe was ruled by monarchs who presided over their subjects from magnificent palaces which became centres of art and fashion. In the latter part of the century minor upheavals erupted in many parts of the western hemisphere, but these were overshadowed by major revolutions in France and America. The French Revolution sent shock waves throughout Europe, changing for ever the relationship between the rulers and the ruled, and precipitating over twenty years of conflict which devastated Europe.

(Below) George Washington commanded the colonial forces which expelled the British from America.
(Centre left) A rebellion against British rule during which a British ship was seized and its cargo thrown overboard.

(Below left) The British 'redcoats' were well-trained professional soldiers.

The American Revolution

Having defeated the French at Québec in 1759, Britain became the dominant power in North America. The original settlements – known as the Thirteen Colonies – now extended along the Atlantic coast. Increased resentment among the colonials against British rule led to war. In 1776 the Thirteen Colonies proclaimed the Declaration of Independence. With the defeat of British forces at Yorktown in 1781, America became independent.

(Left) The American volunteers were largely untrained and often ill-equipped.

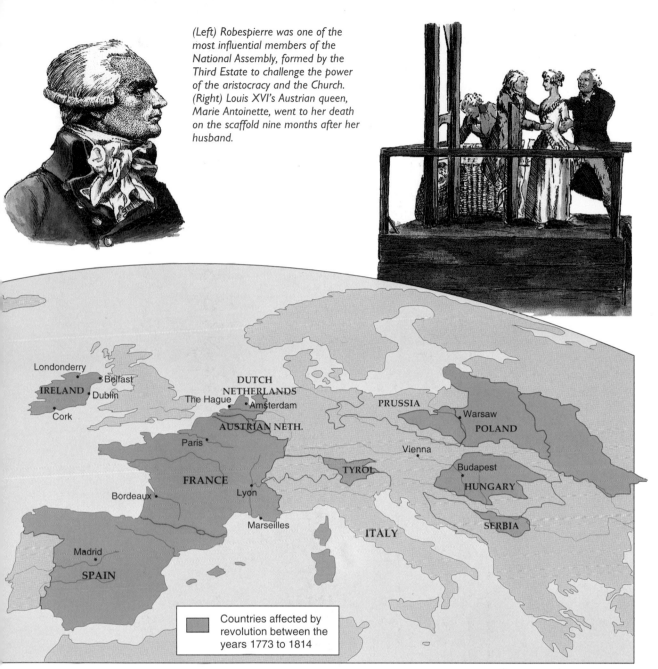

(Left) Robespierre was one of the most influential members of the National Assembly, formed by the Third Estate to challenge the power of the aristocracy and the Church. (Right) Louis XVI's Austrian queen, Marie Antoinette, went to her death on the scaffold nine months after her husband.

Countries affected by revolution between the years 1773 to 1814

The French Revolution

While the French aristocracy lived in luxury, the peasants, who made up over 90 per cent of the population, existed in a state of abject poverty. Opposition to the old order grew, erupting into full-scale revolution when a Paris mob stormed the Bastille prison. The monarchy was overthrown, the king executed and a republic established. These cataclysmic events were followed by the Terror, in which some 40,000 people were guillotined. For the first time in history, the middle and lower classes had taken power into their own hands. Here, citizens march through Paris with a banner proclaiming 'Liberty or Death'.

The Napoleonic Years 1799–1815

Alarmed by the Revolution in France and the execution of Louis XVI, neighbouring states, including Britain, formed a coalition against France. The French then mobilized an army of some 750,000 men and went on the offensive. Led by Napoleon, the French forces defeated one European state after another but failed to drive the British out of Egypt. The first coalition broke up, leaving Britain as Napoleon's only opponent. A second coalition was formed, this time including Russia. In 1799, Napoleon seized control of the French government and appointed himself First Consul. After a brief period of peace, war was renewed in 1803. A year later Napoleon crowned himself Emperor of France. The French armies continued their inexorable progress, and by 1810 Napoleon was at the peak of his power. Only Britain continued to withstand his ambitions to dominate the whole of Europe. In 1805 the British navy confirmed its superiority at sea by defeating the French at Trafalgar, thus frustrating Napoleon's plans for invasion. When French forces invaded Spain, Britain sent an army commanded by Wellington to confront them. After six years of conflict, the Peninsular Wars ended in a French withdrawal. In 1812 Napoleon made the fatal decision to invade Russia. The French army's subsequent retreat from Moscow, and its crushing defeat by the allies at Leipzig, forced Napoleon's abdication and exile to Elba. But he escaped, gathered up an army and confronted the British and Prussians, commanded by his old enemy, Wellington, at Waterloo. The French were defeated. Napoleon again abdicated and was exiled to St Helena where he died in 1821. The French monarchy was restored, and Louis XVI's brother was crowned Louis XVIII. After nearly 23 years of war, the victorious powers met at the Congress of Vienna and began the task of reorganizing Europe.

(Left) Napoleon Bonaparte (1769-1821) was a man of magnetic personality and vaunting ambition and was a military genius. Not only a brilliant general but a skilful administrator, he introduced reforms that shaped modern France. The Code Napoléon reorganized the French legal system and is still used by a large part of the world today.

(Right) Napoleon's invasion of Russia in 1812 was the turning point in his fortunes. Prophesying a quick victorious campaign, he marched his armies over the frontier. After one of the bloodiest battles of the Napoleonic Wars, at Borodino, the Russians withdrew towards Moscow, luring the French deeper into Russian territory. When Napoleon reached Moscow, he found it almost deserted. A day later the Russian holy city was virtually destroyed by fire. Napoleon, with his goal in ruins, his supply lines threatened and the terrible Russian winter approaching, retreated. The retreat became a disaster: short of food, transport and adequate clothing, and hounded by the Russians, the exhausted troops struggled through deep snow and icy winds towards the frontier. Of the 400,000 French soldiers who entered Russia, only 25,000 survived. For Napoleon, it was the beginning of the end of his empire.

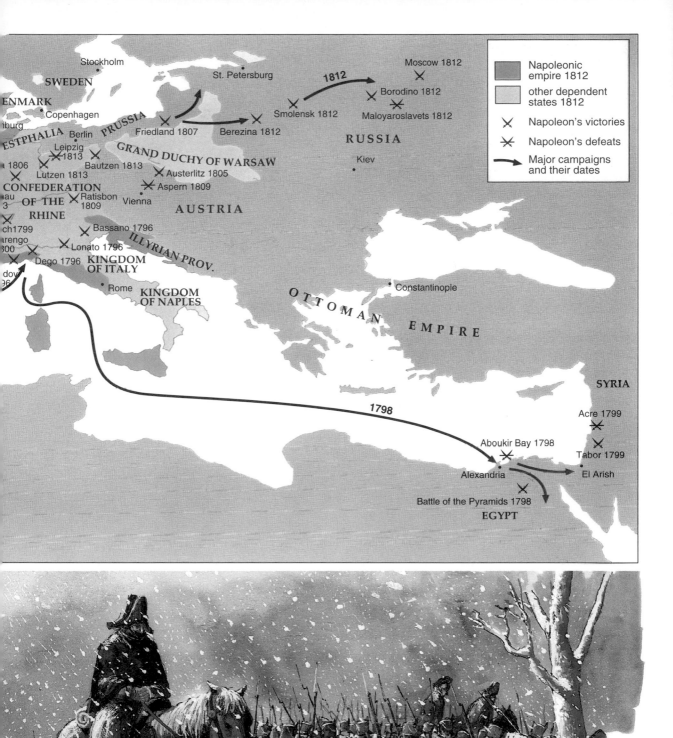

Stockholm

SWEDEN

St. Petersburg

Moscow 1812

1812

ENMARK

Copenhagen

Smolensk 1812

Borodino 1812

burg

PRUSSIA

Friedland 1807

Berezina 1812

Maloyaroslavets 1812

ESTPHALIA

Berlin

RUSSIA

GRAND DUCHY OF WARSAW

Leipzig

1813

Bautzen 1813

Kiev

1806

Lutzen 1813

Austerlitz 1805

CONFEDERATION

Aspern 1809

au

OF THE

Ratisbon

3

RHINE

1809

Vienna

AUSTRIA

ch1799

Bassano 1796

arengo

Lonato 1796

ILLYRIAN PROV.

300

Dego 1796

KINGDOM

dova

OF ITALY

96

Rome

KINGDOM OF NAPLES

Constantinople

O T T O M A N   **E M P I R E**

Napoleonic empire 1812

other dependent states 1812

✗ Napoleon's victories

✗ Napoleon's defeats

→ Major campaigns and their dates

SYRIA

1798

Acre 1799

Aboukir Bay 1798

Tabor 1799

Alexandria

El Arish

Battle of the Pyramids 1798

EGYPT

51

The Making of America 1800–1900

During the 19th century, the United States grew from the Thirteen Colonies strung out along the North Atlantic Coast to become the world's most powerful and prosperous nation, stretching 'from sea to shining sea'. The push westwards began with the sale of Louisiana by the French to America. It cost the US government $15 million and immediately doubled the country in size. The opening up of the far west was a more gradual process: hunters in search of game, and settlers seeking land to farm, drifted ever deeper into the interior. This relentless progression was disastrous for the American Indians, whose ancestral lands were overrun by settlers, miners and cattlemen, and their game – particularly the buffalo – slaughtered. Some Indian tribes fiercely resisted these incursions, but by 1890 they had been confined to reservations. The construction of the railway did much to open up the west, the gleaming rails penetrating the wilderness until by 1869 the east coast was joined to the west by 85,000 km of track. The midwest was largely populated by immigrants from Europe in search of a new life and freedom from political or religious persecution; many found work in the industrial cities of the north. Further west, from Texas to Montana, the plains became home to the cowboy and the cattle barons, who sent countless head of cattle by train to feed the growing populations of cities like Chicago. In the deep south slaves worked the cotton and tobacco plantations. Despite the horrors of the Civil War (1861–65), by the end of the 19th century the 48 separate states in North America had become the United States of today, with a population of 90 million.

Civil War

The disparity between the rich industrial states in the north and the poverty of much of the population in the south was one of the main causes of the Civil War. So too was the north's hatred of slavery, and its fear that it would be extended into the western states. When Abraham Lincoln became president in 1860, his declared opposition to slavery led to the withdrawal of 11 southern states (the Confederacy) from the Union. The war, which began in 1861, raged from Pennsylvania to Mississippi. It ended with the Confederacy's defeat in 1865; slavery was abolished. More Americans died in the Civil War than in all the country's other wars combined.

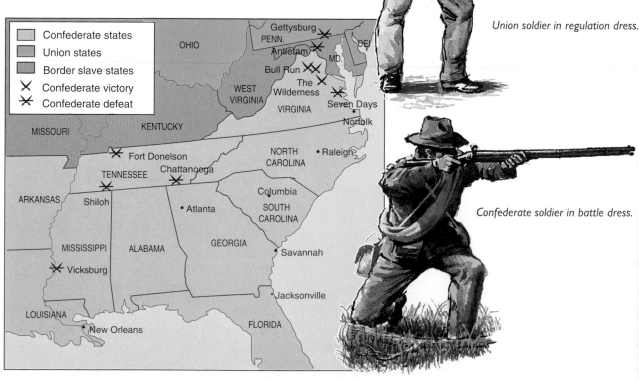

The Union soldier was better equipped than his Confederate opponent, but the Confederates were better led.

Union soldier in regulation dress.

Confederate soldier in battle dress.

Confederate states
Union states
Border slave states
X Confederate victory
✷ Confederate defeat

OHIO

Gettysburg ✷
PENN.
Antietam ✷
DEL
Bull Run ✷✷
MD.
The ✷
Wilderness
Seven Days ✷
Norfolk

WEST
VIRGINIA

VIRGINIA

MISSOURI

KENTUCKY

NORTH
CAROLINA
• Raleigh

✷ Fort Donelson

Chattanooga ✷
TENNESSEE

Columbia

ARKANSAS
Shiloh
• Atlanta
SOUTH
CAROLINA

MISSISSIPPI
ALABAMA
GEORGIA
• Savannah

✷ Vicksburg

• Jacksonville

LOUISIANA
• New Orleans
FLORIDA

Settlers

Pioneers returned from the far west with tales of limitless fertile land to be had for the taking. Families loaded their possessions into covered wagons and set off on the long hazardous journey. As the trails became established, forts were built as staging posts and to provide refuge from hostile Indians.

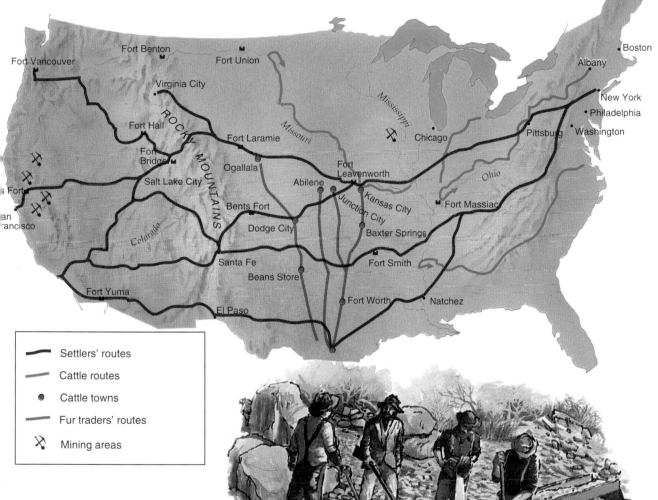

Fort Vancouver
Fort Benton
Fort Union
Boston
Albany
Virginia City
Mississippi
New York
Philadelphia
Fort Hall
ROCKY MOUNTAINS
Fort Laramie
Missouri
Pittsburg
Washington
Fort Bridger
Ogallala
Fort Leavenworth
Chicago
Ohio
s Fort
Salt Lake City
Abilene
Kansas City
Bents Fort
Junction City
Fort Massiac
ancisco
Colorado
Dodge City
Baxter Springs
Santa Fe
Fort Smith
Beans Store
Fort Yuma
Fort Worth
Natchez
El Paso

Legend

— Settlers' routes

— Cattle routes

● Cattle towns

— Fur traders' routes

⚒ Mining areas

Gold Rush

In 1848 a settler found a lump of gold in a stream in California. As news spread, gold-hungry adventurers from all over America and the world converged on California. In five years, half a billion dollars of gold were dug from the Californian mud. In 1850 the state became part of the Union.

Age of Empire 1800–1914

Until the early 19th century European imperialism had been motivated by trade. But the Industrial Revolution, which began in Britain in the mid-19th century and spread throughout Europe, required cheap raw materials to feed its hungry machines. Countries like China and Japan, which had been closed to outsiders, now opened their doors to European trade. Britain, which had retained trading posts at strategic points around the world – such as the Cape of Good Hope and Ceylon – now added others in the Far East, such as Hong Kong and Singapore, which became thriving British colonies. The opening of the Suez Canal – built by the French – in 1869 gave Britain the justification for adding Egypt to its empire. Britain also laid claim to Australia and New Zealand. Many of Britain's acquisitions were to protect its trade with its most prized possession, India. Since the establishment of the East

Mexican Independence
The people of Mexico, resentful of Spanish rule and inspired by the ideals of the French Revolution, demanded independence. The struggle went on till 1821 when Spain granted independence.

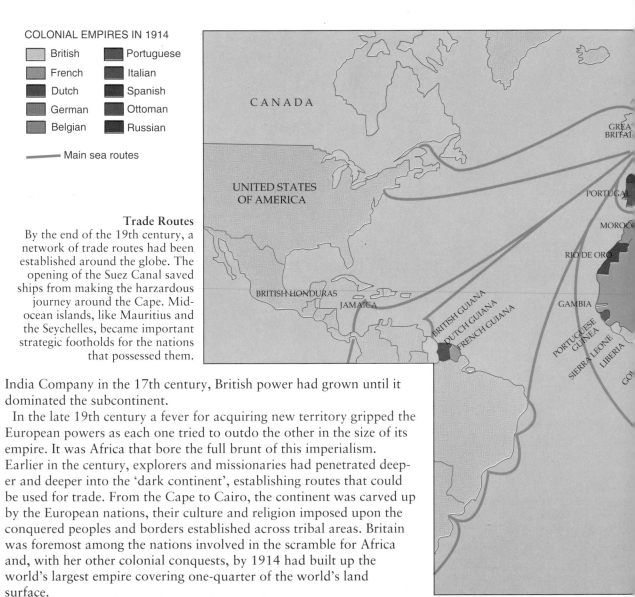

COLONIAL EMPIRES IN 1914

- British
- French
- Dutch
- German
- Belgian
- Portuguese
- Italian
- Spanish
- Ottoman
- Russian

— Main sea routes

Trade Routes
By the end of the 19th century, a network of trade routes had been established around the globe. The opening of the Suez Canal saved ships from making the harzardous journey around the Cape. Mid-ocean islands, like Mauritius and the Seychelles, became important strategic footholds for the nations that possessed them.

CANADA

UNITED STATES OF AMERICA

BRITISH HONDURAS
JAMAICA

BRITISH GUIANA
DUTCH GUIANA
FRENCH GUIANA

GREAT BRITAIN

PORTUGAL

MOROCCO

RIO DE ORO

GAMBIA

PORTUGUESE GUINEA

SIERRA LEONE
LIBERIA

India Company in the 17th century, British power had grown until it dominated the subcontinent.

In the late 19th century a fever for acquiring new territory gripped the European powers as each one tried to outdo the other in the size of its empire. It was Africa that bore the full brunt of this imperialism. Earlier in the century, explorers and missionaries had penetrated deeper and deeper into the 'dark continent', establishing routes that could be used for trade. From the Cape to Cairo, the continent was carved up by the European nations, their culture and religion imposed upon the conquered peoples and borders established across tribal areas. Britain was foremost among the nations involved in the scramble for Africa and, with her other colonial conquests, by 1914 had built up the world's largest empire covering one-quarter of the world's land surface.

The Boer War

In 1814 the British took control of South Africa from the original Dutch settlers – known as 'Boers' (farmers). Determined to maintain their independence from Britain, the Boers trekked into the interior and founded two republics, the Orange Free State and the Transvaal. When gold and diamonds were discovered in Boer territory, the massive influx of prospectors, and Britain's refusal to withdraw its troops from the Transvaal, led to war. Although British forces were superior in numbers, they were steadily out-fought by the brilliant guerilla tactics of the Boers. But the arrival of British reinforcements forced a Boer surrender in 1902.

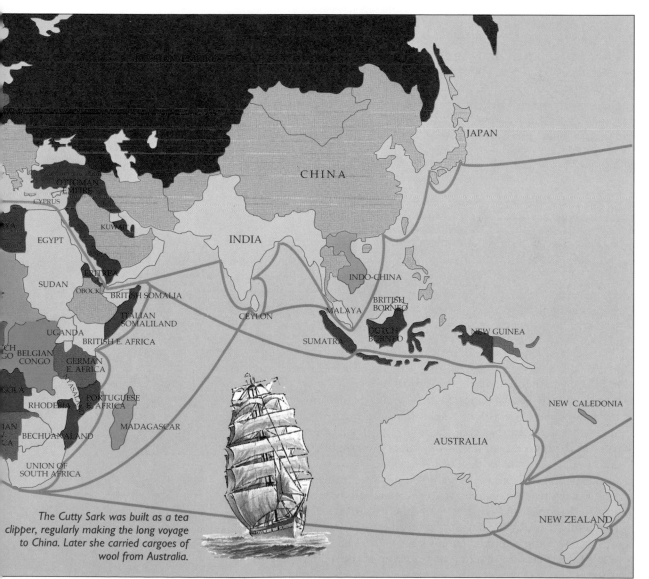

The Cutty Sark was built as a tea clipper, regularly making the long voyage to China. Later she carried cargoes of wool from Australia.

The First World War 1914–1918

By 1900 Germany had become the most powerful industrial power in Europe. Fearing Germany's ambitions to increase its colonial empire, and alarmed by its formidable army and navy, France, Britain and Russia formed an alliance (Allied forces), while Germany allied itself with Austria (Central forces). In an atmosphere of mutual suspicion, an arms race developed. But it was increased tension in the Balkans – which had long been a centre of conflict – that precipitated matters. Serbia's emergence as the strongest state threatened the collapse of Austria's shaky empire in the region, which would isolate Germany in Europe. When the heir to the Austrian throne was assassinated in June 1914 at Sarajevo, Austria blamed Serbia and declared war. By August, all the European powers had mobilized and war was inevitable. Most of the fighting took place in Europe, but campaigns were fought as far afield as Mesopotamia (today's Iraq), the Middle East and in Germany's colonies in Africa and the Pacific. During the course of the war, other countries, like Greece and Italy, joined the war against Germany. At sea, the British navy was faced by German warships and submarines, which caused havoc to ships carrying supplies to the embattled French and British armies in France. In January 1917 American ships were sunk by German submarines. The United States entered the war, bringing massive reinforcements of men and arms to the aid of Britain and its allies. Germany surrendered in 1918 – 10 million had died and over 20 million were wounded. For future generations it became a symbol of the futility and senseless destruction of war.

North Sea

GREAT BRITAIN

London

NETHE
Amsterd

Trench line in the West, 1914

BELGI
Br

Amiens

Farthest German advance in the West, 1914

Paris

Armistice line in the West, November 1918

FRANCE

SPAIN

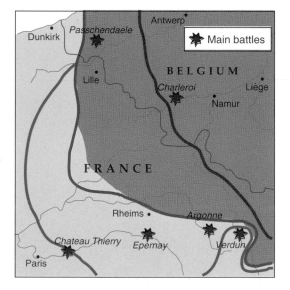

Antwerp

Dunkirk

Passchendaele

⭐ Main battles

BELGIUM

Lille

Charleroi

Liège

Namur

FRANCE

Rheims

Argonne

Chateau Thierry

Epernay

Verdun

Paris

In Western Europe the war took the form of two lines of opposing trenches stretching from the Channel to the Swiss border. The British and French faced the Germans across an area of neutral territory, known as 'no-man's land'. Both sides fought in conditions of unbearable squalor. Living in the trenches, up to their knees in mud, their quarters infested by rats, they were shelled and gassed (right).

Countries of the Central forces
Countries of the Allied forces
Territory held by Central
Powers, December 1917
Neutral countries

NORWAY

FINLAND

Petrograd

SWEDEN

Baltic Sea

Riga

DENMARK

Copenhagen

Vilna

Minsk

R. Elbe

POLAND

RUSSIA

German penetration
of Russia, March 1918

Berlin

R. Oder

Warsaw

Brest Litovsk

Munich

GERMANY

Farthest Russian
advance in the East,
1914–15

Kiev

R. Dnieper

Russian front,
November 1915

Cracow

Vienna

Odessa

R. Danube

Budapest

Sebastopol

AUSTRIA - HUNGARY

Black Sea

Trieste

Belgrade

ROMANIA

ITALY

Sarajevo

Bucharest

MONTENEGRO

SERBIA

BULGARIA

Sofia

ALBANIA

Constantinople

Salonica

OTTOMAN
EMPIRE

Mediterranean Sea

GREECE

War in the Air
*As the first manned flight only
took place in 1903, aeroplanes
played a minor role in the First
World War, being used mainly for
reconnaissance on the Western Front.*

Women at Work
*As the men went to war, the women increasingly took their places
in munitions factories, offices, hospitals and on the land.*

57

Between the Wars 1919–1939

In 1919 a shattered Europe, crippled by the cost of the war, began the struggle toward recovery. The 30 victorious states met at Versailles to work out peace conditions. Germany was blamed for the war and made to pay huge reparations, which led to inflation, high unemployment and resentment against the European powers. In America a loss of confidence in the economy caused the collapse of the New York Stock Exchange: banks closed and thousands were thrown out of work. The American depression sent shock waves round the world. Unemployment in America rose to six million by the end of 1930, while world unemployment doubled. The Great Depression had political repercussions: with promises of a 'New Deal' which would get people back to work, F. D. Roosevelt became US president. In Germany mounting unemployment and fear of social chaos created support for the National Socialist (or Nazi) Party, led by Adolf Hitler. The Nazis created jobs in the armed forces and munitions factories. Nationalism swept through Europe. In Italy the fascist dictator Mussolini rose to power, pledging to increase Italy's prestige in Europe. In Spain a conflict erupted between republicans and nationalists – who were supported by Italy and Germany – which developed into three years of civil war. The failure of Britain and France to aid the republicans encouraged Italian and German expansion in Europe. In the Far East, Japanese economic growth threatened the region's stability. The stage was set for the Second World War.

(Right) To the German people, suffering the aftermath of the First World War, Hitler's promises of a return to prosperity ensured his rise to power. Hitler believed that Germans were a 'master race' and that people – such as the Jews – who were not members of the master race must be eliminated.

(Far right) Thousands of panic-stricken investors throng Wall Street after the collapse of the New York Stock Exchange. In the next three years 5000 American banks closed and thousands lost their savings.

The Chinese Revolution (1911–49)

With the end of imperial rule, provincial warlords controlled China. The misery they caused precipitated an upsurge of nationalism. Chiang Kai-shek united much of China, ruling from Nanking with his Nationalist Party. But his Republic of China collapsed in the face of the Japanese invasion of Manchuria and civil war with Chinese communists. Led by Mao Tse-tung, the remnants of the communist forces set off on the Long March, gathering widespread support. After a brief truce, civil war resumed. The nationalists were defeated and the People's Republic of China was proclaimed in 1949.

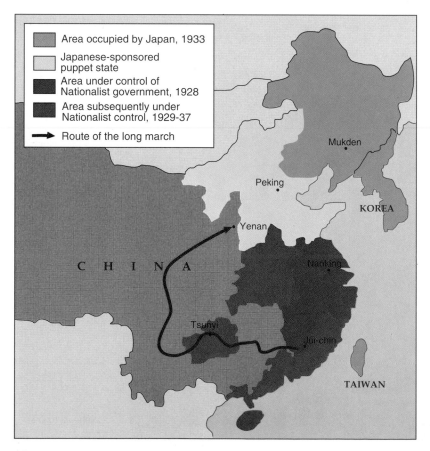

Area occupied by Japan, 1933

Japanese-sponsored puppet state

Area under control of Nationalist government, 1928

Area subsequently under Nationalist control, 1929-37

→ Route of the long march

Mukden

Peking

KOREA

Yenan

CHINA

Nanking

Tsunyi

Jui-chin

TAIWAN

The Russian Revolution (1917–21)

The First World War brought great hardship to the Russian people, and a loss of confidence in the government. In 1917 there was an uprising in St. Petersburg and Tsar Nicholas II was forced to abdicate. A provisional government was formed, but the Bolsheviks (Communists), led by Lenin, seized power, declared Russia a Soviet republic and made peace with Germany. The Revolution was followed by a conflict between anti-communist forces (the Whites), supported by certain Western powers, and the communists (the Reds). The conflict became widespread. The Whites were defeated. In 1921 the new Soviet Union was established.

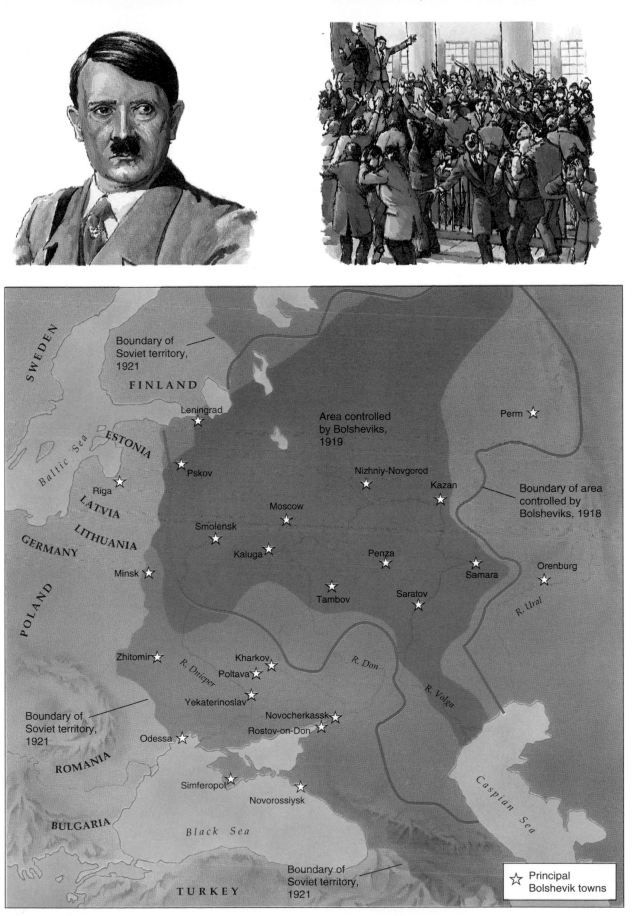

Boundary of
Soviet territory,
1921

SWEDEN

FINLAND

Leningrad

Area controlled
by Bolsheviks,
1919

Perm

Baltic Sea

ESTONIA

Pskov

Nizhniy-Novgorod

Kazan

Boundary of area
controlled by
Bolsheviks, 1918

Riga

LATVIA

Moscow

LITHUANIA

GERMANY

Smolensk

Kaluga

Penza

Samara

Orenburg

Minsk

Tambov

Saratov

R. Ural

POLAND

Zhitomir

R. Dnieper

Kharkov

Poltava

R. Don

R. Volga

Yekaterinoslav

Novocherkassk

Boundary of
Soviet territory,
1921

Odessa

Rostov-on-Don

Caspian Sea

ROMANIA

Simferopol

Novorossiysk

BULGARIA

Black Sea

TURKEY

Boundary of
Soviet territory,
1921

☆ Principal
Bolshevik towns

The Second World War 1939–1945

Hitler's ambitions for a Greater Germany were demonstrated by his annexation of Austria in March 1938, followed by the seizure of Czechoslovakia. British and French attempts to curb German aggression by negotiation (the Munich agreement) failed. Fearful that Germany would overrun central Europe, Britain and France guaranteed to protect Greece, Poland and Romania. When Germany invaded Poland, Britain and France declared war. Surprised but undeterred, Hitler invaded Denmark, Norway and the Low Countries. The French, British and Belgian forces (the Allies) were forced to retreat into northern France and to evacuate their armies from Dunkirk. The Germans pressed inexorably into France. Italy joined Germany in the war and France surrendered. By June 1940, with little cost in either men or equipment, Germany dominated Western Europe. Only Britain remained at war with Germany. Hitler's attempt to bomb Britain into a surrender in August-September 1940 failed. The war now spread farther east; Yugoslavia fell and Italy attacked Greece. In June 1941, confident of victory, Hitler invaded Russia. Instead of yielding to German

(Right) The Germans were masters of tank warfare: fast-moving tanks and mobile infantry, supported by dive bombers, were used to great effect in Poland, France and Greece. But by 1942 the Allies were better equipped, winning decisive battles in the deserts of North Africa. In 1943, the Russians successfully stemmed the tide of German invasion in a massive tank battle at Kursk.

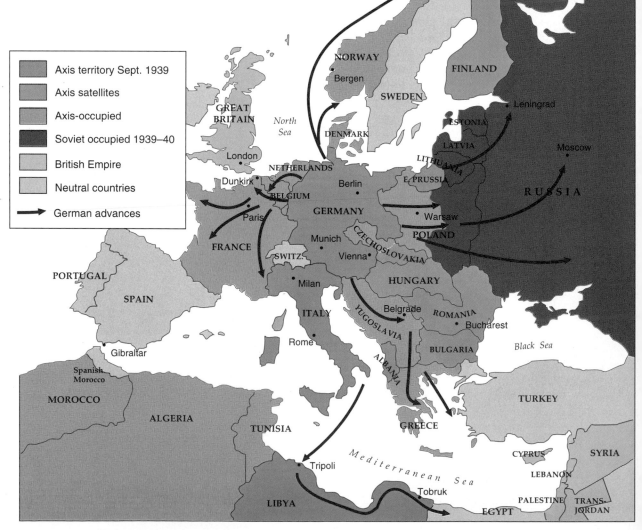

Legend:
- Axis territory Sept. 1939
- Axis satellites
- Axis-occupied
- Soviet occupied 1939–40
- British Empire
- Neutral countries
- → German advances

aggression, the Russians resisted fiercely and in December 1941 began a counter-offensive. At the end of 1941 an event took place that altered the course of the war: Japan bombed the US naval base at Pearl Harbor. The US had been reluctant to become involved, but Japan's unprovoked attack was decisive and America entered the war. A series of crucial battles in late 1942 and 1943 gave the initiative to the Allies on land and at sea. In June 1944 the Allies invaded France and liberated Western Europe, while Russia advanced on the eastern front. War in Europe ended on 8 May 1945.

In no previous conflict had civilian populations become so deeply involved. The bombing of Europe's cities took the war into people's homes. In the first four months of the German air raids on London – the Blitz – over 30,000 people were killed or injured. Hitler's persecution of the Jews caused the death of 6 million in the concentration camps.

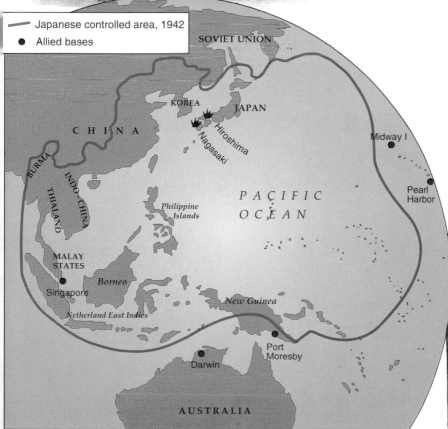

Japanese controlled area, 1942
● Allied bases

SOVIET UNION
KOREA
JAPAN
CHINA
Hiroshima
Nagasaki
BURMA
INDO-CHINA
THAILAND
Midway I
Philippine Islands
PACIFIC OCEAN
Pearl Harbor
MALAY STATES
Borneo
Singapore
New Guinea
Netherland East Indies
Port Moresby
Darwin
AUSTRALIA

With the collapse of European empires in the Far East, Japan saw its chance for expansion, bombed Pearl Harbor and overran much of southeast Asia. War in the Pacific now became crucial. At Midway in 1942 Japanese naval power was shattered by the US fleet. Japanese land forces, however, fought on. Fearing Japanese resistance would continue indefinitely, the Allies dropped atomic bombs (below) on Hiroshima and Nagasaki, causing the death of 155,000 people in Hiroshima alone. Japan surrendered in August 1945.

The Postwar World 1946–1997

At the end of the war much of Europe lay in ruins and thousands were left homeless. Germany was divided into four zones, controlled by the victorious nations. Under the dictator Stalin, the Soviet Union (USSR) took control of the eastern part of Germany and regained much of the territory it had lost at the end of the First World War. Repressive one-party (communist) regimes replaced the previous democracies. Fears that the Soviet Union would extend its control of Eastern Europe into the West accelerated the division of the continent into two armed camps. Mutual suspicion was aggravated by the formation in the West of the North Atlantic Treaty Organization (NATO) – which included the United States of America – and the Warsaw Pact in the East. What became known as the Cold War developed between the two opposing blocs. The Western economies, stimulated by American aid, began to recover. In 1957 a number of them became trading partners as founding members of the European Economic Community (EEC). But in the east, recovery was painfully slow. Harsh conditions led to widespread strikes and unrest. There were uprisings in Hungary (1956) and Czechoslovakia (1968) – both brutally suppressed by

(Below) After the war the Soviet Union rapidly increased its hold on eastern Europe and extended its control into the Baltic states. Berlin, the German capital, was divided into four zones and became the focus of much of the tension generated by the Cold War. In the arms race between the United States and the Soviet Union, each side stockpiled nuclear weapons like the Atlas missile below.

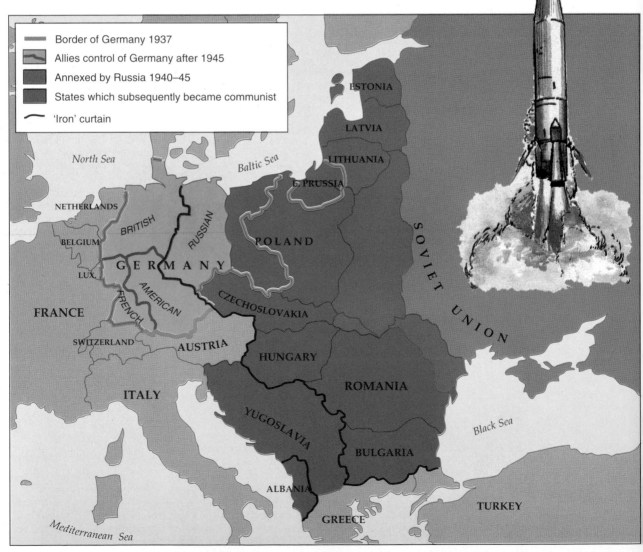

Legend:
- Border of Germany 1937
- Allies control of Germany after 1945
- Annexed by Russia 1940–45
- States which subsequently became communist
- 'Iron' curtain

North Sea · Baltic Sea · ESTONIA · LATVIA · LITHUANIA · E. PRUSSIA · NETHERLANDS · BRITISH · RUSSIAN · POLAND · BELGIUM · GERMANY · LUX. · AMERICAN · FRENCH · CZECHOSLOVAKIA · FRANCE · SWITZERLAND · AUSTRIA · HUNGARY · SOVIET UNION · ITALY · ROMANIA · YUGOSLAVIA · Black Sea · BULGARIA · ALBANIA · TURKEY · GREECE · Mediterranean Sea

Soviet troops. The West's fear of the spread of communism caused a series of confrontations around the world. In the civil war between communist North Vietnam and non-communist South Vietnam, America became involved on the side of the South, while China and the USSR supported the North. After enormous losses, America withdrew in 1975. When Gorbachev became leader of the USSR in 1985, a new era in East-West relations began. With the USSR on the verge of economic collapse, it could no longer afford to maintain its place in the arms race, and agreements were reached between the USSR and the US to reduce nuclear weapons. Discontented with communist rule, the republics within the USSR began to demand independence, and in 1991 the USSR officially ceased to exist. In the east, China had experienced two major upheavals: Mao Tse-tung's reforms embodied in the Great Leap Forward (1958–9) met with opposition that Mao sought to suppress with the Cultural Revolution. A decade of chaos and political unrest followed, which caused the death of millions of Chinese.

Within a few years of the end of the Second World War, virtually all Europe's empires had collapsed. France lost Indo-China and Algeria; Indonesia regained the territories previously under Dutch control. India's long struggle for independence from Britain came to a successful conclusion in 1947. Independence for Burma, Sri Lanka (Ceylon) and Singapore followed. In Africa, all the European colonies except South Africa and Namibia won independence during the 1950s and 60s.

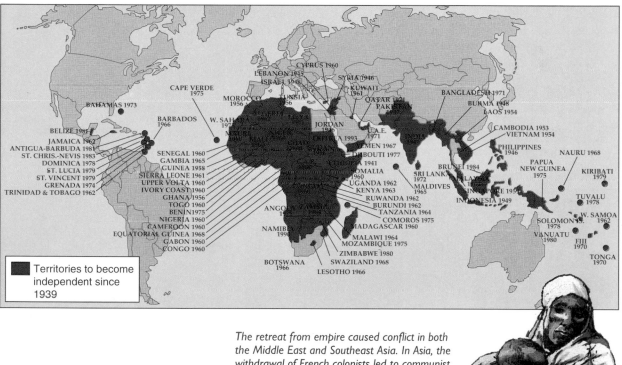

Territories to become independent since 1939

The retreat from empire caused conflict in both the Middle East and Southeast Asia. In Asia, the withdrawal of French colonists led to communist takeover in North Vietnam. The USA's involvement in the conflict, despite a huge injection of men and arms, was ultimately to lead to humiliation (left).

In 1947, when Palestine was partitioned into a Jewish and an Arab state, the plan was disputed by the Palestinians and war broke out in 1948. Since then, three further wars have erupted between Israel and her Arab neighbours. For some African nations, independence brought new and terrible problems Old tribal enmities, suppressed by colonial rule, resurfaced and boiled over into civil wars. In Ethiopia, civil war caused an appalling famine (above) which shocked the world.

The World Tomorrow?

Despite huge strides in technology in the 20th century, with an estimated global population of eight to ten billion by the year 2000, many basic problems remain. Urban populations have exploded, especially in Latin America; soon more people will live in towns than in the country. Engulfed by shanty towns and poisoned by pollution, Mexico City's population of 20 million is expected to double by 2025. The world is faced with the consequences of global warming: 'holes', caused by atmospheric pollution, have appeared in the ozone layer that protects us from the sun's lethal ultraviolet light. There is already a new awareness – highlighted by the Earth Summit in Brazil in 1992 – of the need to conserve the planet's natural resources, such as wildlife and the rainforests. It is estimated that if rainforests continue to disappear at their present rate, there will be none left by 2050. Oil consumption is now so great that if alternative sources of energy are not further developed, oil supplies will also run out by 2050. Although the ending of the Cold War led to a reduction of nuclear weapons by the superpowers, an increasing number of countries possess them, not all of them politically stable. The world's previously most successful nations are being superseded by countries of the Pacific Rim, like Japan. Technological advances, such as virtual reality, are being used in space exploration. Already space stations orbit the earth and in 1997 the first pictures were received from Mars. The question 'is there anybody out there?' no longer seems impossible to answer, and the colonization of other planets no longer just a dream of science fiction writers.

World History
An Overview

Early Civilizations of Asia

Before History

Origins

Scientists estimate that the earth was formed some 4600 million years ago. Fossils of the simplest animals and plants have been found in rocks dating from 1000 million years later. The early development of life within those ancient seas was inconceivably slow. The first land plants and animals evolved in the Silurian age, over 400 million years ago. The great dinosaurs ruled the earth for the 160 million years of the Mesozoic Era, which ended some 65 million years BC. The extinction of these giants provided the opportunity for the family of mammals to begin their colonization of the planet.

Some two million years ago, several groups of primates living around the forest edge in Africa began to show characteristics that might be called 'human'. These creatures began to plan their hunting expeditions and their use of weapons. Other animals use tools – no other animal makes tools for something it plans to do tomorrow!

Still, the development of man into the species *homo sapiens* remained immensely slow. Some evolutionary pathways proved to be dead ends. But the spread of the family of man was relentless. For hundreds of thousands of years, small bands of these evolving people moved into new environments, hunting and gathering their food as they went. The animal, man, proved remarkably adaptable, surviving the cold of the ice ages and the heat of the tropics.

The First Agricultural Revolution

The last ice age rolled back some 12,000 years ago, leaving the world with much the same climate that it has retained until today. Comparatively shortly afterwards some people began to introduce major changes into the timeless pattern of life.

Wheat and barley live naturally in the area between eastern Turkey and the Caspian Sea. At some time people – probably the women – learnt that it was possible to plant the seeds and so reduce the work of gathering. Soon these new farmers began to select which seeds produced the best crop, and so improved the quality of the crops.

The introduction of cereal farming had radical effects on human life. Tribal groups lost their mobility as they had to settle in one place to tend the crops. When, in time, one group began to produce a surplus, it had to defend its goods against attack. Settlements then needed to be fortified and a military class grew up within the community. Once a community was producing a surplus of food, some people could undertake specialized roles within the community.

The domestication of animals was, no doubt, a long process. There was no sharp dividing line between the time when the people followed herds of wild animals as hunters, and the time when they drove the animals as herders. During the same years after the last ice age, people of southern Asia and Europe domesticated sheep, cattle and pigs. In the millennia that followed, tribesmen from the mountains of northern Iran and the steppes of Central Asia tamed the horse and camel.

Scholars differ about the pattern of development of settled agriculture. The traditional view was that all innovation happened in the Fertile Crescent of the Middle East, and skills spread outward, like ripples on a pond. Others hold that settled agriculture was discovered in many different places as conditions favoured it. Certainly the new methods appeared across Europe, as well as in India and Africa in the millennia that followed. Developments in the Far East and the Americas, at least, were independent of those in the Fertile Crescent. Millet and rice were cultivated in China and South East Asia from about 6000 BC. Here chicken, water buffalo and, again, pigs were domesticated. Change came later in the Americas, where maize, potatoes and other important crops were added to the world's store.

The Growth of Cities

As the agricultural age continued, so people began to gather into yet larger communities. The earliest discovered is Jericho, which grew up before 8000 BC. Two thousand years later, Catal Hüyük, in Anatolia, covered 32 acres. These cities provided protection and allowed for greater specialization of role for the inhabitants.

New skills were, indeed, needed. Copper was smelted in Anatolia in about 7000 BC, introducing the age of metals. The earliest known pottery and evidence of the first woollen textiles have both been found in Catal Hüyük.

City life also provided a centre for religious worship. A temple lay at the heart of the community, and religion and government were always closely allied to each other. The change in lifestyle brought with it a change in religious practice. Cave paintings, such as those of southern France give a glimpse of the cults of the hunter gatherers, which focused on animals and sacred places. These have much in common with the practices of people, like some North American Indians, who lived similar lives within historical times.

Settled agriculture brought with it a new emphasis on birth and fertility, symbolized by the mother goddess figures found from widely dispersed areas of this early civilized world.

Sumerian Civilization

Irrigation

As would be expected, the earliest developments in city life happened in regions that had adequate natural rainfall. Some time after 5000 BC, however, groups from the north began to settle in the dry land of Mesopotamia. Here they drained the marshes and used the water from the twin rivers Tigris and Euphrates to irrigate the fertile land.

The Rise of the Sumerian Cities

It appears as though two of the most vital inventions in the history of humans – the wheel and the plough – were made in Mesopotamia in around 3500 BC. These enabled farmers to cultivate the irrigated land in a more concentrated manner, so increasing the surplus production, leading to a spectacular flourishing of cities.

The most famous city, Ur of the Chaldees, was only one; also prominent were Eridu, Uruk, Badtibira, Nippur and Kish. Each city had its own special deity, and it served as the centre for a surrounding region of villages and farm land.

The Evolution of Writing

In about 3100 BC the people of these Sumerian cities learnt how to represent their spoken language by the use of writing. The earliest characters were pictographic, and remain largely undeciphered. The Sumerians later developed the more flexible cuneiform script. The invention of writing marks the beginning of history, but the earliest documents were unremarkable. Written on the tablets of clay are lists showing the ownership of jars of oil and bundles of reeds. They do show, however, that some of the inhabitants were gathering serious wealth, which could be measured in hundreds and thousands of units.

Life in Sumeria

The cities were walled, but it appears that, in the early centuries, this was not a world of warring cities. Disputes were controlled by the exchange of embassies and by dynastic marriages, rather than by conflict. The laws that governed behaviour were not particularly strict.

The area was short of both wood and stone, and the Sumerian people depended heavily on clay for building and many other functions. The skills of the artisans became ever more refined. Gold, silver, bronze and polished stones were made into fine objects for the decoration of people, homes and temples. Weavers, leather workers and potters followed their specialized crafts. The scribes of later centuries wrote down a fine oral tradition of myths, epics and hymns. The world in which small family groups of hunters lived in cooperation had now been left far behind. Everyday life was controlled by a highly developed bureaucracy, which – for good or ill – was to become a hallmark of civilization. Kings were now divine beings, who were buried, not only with treasure, but also with their whole retinue to see them safely into the next life.

Egypt

In about 3200 BC, King Menes united the whole of the land of the lower Nile. The deserts that stretched on both sides of the river largely protected the Egyptians against the invasions that plagued Mesopotamia. Egyptian rulers had to face the armies of Assyria and 'The People of the Sea' from the Mediterranean, but the remarkable endurance of Egyptian civilization owes much to its isolation. Despite this, the Egyptians owed much to the Sumerians. In particular, they borrowed the early Sumerian system of writing, and adapted this into their own pictorial script. *Hieroglyphics* means 'the writing of the priests' and the art remained a closely guarded secret within the priestly caste.

For more than two thousand years dynasties followed one another; the country experienced bad times as well as good, but a continuity was maintained, unparalleled in the history of the world. Even when the land later fell under foreign rulers, Egyptian culture retained its remarkable integrity.

The Nile Waters

Egypt depended on the Nile. This was a kindlier river than the Tigris and Euphrates because each year it flooded the land on either side, providing natural irrigation for the fertile soil. The whole of Egyptian life was attuned to the rise and fall of the great river. The ruler – or pharaoh, as he would later be called – was the owner of the land and the giver of its life, and the ceremonials of kingship centred on the fertility of the land. The Book of Exodus describes how the rulers of Egypt were able to organize the storage of surpluses from good years to guard against crop failures in bad years.

The Calendar

The Egyptians studied the movements of the sun and stars, and they were the first to work out the year, consisting of $364\frac{1}{4}$ days. For the Egyptian farmer, this year was divided into three parts, each of four months – one of flooding, one of planting and one of harvesting.

The Capital Cities

Menes set up his capital in Memphis. Later pharaohs moved it to Thebes, but neither were true cities, like those of Sumeria. Their role was more as a centre of religion than a focus for daily life.

The wide deserts provided more protection from enemies than any city walls. Because of this physical isolation, Egyptian life could remain focused on the villages, rather than on larger centres of population.

Monuments and Art

The massive monuments of ancient Egypt remain objects of wonder. Imhotep, builder of the Step Pyramid at Saqqara, has left his name as the first architect known to history. Many thousands were marshalled to build these tombs for the rulers, working without winches, pulleys, blocks or tackles.

A modern visitor will look with awe at the pyramids and other great stone monuments, but it is the more modest paintings that give insight into the daily lives of the people. They show scenes of busy rural life, where peasants gather crops and hunt wild fowl on the banks of the Nile. They are happily free from the scenes of carnage and inhumanity, which are all too common in much of the art of the period. It was a world in which women had a high status and beauty was admired.

No doubt the peasants had to work hard to keep not only themselves but the whole apparatus of royal and priestly rule, but the river was kind and the land was fertile, and there was usually enough for all.

Migration and Trade

Semites and Indo-Europeans

The Semites were herders of sheep who originated in the Arabian peninsula. They were a warrior people, reared in the stern disciplines of life at the desert edge. The most powerful group in those early years them were a people called the Amorites. They founded cities to the north of Sumer – Babylon, Nineveh and Damascus. The Indo-Europeans were mainly cattle herders, who made their way into Mesopotamia from the north. Their gods emerge in the Pantheon of Greece and in the Vedic deities of India.

The Indo-Europeans had learned how to tame horses from their Asian neighbours. Most importantly, they brought iron. Iron weapons and chariots gave them a technological advantage over the earlier inhabitants of Mesopotamia. Control of iron therefore became an essential precondition of political power. The slow spread of iron technology had other important effects. An iron plough could break in land that had hitherto been too hard for agriculture. This created a rise in production, and hence an increase in population.

The Growth of Trade

Newcomers from both north and south were drawn into Mesopotamia by the rich lifestyle of the cities. But it happened that the area had no significant iron deposits, and was generally poor in other metals. This urgent need for raw materials was to be the driving force for the development of trade in the ancient world.

Money

It is remarkable how much trade was carried on before the development of currency as a method of exchange. Merchants from the civilized Fertile Crescent were able to take a range of manufactured goods to exchange for metals and other raw materials. Goods were also moved around the world as tribute, taxes and offerings to temples. The first coins date from about 700 BC, but their use spread slowly. Egypt, for instance, did not introduce a currency until about 400 BC.

Land Transport

The wheel was of no value in a world without roads. Columns of pack animals began to spread out from the Near East into the highlands of Iran and, through the Balkans, into metal rich Europe, opening up trade routes that would be trampled for many centuries.

Sea Transport

Improvements in the design of ships followed. Oars and sails were developed and rigging improved; decks were made watertight. The Red Sea and Persian Gulf became navigable all the year round, and the Mediterranean at least in summer. The growth in sea transport would ultimately change the centre of gravity of early civilizations away from the inland rivers towards the coastal regions. Ideas and empires could now spread along sea as well as land routes.

Against this background, the empires of the ancient Near East rose and fell.

Babylon, Assyria and the Hittites

Babylon

In 1792 BC, a ruler called Hammurabi came to power in the Semite city of Babylon. He can be looked upon as the first great emperor in the history of the world. Hammurabi's armies carried Babylonian power across most of the Fertile Crescent, from the Persian Gulf and the old Sumerian cities in the east, to the edge of mountains of Asia Minor and the borders of Syria in the west. Conquest was undertaken to secure essential supplies by the control of trade routes, and the exaction of tribute. Carvings show endless lines of conquered people bearing products to swell the stores of the great king, and the riches of Babylon became famous throughout the region.

Hammurabi was an absolute ruler, but he was anxious that his subject should know the laws under which they had to order their lives. He therefore set up pillars in the temples on which were engraved all the laws that governed his kingdom, so that his subjects would be able to come and refer to them. This Code of Hammurabi was the first statement of the principle of 'An eye for an eye'.

Astrology played a vital role in all decision taking, and this led to Babylonians to study the stars closely. By 1000 BC their astrologers had plotted the paths of the sun and the planets with great accuracy, and they were able to predict eclipses. They instituted the system under which the circle is divided into 360 degrees and the hour into 60 minutes.

The first great period of Babylonian power ended when the city was destroyed by the Hittites in 1600 BC. After that, Babylon remained an important centre of trade and culture, but a thousand years would pass before the city would achieve a late flowering of political power, under the great king Nebuchadnezzar.

The Hittites

The Hittites, who destroyed the first Babylon, were an Indo-European people who had come into the area from the north, probably through the Balkans. After defeating Babylon, they dominated an even larger empire than that of Hammurabi, across the sweep of the fertile crescent, from their homeland in Anatolia, Asia Minor to the Persian Gulf and the borders of Egypt. The power of the Hittites was based on skill with iron. It was they who carried iron technology across the region.

Hittite power collapsed in its turn under pressure from the 'People of the Sea', who were also harassing Egypt at the same time. These People of the Sea, however, did not follow up their successes by founding an empire. Rather, they left a vacuum that was to be filled by the most terrible of the empires of the Ancient Near East.

Assyria

The centre of power now moved to the city of Nineveh on the middle reaches of the Tigris. Monuments of the great kings of Assyria, like Tiglath-Pileser I and Ashurbanipal show an empire based on brute military force and the use of terror to control conquered people. Whole populations, like the lost ten tribes of Israel, were moved from their homeland and resettled in other parts of the empire. In this way they lost the identity on which national resistance could be built.

Assyrian armies dominated the region from the twelfth to the seventh centuries BC. They marched north into the highlands of modern Turkey and Iran, looking for metals and other necessary supplies. They conquered Syria and Palestine, and, under Ashurbanipal in the mid-seventh century BC, they even drove the Pharaohs of Egypt out of the Nile delta.

The Hebrews

Among the Semite invaders into the Near East was a group known as the Hebrews. The Bible record tells how Abraham, the father of the people, left the city of Ur to return to a purer nomadic way of life. His descendants experienced a period of bondage in Egypt, from which they emerged in about 1300 BC.

The Hebrews made their home in Palestine, and they had set up a monarchy by about 1000 BC. Hebrew power reached its peak under King Solomon, who died in 935 BC. The kingdom then split; Israel, the northern kingdom, was destroyed by Assyria in 722 BC and Judah, the southern, by Babylon in 587 BC.

The Hebrews do not feature in world history by virtue of their political success but because of their religious faith. They proclaimed a single deity whom they called Yahweh. The sacred writings of the Hebrews have been one of the major influences on the subsequent history of the world. Some themes need, therefore, to be identified.

Monotheism

Initially Yahweh was seen as the God of the Hebrews, who was set over against the gods of other peoples of the area. In time, however, Yahweh began to develop a uniqueness that challenged the existence of other gods. A writer from the period of the Babylonian exile pronounced Yahweh to be the god of the non-Hebrew, as well as the Hebrew people.

Divine Law

The rulers of Babylon and Assyria were absolute monarchs, whose word was law and whose actions therefore could not be judged by any superior authority. The Hebrew prophetic tradition, in contrast, made it clear that a king, no less than any other person, operated under a divine law. Here, a ruler, who has unjustly taken a common man's vineyard, can be challenged by a prophet with the words 'Thou art the man!'

Man and Nature

The Hebrew creation myth, which was handed down verbally for many centuries before being written into the Book of Genesis, clearly sets man apart from the rest of creation. He is made in the image of God and given dominion over the beasts. The Bible has been the vehicle that has transmitted this perspective into Western culture.

Male-centred Religion

The Old Testament narrative describes the fierce rejection of female fertility gods of the Fertile Crescent, which the Hebrews described as The Abomination of Desolation. For the Hebrews divinity was uncompromisingly male, and woman is depicted as a secondary creation, born out of man's side. This rejection of the female strand of religion would later be modified in Catholic Christianity in the cult of the Virgin, but it has been influential in defining western attitudes on the relationship of the sexes.

Persia

In about the year 1000, Aryan people moved south into the land that is now Iran (the land of the Aryans). There were two dominant tribes; the Medes occupied the north of the country, while the Persians occupied the south.

In the early centuries the Medish tribes were subject to the Assyrians, but they rebelled against their masters, and in 612 BC Nineveh was sacked and the Assyrian Empire was destroyed by the army of the Medes. The success of the Medes, as of the Persians after them, was based on their successful harnessing of the horse as an instrument of war.

The power centre shifted south when the Persian King Cyrus united Medes and Persians to form what was to become the greatest empire of the Near East. At its height, it extended from Greece and North Africa in the west to the Indus valley and the edge of the Central Asian steppe in the east. Darius the Great had problems at either edge of the empire – with Greeks in the west and Scythians in the east – but the bulk of the empire held together well until 330 BC.

The official Persian religion was Zoroastrianism. This emphasized the struggle of good and evil, and was to give the Semites the concept of angels and hell fire. It did not, however, seek converts, and the people of the empire were left in peace with their own gods. Cyrus was greeted by the Jews as the instrument of Yahweh, and he even rebuilt King Solomon's temple.

Darius was not as successful a conqueror as Cyrus, but he was an administrator of genius. Once a region had been brought within the empire, the royal satrap worked to win the trust and loyalty of the conquered people. Regional traditions were respected and local people were given responsibility in managing their own affairs. The country was bound together by roads, which could be used for trade and even postal services, as well as for armies.

At its peak, the Persian Empire reached as far as the Indus valley. This was the home of another, distinct Asian civilization.

India

The Harappa Culture

Remains have been found in the Indus Valley of cities, dating from about 2550 BC. The pictogram writing of these early Harappa people has not been deciphered, but archaeologists have discovered houses, with bathrooms, built of burnt brick. There are remains of canals and docks, and Indian products from this period have been excavated in Mesopotamia. Rice was grown, which may indicate that the cities had contact with the Far East. Here is the first evidence of cultivated cotton.

The Harappan cities had houses, granaries and temples, but no palaces. This suggests that the civilization was centred around the priests, rather than around warrior kings. They were therefore probably ill equipped to meet the challenge of invaders.

The Aryans

In about 1750 BC Indo-European Aryans began to penetrate into the land from the north. They herded the cattle, which were to become sacred creatures. Their religion is enshrined in the oldest holy books of the world, known as the Vedas. From these it is possible to get an image of nomadic people, standing round their camp fire at night, chanting hymns to the sun and other forces of nature.

The Aryans overran the northern part of the continent, but they did not completely destroy the people who had been there before them. They slowly spread from the Indus, clearing the dense forest of the Ganges Valley and founding cities, such as Benares.

Hindu Castes

The racial structure of Aryan and non-Aryan people became enshrined in the caste system of India. There were three 'twice born' castes, which are assumed to originate from the Aryan invaders. The *Brahmins* were the priests, the *Ksahiyas*, were warriors and the *Varsyas*, were farmers and merchants. Only members of these castes were permitted to take part in the Vedic rituals.

The *Sudras*, who came below the lowest member of the twice-born castes accommodated the conquered people. Below them were the unclean *outcasts*, who did not enjoy any caste status.

The Cults

As time passed, people looked for religious expressions that could engage the emotions more fully than the Vedic hymns. The cults surrounding the gods *Vishnu* and *Shiva*, with their consorts, fulfilled their needs. It appears that Shiva, at least, was drawn from older pre-Aryan India. The cult of Shiva, who represented the great cycle of birth and death, life and destruction, was to express the Hindu world view most completely.

Buddhism

In the early part of the sixth century BC a prince of the warrior caste, called Siddartha Gautara, later entitled Buddha, left his home to seek enlightenment. He first followed the strict Hindu practice of fasting, but he did not achieve his objective. In the end he found that true enlightenment could only be discovered by 'letting go' of his own self, and accepting that, in life, all things are changing. The Buddha rejected the caste system and his teachings took his followers out of Hinduism.

Although Hinduism and Buddhism separated, any contest for supremacy lay in the mind, for there were no wars of religion, like those that were to mark the West. The two religions share the same root. Both see man as an integral part of the natural world, not as a creature set apart from, and above it, as in the Hebrew tradition.

Buddhism received a great impetus with the conversion of the north Indian king Ashoka in 260 BC. He abandoned his career of conquest and administered his kingdom in the light of the teaching, providing the people with social works and good laws. In the end, Hinduism was to retain its hold on the subcontinent, apart from Ceylon (Sri Lanka) in the south and the mountains of Tibet in the north, while Buddhism made its impact further east.

Central Asia

Across the Himalayas from India lay the great land mass of central Asia. This can be divided into three bands. Furthest north was the great wall of the forests of Siberia. The centre consists of the Asian grasslands. In the south are the deserts and mountains. The last two are influential in world history from the earliest times until about 1500 AD.

In the grasslands of the steppe lived a selection of nomadic tribes. They survived in marginal land, much as, in later times, the Plains Indians would survive on the American prairie. The nomadic life could take peoples right across the grasslands, and they often fought each other for the control of land. Because the plain could only support a small population, drought, war or other impulses could set whole peoples on the move. This would produce a knock-on effect. Ripples could grow to waves. These would then break onto the boundaries of the lands that bordered on the steppes.

These were illiterate people, so their names and history are confused, but they appear in history as the Hsiungnu or Huns, the Avars, the Scythians, the Turks and the Mongols. They were terrible foes, who won their battles by great mobility and superb mastery of the horse.

Further south, in the desert region, lay the trade routes. From very early times Bactrian camels and horses carried goods along these trade routes, creating a link between Europe and the Near East to the west and China to the east. Most of the goods moved from east to west. At an early date, the Chinese learnt to make fine fabric from the web of the silk worm. Pepper and other spices also made light and high value loads. It was an immense and dangerous journey, but the profits were incentive enough to keep the caravans moving.

China

Isolation and Contact

The people of China have long known their nation as *Chung-hua,* the Central Nation. Educated people knew well of the existence of other cultures, but they were looked on as subordinate, and, indeed, tributaries of the great nation. Although the Chinese did maintain contact with the outside world, they were little influenced by it. Chinese culture was therefore able to establish a structure in the early centuries, which remained little altered throughout history.

The immediate concern of Chinese rulers, again from very early times, was to defend the northern borders against the steppe nomads. This border, which would be marked by the world's greatest building work, The Great Wall, lay along the line where the decline in rainfall made settled agriculture impracticable.

Culture and Language

The huge country centred on three rivers, the Hwang-Ho, the Yangtse and the Hsi. They were divided by great mountain ridges. A wide range of climates could be found within the nation. China has been politically divided for long periods, but she has maintained a unity of culture, beyond that achieved by any other people. An important reason for this is that, while the people of the west came to use to a phonic script, China retained the use of pictograms. The difference is fundamental. A phonic script is easily learned, but it needs to reflect the sounds of a language. People of different languages are therefore unable to communicate with each other without learning each other's language. This is inevitably culturally divisive. A pictogram script, in contrast, is hard to learn, but it is not linked to the sound of language. It can therefore be used to bind people who speak differently. China therefore developed a power to absorb and civilize the conquerors who, from time to time, spilled over her frontiers.

Literacy was the property of a cultured elite, whose whole education had, of necessity, been centred on diligence rather than creativity. This gave Chinese culture the twin characteristics of breadth and stability.

The State

Around 1700 BC, the first historical dynasty, the Shang, gained control of the northern Hwang-Ho river valley. Even at this early stage, the court had archivists and scribes. Like their successors of later dynasties, the kings saw themselves as the bringers of civilization to barbarian peoples.

About 1100 BC the Shang were overthrown by the Chou who carried royal power to the central Yangtse river valley. Then, around 700 BC, the Chou in their turn were overthrown by pastoralists from the north. This brought in the time graphically known as the Period of the Warring States.

Confucianism

During this period there lived K'ung-fu-tsu, who became known to the world as Confucius. He looked back from that period of unrest to an earlier time when the world was at peace and believed that the problems of his times arose from the fact that people had forgotten their proper duty. In an ordered world, everyone had a place in society. Some – rulers, parents, husbands – were 'higher'; others – subjects, children, wives – were 'lower'. Everyone, high and low, was bound together in ties of mutual duty and respect. The high had no more right to oppress the low than the low had to be disrespectful of the high. When these bonds were broken, the times became out of joint.

Confucianism therefore placed emphasis on 'conservative' institutions – the state, the civil service, scholarship, and, above all, the family. It was not a religion, in the sense of teaching about God, but it brought a religious dimension to the worship of ancestors.

Social Structure

K'ung-fu-tsu accepted the most fundamental division in Chinese society. The common peasants were not allowed to belong to a clan, and they therefore had no ancestors to worship. Their lives consisted of an endless round of toil.

For those who were, more fortunately, born into a clan, China would become a land of opportunity. Even boys from poor homes could study to pass the necessary examinations, which would open up the coveted civil service jobs. For those with more modest aspirations, growing cities offered opportunities in trade and the crafts.

The fortunate lived in an assurance that Chinese customs and the Chinese way offered the model of excellence, and all other people had to be judged according to the way in which they measured up to this standard.

Mediterranean Civilization

Early Seagoing People

Conquering the Oceans

The earliest civilizations centred on major river valleys. The rivers provided water and arteries of communication. Then the technology of sails and shipbuilding improved to a level that enabled men to venture onto the oceans. From early times, the Red Sea and the Persian Gulf provided important communication routes, which were orientated towards the east. The Mediterranean, particularly in winter, is subject to violent storms. Further advances in marine engineering, such as the construction of watertight holds and improvements in sails and rigging, were needed before sailors could master this environment.

By about 500 BC ships were able to move freely in the Mediterranean, at least in summer, so providing easier communication than was possible on land. There was then no distinction between a fertile north and an arid north shore. The whole region was fertile. Traders and rulers therefore saw the Mediterranean basin as a single unit, bound together by its ocean highway.

Minoa and Mycenae

In about 2200 BC a civilization grew up on Crete, which has been named after its King Minos. Its earliest writing has not been deciphered, but excavations reveal fine palaces and developed communities. Their cities stood beside the sea, and the builders were already confident enough in the control of their ships over the eastern Mediterranean to dispense with fortifications.

Objects found in Crete and Egypt show that there was a lively trade between the two cultures. The Minoan sailors probably traded in timber, wood, olive oil and grapes over the whole of the Mediterranean area.

Inhabitants of the Minoan cities were the first people to enjoy the benefits of piped drains and sewers, and wall paintings show them dancing and playing sports, including the Minoan speciality of bull leaping.

The Minoans set up colonies on the mainland, of which the most important seems to have been at Mycenae. This is the name that is given to Minoan civilization as it is found on the mainland. The culture spread across the Aegean to the coast of Asia Minor and to the city of Troy at the mouth of the Bosphorus.

The first Minoan civilization was destroyed by Indo-European people who poured into the region from the north. Some of these invaders settled in the Ionian peninsula to become Greeks. A later resurgence of Minoan civilization is thought to have been under Greek influence.

The stories written down centuries later by the poet Homer tell of the struggles between the Mycenaens of Troy and the less advanced Indo-European invaders.

The Phoenicians

Semite people, in general, liked to keep their feet on dry land. The exception were the people who lived in the area known as Phoenicia, which is now Lebanon and southern Syria. They developed remarkable skills as sailors and for centuries their ships dominated the trade routes. Phoenician sailors reached the Atlantic Ocean and traded with tin miners in distant Cornwall. The Greek historian Heroditus even reports that one expedition rounded the southern cape of Africa.

The Phoenicians planted colonies to protect their trade routes. Most important, in about 800 BC they founded the city of Carthage. The colony was strategically placed to protect the ships that brought metal from Western Europe.

Phoenicia was never a power on land and, when, in 868 BC the Assyrian king 'washed his weapons in the Mediterranean' Phoenicia lost its independence. But the rulers of the great empires needed these fine sailors, and the Phoenicians therefore exercised influence beyond their military power.

Phoenicia is best known for its sailors. It did, however, make another major contribution to western culture, by creating a phonic alphabet. The words alpha, beta and gamma are derived from the Phoenician words for an ox, a house and a camel.

The Greeks

In Mycenaean times, an iron-working Aryan people were moving south into the Greek peninsula. Myths of early battles with Mycenaean Troy are preserved in the works of the storyteller – or tellers – given the name of Homer.

The early culture was oral, but, in around 750 BC the Greeks adopted and modified the Phoenician alphabet and committed the ancient legends to writing. These were to provide the starting point for the world's first great literary culture.

The beginning of Greek civilization was dated from the first Olympian Games, held in 776 BC. This event, held once every four years, drew together people who shared the Greek language and culture. The participants did not, however, come under one unified government.

Government

The Greek political structure was dictated by the geography of the region in which they settled. This was a land of mountain ranges, with small coastal plains that faced outwards to the sea. Each of these plains was settled by a self-governing community, which initially contained only as many people as the land would support. This was the basis of the *polis*, or city state.

Homer's *Iliad* provides a picture of an early feudal society of kings, nobles and common fighting men. Each city then followed its own course in working out the structure of government. The first struggle lay between the kings (monarchy) and the nobles (aristocracy). Then pressure came from other influential citizens (oligarchy) and from the general mass of free male citizens (democracy). When a state plunged into chaos, a strong man (tyranny), who was often benevolent and public spirited, would emerge to bring order to the polis.

The Greek concept of democracy was specific to the confined structure of the city state. It did not operate through representative institutions, but through the direct participation of citizens in the decision taking process. The meeting place, or *agora*, not the temple or the royal palace, was now the centre of city life. The citizens who met here provided the city with its law courts and its political assembly. Debate and persuasion became vital skills. People could on occasion be swept away by the power of a demagogue, but within this forum they learned to listen and to analyse argument.

The fractured nature of Greek society did not provide peace and stability. The city states might join together in games, but they were as often at war with each other. For both good and ill, the people remained fiercely independent, more ready than any other people before, and perhaps even since, to question the structure of the society within which they lived.

Colonization

Since geography prevented expansion inland, the Greeks had an impetus to expand outwards, along the sea routes. Greek communities were established along the west and south coasts of Asia Minor, on the islands of the Aegean and as far east as Cyprus and westwards to Sicily and southern Italy, and even further into North Africa, France and Spain. These colonies were self-governing, but they often had links with powerful city states, such as Corinth or Athens. They served both as an overspill for excess population and also as trading bases across the Mediterranean Sea.

The Persian Wars

The conflict between Greece and Persia has been depicted as a struggle between an oppressive empire and a freedom loving people. Reality is more complex. Close links had long existed between the Greeks and the Persians and many Greeks served within the Persian army. The trouble started when Greek city states in Asia Minor rebelled against Persian rule and Darius moved to put down the insurrection. The Asians were supported by the European Greeks, and this brought the Persian Empire into conflict with an alliance of Greek cities, led by Athens and Sparta. The army of Darius was defeated at Marathon in 490 BC and the navy, led by his successor Xerxes, failed ten years later at Salamis. This war drew the boundary of the Persian Empire to the east of the area of Greek settlement.

Athens and Sparta

The alliance that had defeated Persia did not survive the victory. Athens was much the largest of the city states, with a larger population than its farm land could support. Prosperity was based on the control of silver mines, which were worked by thousands of slaves. The city's very survival therefore depended on a structure of trade and colonies. Whatever freedom may have been enjoyed by Athenian citizens within their city, their rule of others was often oppressive. The Athenians demanded heavy tribute from client states and put down rebellion as violently as any Persian army.

Other trading states, like Corinth, felt themselves continually threatened by Athenian power. They found allies in the conservative, agricultural state of Sparta. The Peloponnesian War lasted for 27 years, and ended with the defeat of Athens in 404 BC. This led to a reaction against an over-mighty Sparta, and the destructive sequence of wars continued into the fourth century. The Greeks may have provided the world with a vocabulary of politics and an ideal of democracy, but its outstanding achievement lies, not in politics, but in broader fields of culture.

Religion

Greek myth is drawn from the common Indo-European root, which created the Vedas (the sacred writings of Hinduism) in India. It has provided a fertile source of inspiration for western art and literature for more than 2000 years, but it is harder to look back through the twin filters of Semitic religion and rationalism, which have shaped modern attitudes, to understand what the world of gods meant to the Greeks themselves. On the one side, there was a piety of the common man, which condemned Socrates for blaspheming against the gods; on the other side there was a freethinking strain, expressed by Miletus a philosopher of the seventh century, who declared 'If an ox could paint a picture, its god would look like an ox'. The Greek religious tradition was real, but it was not an all-demanding way of life, like that of the Hebrews.

Philosophy and Science

The Greeks invented organized abstract thought and took it to a level that would dominate the philosophy of the Near East and Europe until very recent times. In the Greek perspective, there was no distinction between the arts, the sciences, and, indeed, religion. All were a part of the search for truth. In the sixth century, Pythagoras did not distinguish mathematics from philosophy and religion. The two greatest Greek thinkers defined the twin, often opposing, channels through which all philosophy, and later, all theology, would flow.

Plato, a pupil of Socrates, was 23 years old when his home city of Athens was defeated by Sparta. His attempt to achieve a mental order was therefore born of the political disorder of the post war years. Plato is the apostle of the *ideal* – the abstract of perfection, whether it be for the state, the individual, or in a mathematical equation. In his philosophy, all life is a striving towards an ideal of the good, containing truth, justice and beauty, which was the only reality in an imperfect world. Plato's Academy can lay claim to being the world's first university.

Aristotle came to Plato's Academy at the age of 17 and remained his master's devoted disciple. His interests, however, took him in the opposite direction, as he came to emphasize enquiry and experiment as the source of knowledge. While Plato stressed the *ideal*, Aristotle stressed the *real*; while Plato was drawn into the abstractions of mathematics, Aristotle found himself fascinated by the complexities of biology and literary criticism. For him, truth lay not in a distant abstract, but in a 'happy medium'. Aristotle is therefore seen as the father of the scientific method.

The Arts

Fifth-century Athens provided the most fertile environment for classical Greek culture. The architecture of the Parthenon, the sculptures of Praxiteles and Pheidias provide an illustration in stone of the Platonic ideal. They provided generations of architects and artists, particularly from Europe, with a standard of perfection. Literature also flourished. Aeschylus, Sophocles and Euripides used the ancient myths to explore depths of the human experience and create tragic drama, while the irreverent Aristophanes pioneered the tradition of comedy. The disasters of the Peloponnesian Wars also inspired Thucydides to become the world's first scientific and literary historian.

The contribution of Greece to the world's cultural store is a fundamental theme of history. By the middle of the fourth century, however, the advances were largely confined to the Greek speaking world. The diffusion of Greek culture into a wider world would be the work of a young and brilliant student of Aristotle.

The Hellenistic World

Alexander the Great

The state of Macedon lay to the north of Greece. It crossed the boundary that divided the civilized world from the barbarians. Philip II of Macedon developed his army into an efficient fighting machine and conquered the Greek city states. Philip died in 336 BC and was succeeded by Aristotle's pupil, his son, Alexander.

Alexander inherited his father's army and the Greek power base. The problem he faced was how he coul pay the soldiers who had served Macedon so well. This search for money took Alexander the Great o spectacular campaigns. There was ample booty to be won across the Aegean in the Persian Empire. In 33 BC the Macedonian army defeated the Persians under their king, Darius III, at Issus. The army the marched south into Egypt, where Alexander founded the city that was to carry his name, Alexandria. H returned north, defeated the Persians once more and sacked the capital of Persepolis. Not content, he too his army eastward into Afghanistan and the Punjab. He would have gone further, but his soldiers insiste that the time had come to turn back.

The young man was one of the great soldiers of all time. The importance of his conquests, however, wa that they were the catalyst that brought together the old civilizations of the Near East and the newer Gree culture. Alexander was Greek, but he was drawn to Eastern ways. He himself married the Persian emper or's daughter, and, in a great symbolic gesture, he married nine thousand of his soldiers to eastern womer

The Division of the Empire

Alexander died in Babylon in 323 BC at the age of thirty-two, leaving no heir to succeed to his enormou empire. The land was divided between his generals. The Ptolemies based their power in Egypt, th Seleucids in the region of Syria and the Attalids around Pergamum. Parthia later became independent o the Seleucids. These were centralized states under absolute monarchs. The age of debate and democrac was certainly past. Over most of the Hellenistic world, this was a time of economic growth, but the Gree cities themselves declined.

Hellenistic Culture

Greek was now the official and commercial language of the whole area. The learning of the scholars be came widely known and great libraries were set up at Alexandria and Pergamum. Among the books pre served were many of the writings of Plato and Aristotle. Scholars in the Greek tradition worked in differer parts of the Hellenistic world. Science flourished, as it would not do again for over fifteen hundred year In Alexandria Euclid laid the foundation of geometry. Aristarchus correctly deduced the structure of th solar system eighteen hundred years before Copernicus and Eratosthenes measured the circumference c the earth. Archimedes of Syracuse had the widest ranging genius of all.

Philosophers, such as the Stoics, could no longer question the ways of government, so they turned thei thoughts towards the inner life of man. They led a quest for virtue and true contentment. Classical Gree styles provided powerful models for painters and sculptors, but Hellenistic artists retreated from the Pla tonic search for an ideal and worked instead to project the humanity of their subjects.

Religion

Greek religion was too restricted a vehicle for this new, expansive world. Mystery cults began to spreac which demanded a more active devotion from their followers. Two of these became increasingly dominan From Egypt came the myth of Isis and Osiris. This told of a dying and a rising god. From Zoroastrianisi came the mystery of Mithras, with its powerful image of redemption through blood.

The End of the Hellenistic World

The Hellenistic empires in their turn fell to a new power from further west in the Mediterranean. The Rc man victory at Actium in 31 BC marked the end of the era. No battle, however, could put an end to Gree culture. The Roman poet Horace summed it up by saying that, although Greece was defeated, it took it conquerors prisoner.

Republican Rome

The Etruscans

In the years before 509 BC, central Italy was dominated by a people called the Etruscans. They can be see in lifelike tomb sculptures, but little is known about their culture. They appear to have been an Indo-Euro pean people, who achieved dominance over other people by bringing iron working to a high level of pe fection. Etruscan kings, the Tarquins, ruled in Rome until they were expelled, according to tradition, in 50 BC. The expulsion of the kings remained a powerful myth within the Roman state. Men looked back to th days of the Tarquins as the time when the rights of the citizen were subjected to the will of a single individual

The Structure of the State

The new Roman state was based on agriculture. Indeed, *pecunia*, the name for a flock or herd of animal: became the Latin word for money.

There were different groups within society. The old families who took pride in their status as *patricians*, assumed power in place of the deposed kings. The remaining free people were known as the *plebeians* or *plebs*. At first they were poor farmers, with little say in affairs of state. As Rome grew, however, many plebeians became more wealthy and they began to look for a share in the running of affairs.

Romans, be they patricians or plebs, took immense pride in their status as citizens. Roman citizenship became a unique badge of belonging to a pure and strong society, free from the softness and corruption of the Hellenistic world around them. Every man was liable to military service, which could be for as long as sixteen years in the infantry or ten years in the cavalry. Warlike virtues were admired by society and inculcated in boys through the home and education. At best, this could breed a self-sacrifice to the common good; at worst, it could bring a lust for battle and bloodshed.

The organization of the Roman Republic was not unlike that of a Greek polis. The Roman *forum* took the place of the Greek agora. The *senate*, which was an assembly of patricians, wielded the real power. Two consuls, elected from its ranks, commanded the army in war and were responsible for government in time of peace. The demand of the plebs to be represented was met by the appointment of two tribunes. It therefore became possible for an unusually talented man, from a low family, to rise in the state. This structure lasted for 450 years. It carried Rome from being a small city state to dominance in the Mediterranean basin.

Early Expansion

In the early centuries, Roman armies were occupied with winning control over the Italian peninsula. If there was a ruthless character to Roman expansion, there could also be generosity in the terms given on surrender. Conquered people were given Roman citizenship and allowed a large measure of self-government. Once within Roman rule, they too were expected to provide troops for the army.

The Punic Wars

As Rome expanded, she had only one serious rival. Carthage had expanded beyond North Africa. Her ships controlled the sea and Carthaginian colonies were established in Sicily, Southern Italy and Spain. The two powers were bound to clash for supremacy in the western Mediterranean. The Romans built up a navy, and in the First Punic War (264–241 BC) they defeated the Carthaginians at sea and won Sicily.

The Second Punic War (264–241 BC) marked the decisive struggle between the two powers. When Hannibal crossed the Alps and defeated Roman armies at Lake Trasimene and Cannae, it seemed as though Roman power would be broken. In 202 BC, however, Hannibal was in turn defeated at Zama and Carthaginian power was destroyed. In 149 BC Rome took an excuse to fight a third Punic War. This time Carthage was flattened and the ground on which the city had stood was ploughed over.

The Rise of the Generals

Victory over Carthage had been bought at a high cost, and that cost was paid by the poor. Many peasant farmers, who were citizens, sold their land to the rich and so lost their means of support. This led to a period of internal unrest.

Wars were now being fought far from home, in the Hellenistic east and to the north in the land they called Gaul. Roads were built across the empire, which enabled the army legions to move swiftly from one trouble spot to another. These distant armies could no longer be commanded by consuls, with a term of office of two years.

There therefore arose a new breed of professional generals. These men often became fabulously rich on the booty of war, and, with a loyal army at their back, they could pose a threat to the traditional institutions of the Republic. Marius made his name in Africa and Gaul, and then Sulla in the eastern Mediterranean. Julius Caesar was the most successful in this line of successful generals. In 49 BC he took an irrevocable step when he crossed the River Rubicon, which marked the boundary of Italy, and marched on Rome at the head of his army. By this action he started the chain of events that led to his murder and the founding of imperial Rome.

Christianity

Origins

The early years of the Roman Empire were to see the beginnings of another of the great religions of the world. The Jewish people had maintained a stubborn refusal to dilute their religion to meet the demands of Hellenistic rulers. At the time of Jesus of Nazareth, sects like the Essenes and the Zealots maintained a resistance to Roman rule.

Jesus was a Jew, but he appears to have rejected the path of political resistance and taught instead a message of the relationship of the individual to God and other men, closer to the teaching of some later rabbis. The content of Jesus' teaching was indeed to be influential, but his significance lay not in what he said but in what his disciples declared him to be.

The share of responsibility for his execution can not be determined from the documents preserved, so it is unclear whether he was executed as a danger to the Roman state or as a critic of Jewish practice. Whichever it was, his disciples declared that they had witnessed his resurrection, and proclaimed that he was the Son of God. They picked up the words of the writer from the Babylonian exile and announced him as the saviour of the world, and not just of a chosen people. The holy books of the new religion were written down in the Greek language of the Hellenistic world, rather than in the more restricted Aramaic language that Jesus himself spoke.

Christianity and the Mysteries

Paul of Tarsus carried the message in a series of missionary journeys through the Greek speaking world. There he spoke the language of the popular mysteries – of redemption through blood and of a dying and rising god. With Christianity, however, it was different, he declared. While the mysteries were based in mere images, Christianity was rooted in historical fact.

Paul and other missionaries always sought to found a Christian cell, which they called an *ecclesia*, the word used for the meeting of the Greek polis. Hellenistic culture provided a language for the new religion; Rome provided a structure that enabled it to spread. Missionaries could make use of the Roman roads, and they were not likely to be molested by bandits on the way.

There was no doubting the enthusiasm of the converts, but, for a long time, an outsider would not have readily recognized a fundamental difference between this religion and the mysteries. Heresies, like Gnosticism and Manichaeism were pulling Christianity away from its Semitic roots into the maelstrom of Hellenistic religion. The Roman army generally favoured Mithras. A long path of persecution lay ahead before Christianity would emerge as the dominant religion of the region.

Imperial Rome

The Emperor

At the battle of Actium in 31 BC, Julius Caesar's great-nephew, Octavian, brought Egypt into the empire and ended the years of civil war. Four years later he was given the title of Augustus and made consul for life. He was careful to preserve the honoured republican institutions, but the senate lapsed into impotence and all power now lay with him.

No rule of inheritance was ever established for the position of emperor. In the centuries that were to follow, incompetents would be matched by administrators and generals of ability, imbeciles by philosophers. Most emperors died violently. Succession first passed through the house of Caesar. During one century of good government, it became the practice for an emperor to adopt his successor. For long periods, however, power fell to the general who could command the largest army. But the mass of people would never see the emperor in person. For them, success or failure had to be judged on whether he was strong enough to prevent the huge empire from breaking into civil strife.

The practice of emperor worship was imported from the old Persian tradition. The act of reverence due to the god-ruler was the symbol that bound together the hugely diverse people who now lay under Roman rule. Pious Jews refused to perform this ritual, but this was recognized to be a part of their ancient tradition and it was generally overlooked. The refusal of Christians, who came from all parts and races, was looked upon as a serious threat to the unity of the empire.

Buildings

The great monuments of Rome date from the Imperial age. Augustus himself restored eighty-two temples and boasted, 'I found Rome of brick and left it of marble'. Aqueducts, arches and the huge Colosseum still stand as monuments to Imperial glory. The Romans were content to copy Greek styles to which they added impressive engineering skills.

The more prosperous Roman citizens built homes, such as have been preserved at Pompeii and excavated across the empire. Here they built for comfort, and artists, working in paint and mosaic, expressed a less pretentious view of life with humour and grace.

Natural frontiers

The Roman armies had now carried the empire across Europe, Asia and Africa, until it had ten thousand miles of land frontier. Beyond lay barbarians, ever willing to invade and plunder. The task of defence was made easier by natural boundaries – the African and Arabian deserts and the great rivers Rhine and Danube. This line of defence had two weak points, lying on either side of the Black Sea. In Asia the entrance to the steppes lay open across the land of the Parthians. In Europe generals were tempted to go beyond the Danube, across what is now Romania to the Carpathian Mountains. Roman armies suffered heavy defeats in both of these sectors. Claudius also carried the empire across the natural frontier of the North Sea to Britain. The expedition was designed to bring the glory of conquest and to win control of fabled metal mines of the wild island.

The City of Rome

By imperial times, Rome had grown to be a huge city. Since most of the work was done by slaves, much of the population was unemployed, and the citizens had become accustomed to a lifestyle supported by tribute from conquered peoples. No emperor could contemplate unrest in Rome, so the citizens had to be fed and kept amused on the famous diet of bread and circuses. Entertainments were on a massive scale. The Circus Maximus alone seated 190,000 people. Claudius built the huge harbour at Ostia, where grain, wild beasts and slaves were constantly being unloaded to feed the stomachs and the jaded palates of the people. The city gave nothing back to its empire.

East and West

Gradually a distinction began to emerge between the eastern and the western parts of the empire. The West, centred on Rome itself, covered western Europe and the old Carthaginian lands of North Africa. The east included the old Hellenistic world of Greece, Asia Minor, the Near East and Egypt.

The eastern side of the empire had a better balance to life. It contained ancient cities, but none dominated the region. It was self-sufficient in grain, wood, oil, wine and other essentials, with a surplus to buy in metal from the west and luxuries from the east.

The western part of the empire was not an area of ancient civilization. Since Carthage had been flattened, it had no cities to balance the metropolis of Rome, which constantly sucked in products, so upsetting the economic balance of the region.

In 285 the Emperor Diocletian appointed a co-emperor to rule the western sector. There was now an Empire of the East and an Empire of the West. In 324 Constantine accepted the dominance of the East by taking his capital to his new city of Constantinople.

The Triumph of Christianity

By this time, Christianity had established itself as a growing force. Diocletian tried to stem the tide, but Constantine accepted the new faith. Emperor worship may now have ceased, but even a Christian emperor could not shed the concept that he was the fountain of religion. He declared himself to be the thirteenth apostle and sat as chairman of the Council of Nicea, which established Christian doctrine. This set a precedent for the control of the church by the state.

At about the same time a group of hermits came together in Egypt to form the first monastery in the Christian tradition. This was destined to grow into an influential movement, capable of confronting the ambitions of Christian rulers.

The Barbarian Invasions

The century after Constantine saw increasing pressure on the European frontier of the Western Empire. Far away in the east, the Huns were on the move, and this created pressure on western tribes. The Huns themselves erupted into Europe under Attila in 440, to be defeated at Troyes in 451, but ahead of them, as if a prow wave, came Goths, Ostrogoths, Visigoths, Franks and Vandals.

The Romans found it difficult to defend the long land frontier and they recruited barbarians to strengthen the army. In 376 about 40,000 armed Visigoths were allowed across the frontier. Then in 410 the Goths sacked Rome. Vandals, who left their name for mindless destruction, crossed through Spain into North Africa and then returned for an even more destructive assault on the great city.

In northern Europe, Angles, Saxons and Jutes crossed the North Sea, first to ravage and then to settle in the British Isles. The Celtic inhabitants, no longer protected by Roman legions, were driven back to the highland area of the West, and into Ireland, where the Christian faith survived and flourished.

Byzantium

Her Frontiers

With the ancient capital in barbarian hands, the Roman Empire can be said to have fallen. Those who lived in the Empire of the East, however, recognized no such catastrophe. In 483 Justinian succeeded in Constantinople, and he set about the task of winning back the lost western lands. His armies recovered North Africa, Italy and Southern Spain. It appeared for a time as though the Roman Empire was still a reality. His conquests, however, were ephemeral. From his time onwards, the Empire of the East was under continual pressure.

In the East, Persia was a power of consequence once again, and behind her the steppe nomads were ever menacing. In the south the empire faced growing Arab power. In the north, Slav people were pressing into the Balkans. The Emperor Heraclius led the Imperial armies in more successful campaigns, but the pressure was ever inwards towards what was to be the Byzantine heartland of Asia Minor, Greece, the Balkans and southern Italy.

Cultural Life

The people saw themselves as being direct inheritors of the old empire. Citizens of Constantinople still visited the bath houses; they still followed the chariot races with the passion of a modern football supporter. Justinian completed the work of centuries of Roman jurists by compiling the authoritative digest of Roman law.

Byzantium, however, soon developed a distinctive character that set it apart from the old empire. This drew both from the Greco-Roman and from Eastern traditions. Constantinople remained a home of classical scholarship. Plato was particularly popular, but his thinking became overlaid by layers of mysticism. Classical features were used in buildings, but the great dome that rose over Justinian's Church of the Holy Wisdom demonstrated new skills and a new aesthetic. Secular artists still worked within Hellenistic traditions, but religious artists, in paintings and mosaics, were beginning to express a particularly eastern Christian piety.

Religion

Early in the development of the eastern church there emerged a distinction between secular (living in the world) and religious (living out of the world) clergy. Secular clergy worked at the parish level and were allowed to marry. The ideal was set by the many hermits and monks who expressed their piety in extreme self-sacrifice. Religious icons became the focus of devotion for ordinary people.

The emperor maintained Constantine's position at the head of the church. Patriarchs, bishops and priests lay under his power. Emperors decided doctrine and mercilessly persecuted many of their subjects who held 'heretical' beliefs.

In the centuries after Justinian, the eastern and the western churches drew gradually further apart. In the west, the Bishop of Rome claimed primacy and began to build a centralized structure. The church finally divided into western and eastern parts in the Great Schism of 1054. This was partly about authority, partly about abstruse issues of theology, but it mainly stemmed from lack of understanding of each other's piety.

The Arabs

Mecca

The desert land of the Arabian peninsula was inhabited by fierce and independent minded Semitic tribes people, who were known as Arabs. They led a nomadic life of great hardship. One trade route between the Mediterranean and the Indian Ocean went across this land, passing through Mecca. The city was also a centre for pilgrimage to the sacred stone or *kaba*. The citizens of Mecca jealously guarded the revenues of both the trade and the pilgrimage.

Early in the seventh century a merchant, called Mohammed, had a vision and started preaching the message 'There is no god but Allah'. He came into conflict with the citizens of Mecca, and in 622 he left the city to live in Medina. This is the date from which the Arab world numbers its calendar.

Islam

The prophet Mohammed had met Christians and Jews and read many of their books, and the religion that he founded lies within the Semitic tradition. He preached one god, which for him ruled out the Christian concept of the Trinity. The word 'Islam' means 'submission', for the duty of the Muslim is to submit to the will of the one god. He gave his followers the five duties – daily prayers, alms, fasting, the keeping of Friday as a holy day, and the pilgrimage – but the message was one of great simplicity. Very quickly, the feuding tribes of the peninsula were given that sense of community, which has ever since been the distinguishing feature of Islam.

Mohammed taught his followers that Christians and Jews were 'people of the book'. They and their religion had, therefore to be treated with respect. Once they accepted Muslim rule, they might be taxed, but they should not be persecuted or converted by force.

The Arab Conquests

Once the Arabs were united, they started raiding towards the north in search of booty, into the lands controlled by Byzantium and Persia. Their invasions had startling and unexpected success, partly because the two empires had weakened one another by endless warfare. More important, however, was that taxation and religious persecution had made their governments deeply unpopular with the people. To 'heretical' Christians, the tolerant Muslim invaders seemed greatly preferable to either emperor.

The Persian Empire collapsed and Byzantium was pressed ever further backwards. Jerusalem fell in 638. It seemed as though Constantinople itself would fall, but in 717 the Arab armies were driven back from the city walls. By this time the Arabs not only controlled the Near East, but also North Africa and the whole of Spain. Their armies were even crossing the Pyrenees into the plains of Europe. Here, however, they found themselves in an alien environment of cold weather and barbarous people, so they turned back towards the south. The Arab armies carried Islam over this wide empire. Many conquered people converted; indeed Christianity disappeared completely from its old stronghold in North Africa.

The ultimate authority within the Islamic world lay with the caliphs. In 750 the ruling Umayyad house was overthrown and the new Abbasid rulers moved the capital to Baghdad.

Arab Culture

The Arabs possessed a powerful poetic tradition before the time of Mohammed and Islamic culture was founded in literature. The Koran, with its religious message and its classical language, provided a powerful unifying bond for one of history's more stable empires. Since the depiction of the human form was forbidden, art developed as elaborate geometric pattern. As the centre of empire moved out of the Arabian peninsula to Baghdad, so eastern influences became increasingly powerful. The Arabic language remained, however, the cement of the Islamic world. Although local dialects might vary, scholars from all parts continued to use the pure language of the Koran.

The Muslims did not come as the destroyers of civilization. The men from the desert quickly absorbed the cultures that they conquered. Their scholars read the Greek philosophers, and united them with the astronomy, mathematics and medicine of the east, so serving as the main channel for the ancient learning in a troubled world. Muslim civilization reached one of its peaks in Spain, where the university of Cordova was a major centre of learning.

The eastern Mediterranean remained the centre of thriving trade. War might bring temporary disruption, but trading links with the East were never long severed. From India came spices, pepper and sugar; from China came porcelain and silks. The wealthy of Byzantium had an insatiable taste for luxury goods and the Arabs soon came to share these sophisticated tastes. Byzantium controlled the overland routes to China, which ended at the Black Sea ports. The Arabs controlled the sea routes by the Persian Gulf and the Red Sea to India, with links beyond to China and the Spice Isles.

Threats to Arab Civilization

In time, Byzantium ceased to be a threat to the Islamic Empire; indeed it seemed only a matter of time before Constantinople must fall. From the eleventh century, for some 300 years, Arab civilization would be subjected to assaults by Christian crusaders from Europe and successive waves of nomadic invaders from the steppes of Asia. The latter were by far the more threatening of the two, and it was they who finally brought the great days of Near Eastern civilization to an end.

The Formation of Europe

Church and State

The Papacy

In the year 590 a new Bishop of Rome was elected who would later be known as Gregory the Great. He was a Roman from a senatorial family, but, in the chaos of his day, he had made the choice to become a monk. For a devout Christian, the monastic life seemed to be the only safe course to heaven in a violent and turbulent world. But Gregory saw that it was pointless to live with regrets for past glories of Rome or hopes for help from Byzantium. The church now had a mission to the restless and threatening barbarian world. Gregory selected monks as missionaries and sent them to bring Christianity to the barbarian tribes. The best known of these was Augustine of Canterbury. At the same time, missionaries from Ireland were moving south from Scotland into England and northern Europe. The missionaries from Rome, however, succeeded in linking the growing church back to Rome.

For Gregory's successors the first priority was to establish the primacy of the bishopric of Rome, or papacy. Popes claimed that, since they stood in a direct line from St Peter, they had inherited his 'power to bind and loose'. A pope could therefore control men's eternal destiny by the weapon of excommunication. In an extreme situation, he could even place an interdict, which forbade the performance of any sacraments, on a whole country. In an age of faith this was a formidable sanction.

The Popes had first to bring the Christian clergy under their control. Ordinary parish priests were generally illiterate peasants; bishops were temporal lords who used the church as a means of expanding family lands. Most were married men, who expected to pass their lands and livings on to their children. Their prime allegiance was therefore to the king or chief, rather than to a distant pope.

Monasticism

Only the monks were free from these temporal ties. The Rule of St Benedict, which imposed poverty, chastity and obedience, was now widely accepted. The monks were also almost alone in being literate in an uncultured world. This meant that they could reach positions of influence in both church and state.

The popes used monks as their representatives, and, wherever possible, promoted them to high positions within the church. In time the popes worked to extend their control over the secular clergy by forbidding clerical marriage altogether.

A Time of Turbulence

In the early centuries after the fall of Rome, the pope and his monks were able to establish respect and authority because they provided the only apparent stability in a troubled society. Groups of barbarians roamed through Europe, bound to their leaders in simple tribal ties. When they settled down and adopted Christianity, much of the old way of life continued. Society still had no recognizable political structure, in the modern sense. Disputes were still settled by traditional 'rough justice', such as the ordeal and trial by battle.

Change continued slow in the dark forests of Germany. In time, however, the Franks and other groups in the western part of the European mainland adopted a form of Latin as their language, and paid some respect to the Roman legal system. The tribes who were more cut off in the British Isles, continued to speak their own German language, and developed law, based on past rulings, as preserved in the minds of the elders. So developed the divisions between the romance and Anglo-Saxon languages, and between Roman and common law which were to become important in later western civilization.

Political and social order was beginning to emerge by the end of the eighth century, but then Viking ships brought new danger to European coasts. It is never easy to say why a people go on the move, but it appears as though population growth and weather problems disturbed the balance of marginal Scandinavian farming. Certainly the feared Norsemen set off on 'land takings' and voyages of plunder. Their ships spread out across the North Atlantic to Iceland, Greenland and North America; they emerged into the Mediterranean; they sailed down the great rivers of central Asia, setting up the Russian state, and reaching Constantinople;

they won control of northern Britain and Normandy. In 1066 a family of Norse descent won the crown of England.

The Norsemen were not the only raiders. Men from the steppes, this time the Magyars, were pillaging from the east and Muslim Saracen raiders came from the south. Hardly any part of Europe escaped. The unfortunate monks of Luxeil had their monastery burned by Norsemen, Hungarians and Saracens.

The Empire

For a brief period a new power arose in Europe. In 771 the ruthless and talented Charlemagne succeeded to the whole of the Frankish kingdom. For the next 40 years he led his armies to victories on all his borders, even mounting the first counterattack against Islam in Spain. Charlemagne was more than a conqueror. He was a devout Christian, and did much to spread the faith – by the sword if necessary – across Europe. He also respected learning, and he could read himself, although writing defeated him. He encouraged the clergy to respect books and learning, he founded schools and brought the best minds of the day to his court.

On Christmas Day, 800, he was crowned by Pope Leo III in the church of St Peter in Rome. The people cried, 'to Charles Augustus, crowned by God, great and peaceful Emperor of the Romans, Life and Victory.' A new Roman Empire had been proclaimed.

The empire was based on one man's will, and, like Alexander's, it fell apart on Charlemagne's death. It was divided into three parts. The central kingdom did not survive, but the two other halves would ultimately become France and Germany. Charlemagne's eastern successor retained the title of Holy Roman Emperor, but his lands remained a loose confederacy. In 940 the Comte de Paris, Hughes Capet, won the French crown and established a monarchy that was to survive until the French Revolution. His family was the first European dynasty to establish the concept of a hereditary monarchy.

Powers Temporal and Spiritual

After Pope Leo III had placed the crown on Charlemagne's head, he stretched himself on the ground as a sign of honour to the emperor. Later popes would regret this gesture. The first objective of the popes was to win control within the church. This involved taking the right to appoint bishops away from the temporal rulers.

In the eleventh century, Pope Gregory VII and Emperor Henry IV came into conflict in the Investiture Controversy. Gregory was victorious, forcing Henry to stand barefoot in the winter snow as a sign of submission. Gregory then formulated the extreme claim that all power came from the pope, and he therefore had the right to appoint and depose kings and emperors. The Investiture Controversy was the first of a series of disputes between church and state. They involved, not only the Holy Roman Emperor, but also kings of France and England.

King, Lord and Parliament

The Feudal System

In those troubled times, people were prepared to sacrifice liberty in the interest of security. Kings and emperors were remote figures, so free men bound themselves to their local lord, who could give assistance when danger was near. When a man took an oath of loyalty he gave his lands to the lord, and then received them back as the lord's vassal. He had the obligation to follow the lord to war, but as a mounted knight, to set him apart from the common serfs. The lord, in his turn, bound himself to a higher lord, and the king stood at the apex of the pyramid. Only the serfs were nobody's vassal, because they had nothing to give in exchange for protection. These common people were not allowed to leave their villages, to go to school or to get married without their lord's permission.

By the end of the ninth century, this feudal system had spread to all but the most remote areas of Europe. Kings, like other lords, were concerned to extend their lands wherever they could by war and dynastic marriage. The two way nature of the feudal compact served as a check on royal power. In France, the Capetian kings stood at the apex of the pyramid, but for long periods their actual power did not extend beyond their own lands around Paris. So, when the King of England married a French heiress, he did homage to the French king for his lands in Aquitaine, but he did not permit any interference within his territory.

The Hundred Years' War between France and England was fought sporadically from 1337 to 1453. The English king may have laid claim to the crown of France, but it remained in essence a struggle between a dynastic monarch, determined to establish direct control over feudal lands on the one side, and an overmighty subject, on the other. It was one of the catalysts that defined the meaning of the modern nation state. Writing some two hundred years later, Shakespeare would put words of nationalistic fervour into the mouths of John of Gaunt and Henry V. Such sentiments would have been incomprehensible in the time of Charlemagne or William the Conqueror, but they were beginning to have some meaning to their supposed speakers.

King and Parliament

William the Conqueror gave English kings more direct authority within their own realms. The feudal system was constructed to ensure that no lord could become 'over mighty'. Vassals, for their part were concerned that the king should not achieve unlimited power. In 1215 the lords forced King John to sign Magna Carta, which laid down two basic rights – that no free man could be imprisoned without a trial, and the king could not raise taxes without the consent of a Great Council. In 1295, King Edward I called what became known as the Model Parliament, because it set the pattern for future parliaments. Representation was by estates – the Lords temporal, the Lords Spiritual and the Third Estate, with the first two sitting together in an upper house. It was also established that parliament had the responsibility to act as the highest court in the land, to give advice to the king, to make laws and to vote taxes.

The Rise of the Towns

The inclusion of the third estate in Edward's Model Parliament was testament to the growing importance of trade in the European economy. Wealth was no longer the preserve of landowners and the church, so, to achieve maximum income, it was now necessary to consult with the representatives of the growing towns.

As towns grew in importance, kings gave them charters, which assured them freedom from interference by local landowners. Their walls were the symbol of their independence, and magnificent churches the evidence of their wealth. Trade provided a means by which low-born men could rise to positions of power within their own community, and even within the state. Different occupations were organized into guilds, which controlled terms of entry, quality standards and gave members a social structure.

The cities were often natural allies to kings who wanted to centralize power. Over-mighty nobles might flourish in conditions of civil war, but merchants needed the peace that only a strong government could provide. Kings, for their part, recognized that the growing wealth that was the basis for national strength as well as royal revenue was generated not on noble estates but inside the town walls.

The Cloth Trade

The Lord Chancellor of England still sits in the House of Lords on a woolsack. This was a reminder to parliament that the nation's wealth rested on the woollen trade. England, however, stood in the lowly position of a primary producer; the business in finished cloth centred round Flanders. Flemish weavers jealously guarded the trade secrets that made their cloth the most sought after in Europe. From the thirteenth century, the economy of northern Europe became increasingly sensitive to fluctuations in the fortunes of the cloth trade.

The Crusades

The First Crusade

In 1095 the Byzantine emperor appealed to the pope for assistance against the Turks. The pope answered the call by preaching a Holy War. The motives of those, both noble and common folk, who took the cross, were very mixed. Many of the Norman lords who took the lead saw the opportunity of a new land taking, like those of their Viking ancestors. But there was also a real devotion. The two were not incompatible. When the army arrived first in Byzantium and then in the Arab lands, they appeared like barbarians, with nothing to recommend them but their brute courage. Jerusalem fell to the crusaders, who waded through blood to give thanks for the victory.

Outremer

The crusaders established states in the conquered land. The Muslims resented these Christian enclaves in their territory, and they were therefore under constant pressure. In 1187 Saladin reconquered Jerusalem, and the crusaders were unable to win it back. In 1291 the last Christian outpost fell to the army of Islam. The crusades gave the West two centuries of contact with a higher culture. Knights returned home with a taste for oriental luxury goods. Some picked up an interest in learning and mathematics, and methods of castle construction and siege warfare were modernized on Arab models.

The Later Crusades

Eight campaigns between the eleventh and the thirteenth centuries are known as crusades, as well as tragic children's crusades. The movement turned inwards against European heretics. The simple crusaders were not always able to distinguish which enemy they should fight. The Venetians encouraged the fourth crusade to turn on Byzantium. In 1204 Constantinople was captured by the crusaders and the city remained in Christian hands until 1261. Although the rump of empire would survive into the fifteenth century, Byzantium never recovered from the disaster.

Spain

At the same time, Christian forces were counterattacking against the Muslim Moors in Spain. In 1212 the Moors were defeated and driven back to Grenada. The reconquest of the peninsula was completed in 1492. A great culture was replaced by a fanatical Christian state, in which the Inquisition was used as a tool of persecution against Moors, Jews and many Christians whose views did not please the authorities.

Learning, Art and Society

Scholarship and Authority

As long as there was no nation state, there were no sharply defined national boundaries. Latin provided a lingua franca and the church a broadly based structure within which the educated of their day could communicate.

Through the troubled times any learning remained behind monastic walls. The books of early Christian fathers were copied and became the intellectual authorities of the new world. Men had lost confidence in their own ability to reach conclusions, either through logic or through experiment, and all argument therefore referred back to authority. Even quite trivial issues of dispute would be decided by the weight of authority that could be mustered on the one side or the other.

The authors of antiquity were largely unknown until around the twelfth century. Then translations began to be made into Latin from copies preserved in Islamic Spain and Sicily. The ancient dichotomy between Plato and Aristotle began to be reflected in arguments between nominalist and realist theologians. Thomas Aquinas, in particular, baptised Aristotle. This did not, however, lead to an increase in experiment; classical authors joined the Christian fathers as valid sources of authority. In southern Europe, men still lived amidst the ruins of classical civilization. The classical and the Christian came together until, as in Dante's *Inferno* and Michelangelo's Sistine Chapel, they became indistinguishable from each other.

By the twelfth century, learning was coming out from monastic walls into the more open atmosphere of universities. The first was at Salerno, where Islamic and Byzantine influence was strong. Then came Bologna, Paris, Oxford and many others. Crowds would follow teachers, like Peter Abelard, who spoke a new and more restless language. University students were in religious orders of some sort, but the educational impetus continued outwards into the wider population. By later medieval times, an increasing number of lay people, particularly in the towns, were acquiring literacy.

Architecture and Painting

In early medieval times most stone buildings were either castles or monasteries. Many were fine buildings, but they added little to the techniques of antiquity. By the twelfth century, architects were developing their own signature. The Romanesque style of Southern Italy was based closely on a study of classical models. In northern France and England there rose magnificent cathedrals in the Gothic style. Here the pointed arch and the flying buttress enabled them to give their structures both height and light.

Most painting, likewise, remained dedicated to the church. Altarpieces showed the Virgin and child, with patrons and saints; frescoes and stained glass windows reminded illiterate worshippers of Bible stories; monks, copying psalters and books of hours, under no pressure of deadlines, painted exquisite decoration. In Italy, the school of Sienna worked under direct influence from Byzantium. But painters, like architects and stone masons, were craftsmen who were happy to work for any patron, and, as the centuries passed, an increasing number of commissions were available for secular work.

Literature

Medieval literature, like that of any other period, was made up of different strands – folk tales and myths, national histories, historical chronicles, love poems and works of devotion. Early vernacular literature, like Norse sagas and the Anglo-Saxon *Beowolf*, helped to create national language areas. In the early centuries, however, Latin was the language of both secular and religious writing.

By the fourteenth century a new vernacular literature was emerging. The supreme example of in English is *The Canterbury Tales*, written by soldier and customs officer, Geoffrey Chaucer, for an audience of other lay people.

Times of Change

The Black Death

A sickness new to the human race was first reported in the Yangtze Valley in 1334 and, according to one estimate, some thirteen million Chinese died in the following years. Relentlessly it spread from east to west, leaving devastation in India and across Asia. In 1347 the plague spread across Northern Italy and in the following years it is estimated that between a quarter and a third of the population of Europe perished. This first outbreak was the worst, but the disease returned periodically until the second half of the seventeenth century. Although it was a worldwide phenomenon, its effects have been most closely studied in Europe.

Initially it brought economic collapse; prices of all goods fell sharply and much farm land returned to nature. As life recovered, employers were faced with an acute labour shortage. This created strains within the social structure of both town and country. Guild regulations were flouted and the feudal structure began to crumble. There were major peasant uprisings, in France in 1358, in Florence in 1378 and in England in 1381.

The Late Medieval Church

Pious Christians were unable to understand why God could have created such destruction. The plague accentuated a Christian piety that identified God as judge and destroyer and the saints, particularly the Virgin Mary, as protector.

The church, like all institutions, moves through cycles of corruption and reformation. In early medieval times, reformation came from within. The last of these reforming movements was the founding of the friars by Francis of Assisi in 1209. Now the impetus for reform had grown weak. In the fourteenth century popes taxed the faithful heavily to maintain a lavish lifestyle. After the Black Death these taxes fell all the more heavily on a smaller population. One fund raising technique was the offer of indulgences, by which punishment in the next world was remitted in exchange for payment in this world. During the fourteenth century the church lost its independence when it moved under the protection of the King of France in Avignon. The Great Schism, when rival popes competed from Rome and Avignon, further undermined spiritual authority. Some Franciscans denounced papal luxury and were burned as heretics but their message was heard by the people.

Before the end of the fourteenth century John Wycliffe in England and Jan Hus in Bohemia were preaching that man did not need the apparatus of the church to make contact with God. Hus founded what was to be the first protestant church, and Wycliffe translated the Bible into English.

The Reformation

In the early sixteenth century the pope set out to raise money for the building of St Peter's by selling indulgences. In 1517, the German priest Martin Luther challenged the papal representative to a debate by nailing 95 theses to the door of Wittenberg cathedral. The church authorities sought to have him condemned, like heretics of old, but he found protection from German princes. The protestant movement soon won followers, particularly in the trading towns and in Northern Europe.

Luther did not initially see himself as the leader of a movement that would split the western church, but, as he preached the supremacy of the Bible and faith over the sacraments and traditional authority, the division quickly became irreconcilable. He found himself leading a mass movement, based on individual piety. Luther was the catalyst for another round in the ancient struggle between lay and secular powers. He only survived to preach because he was adopted by German princes, who saw his movement as a useful weapon against the power of the church.

Eastern Europe

Russia

It appears as though the Norsemen who settled the rivers of Russia brought no women with them, so the process of assimilation was rapid. In 980 Vladimir established the kingdom of Kiev and he married a sister of the Byzantine emperor. It is said that Russian envoys visited Constantinople and the West to decide which form of Christianity should be adopted. They were overwhelmed by the splendour of Constantinople, and the eastern link was forged. Kiev was destroyed in 1169 and the centre of power was driven northwards to Moscow. Trading and cultural ties with Byzantium were largely lost, and Russia was increasingly isolated until it was overrun by the Mongols in the thirteenth century. Russian independence can then be dated to the victory over the Tartars in 1380. The Grand Princes of Moscow emerged as rulers and Ivan III (1462–1505) adopted the title of Tsar (Caesar) and the double headed eagle, to substantiate the claim that, with Constantinople in Ottoman hands, the Russian monarchy had now inherited the imperial tradition.

Poland

When Vladimir made his choice of the eastern church, the Poles on his western frontier had just turned in the other direction. The missionaries who brought western Christianity to Poland also acted as forerunners for waves of land-hungry German invaders, led by the fearsome Teutonic Knights. In late medieval times, a Polish state lay across the central European plain, with its prosperity based on grain exports to the west through the port of Danzig. It was, however, already showing signs of the damage that would be caused by its geographical location as a buffer between Western Europe, the Scandinavian north, Russia and the East and the disturbed cauldron of Slavs and Magyars in the Balkan south.

In both Russia and Poland the serfs lived in great poverty, under the control of a wealthy landed class. Rulers were faced with a perpetual challenge from over-mighty subjects without being able to look for the support of any considerable middle class.

The Wider World

Asia Before the Mongols

India

For centuries after Ashoka, the Indian subcontinent was divided into warring states. The south, behind its mountain barrier, remained the home of non-Aryan people. They maintained contact with the Mediterranean civilizations through the Red Sea and Persian Gulf trading routes. In the northwest, the frontier and Indus valley remained open to Asian invaders. Invading Hunas, probably Huns, devastated this region, as they did lands both to east and west.

In about 320 AD the Guptas united the whole of northern India. This marked the great age of Hindu culture. In the fifth century, the decimal system was invented, so opening new areas of mathematics. Sculpture and literature flourished, both achieving a broad unity of style, characterized by a warm sensuality. Buddhist culture declined as Hinduism spread across Asia and into the islands of the Pacific. The island of Bali remains today a marker of this great expansion.

The Hindu Empire was in time challenged by the rise of Islam. Muslim traders – always effective missionaries for the Prophet – would have visited the western ports in the seventh century. By the eighth century invaders were crossing the open north western frontier. By the twelfth century, they controlled the Punjab, and a century later they dominated the Ganges valley. The fateful religious divide was now established.

China

China was united more effectively by language and culture than it was by its political structure. The two most powerful dynasties were Han (c. 205 BC-AD 220) and T'ang (618–907). Their empires were comparable to that of Rome at its most powerful. During the T'ang Dynasty trade flourished, and China became a major sea power, with trade reaching from the Persian Gulf in the west to Indonesia in the east. The great Chinese dynasties had an expectation of life of about 300 years. They were founded by a great individual who combined military and administrative skills. In later years, as the succession passed to lesser men, the state would come under pressure from nomads to the north and rebellion at home. Imperial authority was upheld by officials, who preserved the traditions of K'ung-fu-tsu. Their main tasks were to take the census and keep the land register up to date. Beyond that, they maintained only a broad supervision over local lords, who raised taxes and performed the day to day tasks of administration themselves.

Great civil works were undertaken. The country was now bound together by canals, of which the most important was the Great Canal, which linked Peking with Hang-chou. Huge irrigation projects were undertaken to provide food for the ever growing population. The casting of iron, printing, the magnetic compass, the use of paper money and explosives were all pioneered in China, but the conservative structure of society militated against the fullest exploitation of her inventions.

In the periods between the great dynasties, the country relapsed into warring states. There were times of disaster, when armies ravaged large areas, but in general, conditions changed little for the mass of peasants, whose life was always more closely governed by local lords than by distant emperors. But, while Europe remained divided into her warring states, China could always be drawn together once again by a dynamic new dynasty.

The Sung Dynasty (960–1279) was never as powerful as its great predecessors and in 1127 it lost the northern part of the country to Chin invaders. In the following century and a half the Southern Sung Dynasty lacked military power, but the period is viewed by many as the high point of Chinese culture. The Imperial capital of Hang-chou was a centre of wealth, culture and leisured living, far beyond any other city in the world.

Sung art was influenced by the Zen school of Buddhism. Painters, such as Ma Yuan, worked with an economy of line and colour to make a visual statement about man's position within the world order. Potters made dishes that looked 'like ivory, but were as delicate as thin layers of ice'.

The Seljuk Turks

The name 'Turk' is given to widely dispersed people, originating on the Asian steppes, who spoke a common language. In the tenth century, a chief called Seljuk settled with his people near Samarkand and was converted to Islam. The tribe organized an army based on slaves, mainly recruited from southern Russia and the Caucasus, who were known as mameluks. Backed by these fearless warriors, Seljuk's grandsons built an empire, from Azerbaijan and Armenia, into the ancient lands of Middle East. They overran Persia, captured Baghdad, Jerusalem and Egypt and invaded Byzantine lands in Asia Minor.

Later Seljuk rulers found it difficult to hold this vast empire together. While their efforts were largely directed against European crusades, they faced trouble in other parts of the empire. In Egypt, for instance, mameluke soldiers established a virtually independent government. The Seljuk Empire therefore became vulnerable to another and greater threat from the Asian steppes.

The Mongols

Genghis Khan and his Successors

In 1206 a chief called Temujin, better known to the world as Genghis Khan, united the Mongol tribes who lived in the area today called Mongolia. These were wild, nomadic peoples in the tradition of the horsemen who had come from the steppes throughout recorded history. He then established dominance over the more numerous Turkish peoples from the land to the north of the Himalayas. Genghis Khan came to believe that he was destined to rule the world, and he embarked on the greatest programme of conquest in history. His followers were magnificent horsemen. As a nomad people, they could survive on dried milk and the blood of their horses. Released from the constraints of supply, they were therefore uniquely mobile. They were also utterly ruthless. Cities that accepted them were often treated with leniency; those that resisted were liable to be levelled to the ground, and the population massacred. As the reputation of the Mongol horde was carried ahead, rulers capitulated to avoid the dreadful destruction.

By the time that Genghis died in 1227, the Chin Empire of northern China had fallen, and Mongol armies had swept across the open grasslands of Asia as far as Russia and the Caucasus. Still the advance continued. In 1237–38 the Russian state was overwhelmed by horsemen who rode down the frozen rivers, achieving the winter conquest that would later elude both Napoleon and Hitler. When a Great Khan died the armies returned to their homeland to debate the issue of succession. Europe might have been overrun had Genghis Khan's successor not died in 1241. The armies did not again threaten Europe; to the Mongols, it seemed a poor land, hardly worth conquering. They did, however, return to the Middle East, capturing Baghdad and destroying the caliphate in 1258. The tide of conquest finally turned here too when, in 1260, the mamelukes of Egypt organized the armies of Islam to defeat a Mongol army at Ain Jalut, near the town of Nazareth.

Mongol China

The Mongol Empire was now divided into four, with the eastern section the portion of Genghis' grandson,

Kublai. He led a Mongol assault on the Southern Sung Empire, which fell in 1279. Further expeditions were launched into South East Asia and even, unsuccessfully, against Japan. While his grandfather Genghis had devastated the north, Kublai respected the civilization that he conquered. Although he spoke little Chinese, he was a patron of literature and, like conquerors before him, he adopted Chinese ways. Mongol rule had now united the whole territory between Europe and China under a single authority and the ancient overland routes were opened once again. In 1275 members of the Polo family from far away Venice reached the court of Kublai Khan. When the young Marco Polo finally returned to Venice in 1299 he gave the west its first information about the civilization of the east. Readers in the more primitive Europe found it hard to believe that such a land of riches could exist far to the east, but some two centuries later a Genoan sailor called Christopher Columbus would own and make notes on a copy of the Venetian's narrative.

For the Chinese, however, the Mongols remained a dynasty of foreigners. Prosperity declined sharply and there was a wave of unrest, and the Mongols were overthrown in 1367 by a new Ming Dynasty. This survived its allotted three centuries until 1644 when it was in turn overthrown by new invaders from Manchuria, who established the Manchu Dynasty.

Later Mongol Conquests

In about 1370 Tamerlane, a chief from the region of Samarkand, proclaimed that he was the man to revive the Mongol Empire. In the next thirty years, he ravaged the Middle East, Asia Minor, southern Russia and northern India with a brutality matched only by his distant kinsman Genghis Khan. The ancient lands of the Fertile Crescent, so long the focus of world civilization, never recovered from his invasion. The Mongol Khanate of the Golden Horde in Russia was fatally weakened. He died in 1405, when on his way to carry his conquests into China.

In time the Mongol people of Central Asia and the Middle East came to accept the religion of Islam. The weakness in Mongol power lay in the fact that there was no established law of succession. Tamerlane's successors, like other Mongols, were concerned with domestic issues as they contested succession. Fifth in line from Tamerlane was the more attractive Babur, an accomplished soldier who was also interested in literature, music and architecture. The kingdoms of northern India were at that time in a state of permanent warfare. In 1526 Babur won a series of victories, and by his death in 1530 he had established Mongol – or Mogul – rule in northern India.

Mogul India

Akbar

In 1556 Babur's grandson, called Akbar, inherited a weak and divided empire as a boy of fourteen. He also inherited the ancestral belief that no empire can survive unless it is continually expanding, and throughout his reign he kept his armies constantly on the offensive. He continued old Mongol tactics. When a city, like Chittor, resisted it could be utterly destroyed and its people massacred; when people accepted his authority, they found him a generous ruler. By 1600 his Mogul empire controlled the whole of the subcontinent, except for Ceylon (Sri Lanka) and Vijayanagar in the south. Akbar built a huge capital at Fathpur-Siki, which was to be the model for Mogul public buildings of incomparable grandeur, culminating in Shah Jahan's Taj Mahal.

The country was divided into provinces, but all authority sprang directly from the emperor himself. Although a ruthless conqueror, Akbar was anxious to bind his people together effectively, and he was concerned at the religious division that existed between his Hindu and Muslim subjects. He was suspicious of all dogmatism, and devout Muslims accused him of backsliding when he abolished the poll tax payable by Hindus, and worked to find a compromise between the two religions.

The Decline of the Mogul Empire

Akbar was an outstanding ruler, but his empire suffered from weaknesses inherited from his Mongol tradition. In Europe, structures of government were coming into existence that transcended the personality of the ruler. In Mogul India, however, authority continued to be overdependent on the ability of one man. In his last years, even Akbar was plagued by rebellious sons. The instability of the empire can be illustrated by events at the end of the reign of Shah Jahan. In 1657 he fell ill, triggering a ferocious civil war between his sons. The victorious Aurangzeb was a devout and intolerant Muslim, and under his rule the united empire created by Akbar began to fall apart.

The Ottomans

The Foundation of Empire

Mongol successes in central Asia created more movement of nomad tribes out of the grasslands. In the late thirteenth century, one Ertughrul led a band of followers, who were equally devoted to Islam and to plundering, into the Seljuk lands of the Middle East. Ertughrul's son, Othman overthrew the Seljuk sultans, and founded the great empire that was to bear his name.

Othman's successors defeated the Byzantine army. They captured Asia Minor, and, in 1361, crossed into Europe to establish Ottoman power in the Balkans. Constantinople was now an isolated fortress in Ottoman lands, and in 1453 it fell to the Sultan Mehmet II.

The Spread of Empire

Ottoman power reached its peak in the century after the fall of Constantinople. In the early sixteenth century Selim I marched southwards, defeating the Mamelukes of Egypt and capturing Mecca, where he was proclaimed Caliph of the Islamic world. His successor Suleiman I, the Magnificent, turned north. In 1526 he defeated the Hungarian army at the great battle of Mohacs. Three years later his armies laid siege to Vienna.

Africa

Trans-Saharan Trade

Historians of early sub-Saharan Africa are restricted by the lack of written records and the destructive capacity of termites, working on wood and mud brick. The continent, however, was far from isolated. A thriving trade existed across the Sahara trade routes between North Africa and the grassland region that lies across the continent from near the Atlantic to the Nile.

The staple product being carried southward was salt – an essential commodity for people living in a hot climate. The Muslim traders who crossed the desert carried various luxury goods, and also brought their religion and literacy in Arabic script. On the return journey they carried gold, slaves and leather goods. Before the time of Columbus, Europe was heavily dependent on African gold, and 'Morocco leather' has always originated south of the Sahara. A key focal point of this trade was Timbuktu, on the Niger, which became famous as the meeting point of the camel and the canoe. The town was already well enough known to be marked on a Spanish map in the late fourteenth century.

The gold and probably most of the slaves came from the forest region still further south, so trade reached out in both directions. Among the most active traders were the Hausa people, who were based on city states, such as Kano, and Zaria. They would be late recruits to Islam and they never organized into larger political units.

African Empires

Broadly based political structures did, however, come into existence in the Southern Sudan to control the two-way trade. The Empire of Ghana (eighth to the eleventh centuries) was succeeded by Mali (twelfth to fourteenth centuries) and Songhai (fourteenth to sixteenth centuries). Kings like Musa Mensa, who ruled Mali in the early fourteenth century, were well known for their wealth and learning across the Islamic world, and even beyond. The trade in gold appears also to have stimulated the growth of forest kingdoms, such as Benin and Oyo. These would grow in importance with the arrival of European ships on the coast in the fifteenth century. Far to the east, the kingdom of Ethiopia maintained its isolated Christian tradition, again with power based on trade with the north by way of the Nile.

There was also traffic in gold and slaves down the coast of East Africa. The unique stone ruins of Zimbabwe provide evidence to support the reports of inland states in this region.

America

America was the last continent to be settled by man and it remained the most isolated. Traditional hunter/gatherer lifestyles were successfully followed by people of widely differing culture across wide areas of North America and within the many forest regions of North America until they suffered under the impact of European invaders. The cultivation of maize and then of other crops, however, made possible the development of more complex civilizations.

Central America

The earliest civilization was that of the Olmecs, which flourished on the coast of the Gulf of Mexico in the seventh century BC. Many of the characteristics of later civilizations of the region can already be recognized in these people. In their capital of Teotihuacan they built huge pyramids, apparently dedicated to the same gods that would be worshipped by people of the region in later generations.

The most accomplished civilization of the region was the Maya, centred on the Yucatan peninsula, which reached its peak in the sixth century BC. The Mayans used a pictogram form of writing. Like the Babylonians, they laid emphasis on the calendar and the heavenly bodies and they developed great skill in mathematics and astronomy, working out the duration of the year and learning how to predict eclipses. They were the first people in the world's history to achieve a sense of the vast span of time. Mayan sites, like those of ancient Egypt, are not cities, but vast complexes of temples and other ceremonial buildings.

The Maya were succeeded by the Toltecs, and they were overthrown in their by the Aztecs, who dominated the region from the thirteenth century AD. They appear to have introduced mass human sacrifice. This practice came to dominate the whole of Aztec strategy for the region. As victims were best found in warfare, they had no motivation to create conditions of peace, but rather encouraged a general unrest among subject people.

The Aztecs had a tradition that the white-skinned and bearded god Quetzalcoatl would one day return from the east. When the invading Spaniards appeared to fulfil this prophesy, there were many subject people who were prepared to take their side against their feared Aztec masters.

The Andes

The long spine of the Andes is perhaps the most improbable setting for any of the world's civilizations. Between 600 and 1000 AD, a people called the Huari brought some political unity to this area. In the tenth century, the Incas, based on Cuzco in modern Peru, were only one of many smaller groupings. They then conquered an empire that by the fifteenth century stretched 2000 miles from Quito in modern Ecuador to the deserts of Chile.

The Incas were a non-literate people. Instructions were carried to distant parts of the empire by messengers. Again, lacking the wheel, these messengers travelled on foot over a road network, built with great engineering skill. Inca power was centred on heavily fortified cities, where invading Spaniards were to find a wealth of beautiful objects made of gold and stone.

The Incas were not as oppressive to their subject people as the Aztecs, but there were still many who were prepared to support the small force of Spaniards who arrived in 1531 to conquer and loot the empire.

The Triumph of Europe

The Background to Conquest

New Perspectives

The Mappa Mundi, in Hereford Cathedral, illustrates the medieval perspective of the world. Jerusalem lies in the centre of the world, with the three known continents – Asia, Africa and Europe – arranged around the Mediterranean Sea. Phoenician and Viking ships may have sailed the wider oceans, but these lay at the edge of the known universe.

By the fifteenth century, changes were taking place. The reports of Marco Polo's travels in the East were becoming widely known. No profit orientated merchant could ignore his descriptions of markets loaded with silks, velvets and damasks. He had travelled beyond China to the islands of the Pacific and described how cheaply spices could be obtained. It was still impossible to keep meat animals alive through the European winter, so all except the breeding stock was slaughtered and salted down at Michaelmas. By spring it was barely edible without pepper, cinnamon and nutmeg to disguise the taste.

In 1400, a copy of the Hellenistic Ptolemy's *Geography* was brought from Constantinople and published in the west. It contained many errors, but did show that the world was round and not a flat dish. During the century, this became the accepted view of scholars.

The Ottoman conquests helped stimulate interest in alternative routes to East Asia. Through medieval times the majority of luxury goods had been brought by the Asian overland routes. These were now threatened by a hostile power. The Genoese, traditional allies of Byzantium, were particularly threatened by the new developments. Ottomans and Venetians alike combined to shut them out from the profitable business.

Logic demanded that traders should turn their attention to the oceans that lay beyond the enclosed Mediterranean world. Luxury goods were high value and low bulk cargo. Projected returns on investment on one cargo reaching Europe were astronomical.

Technical advance

During the fifteenth century major technical advances were also made in Europe, which brought such a project within the bounds of the possible. Before that time European ships had been square rigged on a single main mast. Such a ship could be manned by a small crew, but could not sail efficiently into the wind. Arab ships used a lateen sail. This could sail into the wind, but such a large crew was needed that it could never go far from land where food could be obtained. Shipbuilders now constructed multi-masted vessels, with both square and lateen sails, which could both be handled by a small crew and sail into the wind.

If ships were to sail far out from land, then navigational techniques needed to improve. By 1500 European sailors were skilled in the use of the magnetic compass, either re-invented or brought from China, and in measuring latitude. Almost 200 years more years would pass before similar advances were made in calculating longitude. Great advances were also made in cartographical techniques, with the Dutch leading the way.

European craftsmen also developed gunnery to new levels. King John II of Portugal took particular interest in the problems of mounting modern guns on board ship. Success in these experiments meant that European ships could command the seas. In previous centuries, ships came together with grappling hooks to allow soldiers to fight a conventional battle. Now the European ship could sink an enemy ship without allowing it to come close enough to bring the soldiers into action.

Population and Prices

The intellectual climate was favourable, commercial incentives were strong, and the required technology was available. As with Norsemen and Mongols, however, a further 'push factor' was needed to trigger off a major movement of European people. Demographers have shown that Western Europe had recovered from the Black Death and a cyclical population increase was in progress. Pauperism was on the increase, and also, in populations organized on the basis of primogeniture, landless younger sons of gentry families were looking for any way of making a fortune.

Historians now link the population rise with an inflationary trend that persisted through the sixteenth century. On average, prices quadrupled between 1500 and 1600. Since wages and savings did not always keep up with the rising prices, this created conditions of hardship that could make emigration attractive.

Religion

Christians of the period generally held that unbelievers possessed no rights. The Pope declared that Christian kings had a right to conquer heathen lands. Some Catholic friars and, later, Jesuits did identify with the cause of the native people, but even their mission stations were instruments of colonial control. The Protestant record was, if anything, worse. Some 300 years would pass before protestant Christians made any serious attempt to protect the rights of and to share their faith with non-European people.

Asia

The Portuguese

By 1400 Portugal was free from Muslim rule and had established itself as a separate country from Spain. Its geographical position made it a natural Atlantic pioneer. In the first half of the fifteenth century, the king's brother, Henry 'The Navigator' established a school for sailors at Sagres, by Cape St Vincent, and sent out expeditions to explore ever further south into the Atlantic. Slowly they pushed the boundaries of exploration beyond the Azores and to Senegal.

In 1487, twenty-seven years after Henry's death, Bartholomeu Dias rounded the Cape of Good Hope and established that the way to India lay clear. In 1498 Vasco da Gama took his ship to Calicut in south India. Indian merchants were happy to sell to the newcomers as they offered higher prices than the Arabs. He returned with a cargo of pepper, cinnamon, ginger, cloves and tin. It was reported that the King of Portugal and Vasco da Gama's other backers made a 6000 per cent return on their investment. A century of human and financial investment had finally paid a dividend. In 1503 the Portuguese established a permanent base in India, at Cochin, followed in 1510 by Goa, and later by Seurat.

In 1509 the Arabs sent a fleet, manned by 15,000 men, to drive the Portuguese from their seas, but the European superiority in ships and gunnery proved decisive in a battle off Diu. From that time European fleets exercised control over the world's oceans. Arab and oriental sailors could no longer confront them in battle, but only operate as pirates.

In 1517 the first Portuguese ship arrived off the coast of China and, according to European custom, fired their guns in salute. The Chinese found these barbaric Europeans 'crafty and cruel', but had to respect their guns, which 'shook the earth'. In 1521 Portuguese ships had reached the Spice Islands. In 1557 they established their trading base at Macao, off the Chinese mainland.

The Dutch

The Portuguese successfully protected their Africa route against encroachment by other European nations until the last years of the sixteenth century. Then in 1594 a group of Dutch businessmen fitted out four ships to sail to the Far East. They carried the products of Europe – woollen and linen fabrics, glassware, ornaments and different kinds of ironware, including armour. The ships reached East Asia and found that the people welcomed their quality goods. In 1602, the Dutch parliament, the Estates, set up the Dutch East India Company to follow up this initiative. The Malacca Strait, in modern Indonesia, became the focus of the empire, with headquarters on the island of Java. The Dutch then set about driving the Portuguese out of their Asian empire. Only a few Portuguese outposts, such a Goa and Macao survived the assault.

Once in control, the Dutch traders ruthlessly set about eliminating all competition. In 1623 ten English merchants were tortured and killed at Amboyna. But they were not content to exclude other European competition from their market. Chinese junks were shut out of their traditional markets as even local trade was channelled into Dutch ships. By now Europe was becoming glutted with spices, so the Dutch governor, Jan Coen set about controlling production to keep prices high. On one occasion he destroyed all the nutmeg trees on the Banda Islands and either killed or sold into slavery the entire population of 15,000 people. He burnt villages along the coast of China in an attempt to control the whole region, but complained that China, like India, was 'too extensive for discipline'.

The English

The English East India Company was founded two years earlier than the Dutch, but it lost the race to control the Spice Islands. After Amboyna, the Dutch and the English were bitter commercial rivals. The English had to accept that the prize of the Pacific trade was closed to them and had to make do as a second best with establishing themselves in India. The trade in coffee, tea and cotton goods was of lower value than that from further east, but as the English trading stations at Madras, Bombay and Calcutta grew in importance tea gained status as a fashionable drink. When Dutch power waned in the later years of the seventeenth century, English ships were able to use their Indian bases for trading with China and the Pacific Islands.

The French

The French East India Company had now replaced the Dutch as the main competition. French merchants, however, operated under difficulties. They came from a nation whose power was centred on its land army. While naval and commercial interests were influential in London, they carried little weight in Paris. In times of war, French ships were exposed to the powerful English navy and French overseas outposts were at all times starved of resources.

It long seemed impossible for any European nation to establish political control in the sub continent. Then the death of Aurangzeb in 1707 marked the end of the Mogul Empire as an effective force, and the subcontinent split into warring states. From that time, the trading companies became increasingly involved in politics.

America

The Spanish

On 2 January 1492 the troops of the 'Catholic Monarchs', Isabella of Castile and her husband, Ferdinand of Aragon, finally drove the Moors out of Grenada. In the cheering crowd was a Genoese sailor, Christopher Columbus. Like another Genoese, John Cabot, he had decided that the Indes could best be reached by sailing westwards. Both turned to western European monarchs, with a natural interest in Atlantic trade. Columbus won the support of Isabella, and in August his three ships sailed from Palos, to reach San Salvador on 12 October.

Columbus was bitterly disappointed that he did not find the eastern markets described by Marco Polo. In later voyages he explored the Caribbean Islands and reached the mainland. He died in 1506, still convinced that he had reached the Indes. Before then, however, another Italian, Amerigo Vespucci, this time in Portuguese pay, had established that this was indeed the continent that subsequently carried his name. In the year that Columbus sailed, the Spanish Pope, Alexander VI issued a bull, awarding to Spain and Portugal all lands already discovered or to be discovered in the West, towards the Indes or the ocean seas, with the dividing line between the two on the line of longitude 45 degrees west. This ruling gave Brazil to Portugal and the rest of the continent to Spain. The Spanish, however, never established effective control to the north of a line from modern Georgia in the east to California in the west.

In 1519 Magellan led an expedition to explore this new world. When the remains of his expedition returned in 1522, having circumnavigated the globe, the basic facts of world geography were finally established.

Meanwhile the Spaniards were establishing their power in the New World. In 1513 Balboa crossed the Isthmus of Panama and reached the Pacific Ocean. In the east, Portuguese guns could win naval battles, but they could never bring down great empires. In the west, however, the Spaniards found that civilizations crumbled before them. There was too large a gap between the technology of the 'New World' on one side and the firearms, horses and armour of the 'Old World' on the other. Perhaps most important, the American 'Indian' people were psychologically ill equipped to confront the brutal European soldiers. Many were killed by the newcomers; many lost the will to live when forced to work in unfamiliar ways; even more died of the plague and other diseases for which they lacked immunity. According to one estimate, twenty-five million people lived in what was to become New Spain when Columbus landed, but only a million and a half survived a century later.

The Spaniards may not have found silks and spices, but they found gold. What to the native Americans was a decorative metal was, to the Spaniards, the basic unit of exchange and measurement of wealth. For gold Cortes and Pizarro destroyed the Aztec and Inca civilizations. Unsuccessful searches for gold established Spanish rule in what is now the south of the United States, from Florida to the Great Plains, and the Californian coast. All kinds of gold objects were melted down and shipped back to Spain, where the new riches funded the emergence of Spain as a major power.

The gold was soon plundered, and no significant mines were discovered. A sustainable flow of wealth was, however, established by the opening of silver mines in Peru. Spain now controlled both sides of the Isthmus of Panama and a merchant fleet was built on the westward, Pacific side. A trading base was established at Manila in the Philippines, and galleons carried trading goods across the wide Pacific. These luxury goods from the Orient, along with silver from Peru, were then carried across the Isthmus of Panama and loaded onto the Atlantic treasure fleet for Spain.

In the early years of colonization few women left Spain for the New World, and settlers took Indian wives. The culture, and even the religion of New Spain therefore developed a syncretism between Spanish and Indian traditions. In time the importation of black slaves from Africa further complicated the ethnic mix. It has, however, remained generally true, even into modern times, that the social position and wealth of any individual could be gauged by skin colour.

The English

John Cabot was convinced that Columbus had got his sums wrong. He believed correctly that China was far out of range of any ship following a southerly route. By his calculation, the journey could be made at a more northerly latitude. Sailors from Bristol, England, were already fishing the Newfoundland banks and knew the North Atlantic well. Cabot therefore won support from King Henry VII of England and in 1496 reached the coast of North America. It was not obvious that the north of the continent was embedded in the Arctic ice and Cabot's son, Sebastian led a long line of English sailors in search of the North West Passage. The English sea dogs, Drake and Hawkins preferred the warm waters of New Spain to the cold northern seas. They first operated as traders, and then, after being attacked by Spaniards, as privateers.

The gold of New Spain and the luxury trade of the Orient offered instant riches. Returns on investment in North America were likely to be less spectacular. By the 1580s, however, Sir Walter Raleigh and others were advocating colonization of the land of Virginia, which was now claimed by England. Attempts were made to establish colonies in 1585 and 1589, but both failed. The first successful colony was established at Jamestown in 1607. In 1620 a group of 'Pilgrim' refugees set up a colony at New Plymouth, Massachusetts, and later moved to the better site of Boston.

The English settlements were based on a farming economy. Disease, spreading from New Spain had recently ravaged the native American tribes, leaving much of the land vacant. The surviving people practised a mixed hunting and farming economy, based on shifting cultivation, so to newcomers much of the land appeared to be empty. As land-hungry settlers kept on arriving and pushing inland towards the Appalachian Mountains conflict with the Indian people was inevitable.

The Dutch

In 1614 the United New Netherlands Company established a colony at the mouth of the Hudson River. The Dutch recognized the potential of the trade in beaver fur and used the Hudson to make contact with Indian people of the interior. This settlement divided the English colonies of Virginia and New England, and hostility between the two Protestant countries, aroused in the far Spice Islands, spilled over into the New World. In 1664 the English drove the Dutch from North America.

At the height of their powers, the Dutch carried their assault on the Portuguese Empire into the New World by annexing Brazil in 1637. The Portuguese settlers rebelled against them and they were driven out in 1654, leaving Brazil as the western outpost of a once great Portuguese Empire.

The French

In 1603 the French explorer Samuel de Champlain sailed into the St Lawrence River. He too was still searching for the elusive route to the east. He later established settlements that were to become Montreal and Quebec and pressed on to explore the inland waterways of the interior. The French settlers were comparatively few in number and they received little support from their home government. De Champlain and those who came after him exploited Indian rivalries to establish a flourishing trading empire, based on the fashion trade in beaver fur. As the animals were hunted to near extinction in the east, the 'beaver frontier' moved west, taking the hardy French after them.

French explorers followed the Great Lakes waterway into the interior and then the Mississippi to the Gulf of Mexico. Here they established the French outpost of New Orleans. The North American empire, named Louisiana, after Louis XIV, now followed the waterways in a huge, but lightly populated arc. At first the French and English colonists only came into contact with each other in the Hudson Valley. The risk of conflict grew, however, when the French tightened the noose around the English colonies by taking control of the Ohio River. At the time, however, colonial wars, which decided the fate of India and North America, were seen as little more than a sideshow beside the main European conflicts.

The Old Colonial System

The Dutch can be credited with the development of mercantilism, which became known as the old colonial system. This was not developed specifically for North America, but, when applied by the English in their American possessions, it became a root cause of later conflict between the colonists and the mother country. It was assumed that overseas colonies existed to promote the interests of the mother country, by extending its economic base. Colonists were expected to produce cash crops. Some, like rice from the Carolinas or tobacco from Virginia, could not be produced in northern Europe. Softwood timber from New England was also of vital strategic importance for shipbuilding at a time when European forests were finally disappearing. Buying these goods from a national source saved the mother country the foreign exchange, which would be required to purchase them from abroad. By selling these crops, the colonists earned money that would be spent on the manufactured goods. This in turn assisted the manufacturing industries and strengthened the merchant marine of the mother country. Any business between the colony and a third country had to be transacted through the mother country. This had the further benefit of boosting customs revenue.

The trade-off was that the mother country was responsible for providing the colonists with protection, be it from local populations or from hostile Europeans. This involved the Westminster government in the expense of funding wars against the French and their Indian allies. The system came under pressure when the colonies began to develop out of their original role as providers of raw materials to develop their own manufactures.

Africa

The Atlantic Slave Trade

The Portuguese were the first to discover that West Africa had human resources, which were to be exploited in a slave trade, which continued for some 350 years. A base was established on the coast as early as 1448, from which comparatively small numbers of slaves were shipped back to Portugal.

An acute labour problem then began to develop in the new American plantations. The obvious solution was to recruit American Indians. Heavy field work, however, proved alien to them. Many died, often by suicide, when forced to work on European plantations. European labour was also brought in, both by the forcible transportation of convicts, and by indentured labour schemes, under which immigrants were bound to their masters for a given number of years. Again, however, expectation of life was short, and the labour problem remained unresolved.

Portuguese ships then began to take slaves directly to their colony of Brazil. In 1562 John Hawkins began the English slave trade between West Africa and the Caribbean. Dutch, French, Danes and later sailors from both North and South America joined in the business. European nations established forts on the West African coast to protect the interests of their slave traders.

It is estimated that some eight to ten million slaves were carried across the Middle Passage to America. The economies of European cities, such as Nantes, Bristol and later Liverpool, were based on slaving, and the business was accepted as a part of the national commercial interest.

The individual suffering of slaves would ultimately receive wide publicity; the impact the trade had on African society is harder to quantify. European sailors rarely penetrated inland to find their own captives. Domestic slavery already existed on the continent, and Africans initially sold their own slaves to purchase European goods. In time, however, demand outstripped this source of supply. Military confederacies, such as Dahomey and Ashanti, grew up to fulfil the double function of protecting their own members, and feeding slaves to the European forts. When Europeans later penetrated the continent, they discovered that these states often acted with a savagery untypical of African society further inland. The demand for slaves created an endemic state of war that penetrated inland, far beyond any direct European contact. The resulting depopulation appears, however, to have been largely balanced by improvements in the African diet as a result of the importation of American crops, such as the yam and cassava.

Colonization

The first African colonies had the prime function of protecting and providing staging posts for national ships on the eastern trade routes. The Portuguese previously established the outposts in Mozambique and Angola that would achieve the distinction of being the longest lasting European overseas colonies. In 1652 Jan van Riesbeck set up the Dutch colony at the Cape of Good Hope, to serve the eastern convoys as a 'tavern of the seas'. In the eighteenth century, the French established an interest in the Indian Ocean island of Madagascar, along with Mauritius, and Reunion. The slave coast of West Africa remained unattractive for colonization. European slavers and soldiers themselves suffered a high mortality rate from tropical diseases, particularly yellow fever and malaria.

East Africa

At this time, East Africa lay off the main trading routes, and the region offered little to attract European merchants. Arab dhows still sailed undisturbed to Zanzibar and their caravans penetrated deep inland. Here again, slaves featured prominently as a trading commodity alongside gold and ivory. The area remained an Arab area of influence until European missionaries and traders penetrated the area in the nineteenth century.

The Nations of Europe

Italy and the European Powers

The City States and the Papacy

In the fifteenth century, the northern half of Italy was the most advanced part of Europe. The great trading cities of Genoa and Venice brought in wealth and broad contact was maintained, both through trade and cultural exchange with Arab and Byzantine civilizations. The country probably benefited from the fact that it was never brought under unitary political control.

The broken terrain of Tuscany and Umbria suited the development of independent city states, not unlike those of ancient Greece. Florence and Siena, like Athens and Sparta of old, built up confederacies to counterbalance the power of the other. In the late fourteenth century, the banking family of Medici took power in Florence. Times were not always easy, but they led the city to its unique flowering of culture.

In the north, another ring of states, with Milan as the most powerful, controlled the trading routes across the Alps. In the centre, the pope ruled the Papal States as any other temporal monarch, and involved himself in the politics of the peninsula, attempting always to extend the patrimony of St Peter. During this period the lifestyle of the popes was little different from that of any other monarch. They led troops into battle, promoted family interests, including those of their children, and built themselves enormous monuments. Julius II's decision to build himself a tomb set off the chain of events that triggered the Reformation in distant Germany; the tomb would be too large for St Peter's, so the church had to be rebuilt; this involved raising money by the granting of indulgences.

The Theory of Kingship

Within this turbulent world of Italian politics, only the fittest survived. Niccolo Machiavelli worked for the Florentine state, travelling widely as a diplomat. He wrote a book, called *The Prince*, which was based on these experiences, which contained advice for the Medici family on the theory and practice of government. Political decisions, he argued, could only be taken on a cool, indeed callous, assessment of the security needs of the state and of its ruler. Medieval concepts of the mutual duties of ruler and subjects were cut away in this first exposition of what would later come to be called 'real politik'.

Medieval monarchy was based on a feudal alliance between king and his tenants in chief. In the sixteenth century, power was being drawn to the centre at the expense of both the magnates and of representational institutions. For Machiavelli's prince, power was its own justification. The theory of centralization was later taken further with the formulation of the concept of the divine right of kings. Rulers, it was said, held power directly from God. Rebellion was a sin and criticism of the royal will was tantamount to treason.

Foreign Invasion

In 1494 Charles VIII of France crossed the Alps at the head of an army of 30,000 men. He laid claim to the Kingdom of Naples and on his way south, through Rome itself, his army left a trail of destruction. Other foreign armies followed. Artists still worked on, producing some of the greatest works known to man, but the days of the city state were over and Italy would henceforth be a pawn in the real politik of the great powers. In 1527 the ragged, unpaid and hungry army of the great emperor, Charles V, ran wild in the streets of Rome, and the city was sacked for the first time since the barbarian invasions.

The Empire of Charles V

Throughout medieval times, kingship was fundamentally a matter of family inheritance. Charles was the ultimate beneficiary of this dynastic system. From his mother, the mad Joanna, he inherited his grandparents' crowns of Castile and Aragon. On the paternal side, he inherited from his grandfather the title of Holy Roman Emperor, and from his grandmother the lands of the Duchy of Burgundy. As king of Castile he controlled Spanish land in the New World; as Emperor he ruled Austria, Hungary, Bohemia and much of Germany; as Duke of Burgundy he possessed the Netherlands, which was the richest part of all Europe. His empire was larger than that of Charlemagne.

France was now shut in on all sides, and its king was determined not to let Italy fall to Charles' empire. The crusading spirit was finally laid to rest as Pope and King of France allied with the Ottoman Turks against Charles.

This great empire, like that of Charlemagne, carried the seeds of its own destruction. Charles was unable to function adequately as ruler of such dispersed lands, and resentment grew, particularly in the Netherlands, at the taxes raised to support Italian wars. Charles was also depressed at his inability to control the spread of Protestantism within his own lands. He abdicated in 1556 and the empire was divided. The title of Emperor passed to his brother Ferdinand I, while the more valuable western share, consisting of Spain and the old Burgundian lands, went to his son, Philip II. There were now two Hapsburg dynasties in Europe.

Protestantism and the Counter Reformation

The Spread of Protestantism

Luther's new beliefs found most followers in northern Europe, particularly in Germany itself and in Scandinavia. The impetus behind the further spread of Protestantism came, not from Germany but from Geneva. John Calvin was French, but he achieved prominence in the Swiss canton. He preached a harsh form of Protestantism; since God was all-powerful, he had predestined a minority of people – the elect – to salvation and the rest to damnation. The elect had to show their status by a strict adherence to a way of life. Within Geneva, moral sins like adultery and even disobedience by a child to parents, were severely punished. Calvinism proved to be a more militant faith than Lutheranism. It appealed in the Netherlands, in England and on the west coast of France, in Scotland and later in the Lutheran heartland of Germany.

All Protestantism stressed the direct communion of the individual with God, and it is not therefore surprising that it quickly showed a capacity to fragment. In 1532 an extreme group, the Anabaptists, took control of the German city of Münster, preaching not only rejection of infant baptism, but polygamy and a radical social gospel. In the extreme Protestant sects, authority lay not in any higher political or ecclesiastical power, but in the local 'gathered church'. These separatist churches were persecuted in Protestant and Catholic countries alike, but it was this tradition that would ultimately implant itself in the New England colonies of North America, and profoundly influence the development of American society.

Tolerance was not a cherished ideal in sixteenth century Europe, but by 1530 it had become clear that Protestantism was too powerful a movement to be readily suppressed. In that year the Peace of Augsburg laid down the principle of 'cuius regio, eius religio' – the country would follow the religion of the ruler. This left rulers free to persecute within their own dominions.

Sweden and England Break with Rome

Two European monarchs took their nations out of communion with the Roman church. Both were motivated by national and financial, rather than by religious reasons. In 1523 the young Swedish nobleman Gustavus Vasa, succeeded in his struggle to make Sweden independent from Denmark, and was proclaimed king. Lutheranism had already made progress among his people. In 1527 he broke with Rome as a symbol of the new national independence, and he enriched his hard pressed government with church lands.

Henry VIII of England had showed no personal inclination towards the reformed religion; indeed he had written a pamphlet attacking Luther, and had persecuted Protestants. In 1530, however, he became involved in a dispute with the pope over his divorce to Catherine of Aragon. Using selective intimidation, he won the support of parliament for a breach with Rome, and then for the plundering of the monastic lands. The Church of England, reformed in doctrine, but conservative in practice, was the creation of Henry's Archbishop of Canterbury, Thomas Cranmer. After a short return to Catholicism under Mary I, Henry's daughter, Elizabeth, declared that the English church should be a home for all men of goodwill. Separatist Protestants and politically active Catholics were still persecuted, but England did escape the worst violence of these years.

The Counter Reformation

The Roman church had been on the defensive against an aggressive Protestantism for twenty-five years when Pope Paul III called his bishops together for the Council of Trent. Paul represented a new generation of Popes, anxious to clear away the scandals of the past, and re-establish the western church on a firm footing. The discussions were dominated by bishops from Spain and Italy, where Protestantism had found no foothold. The Council brought in reforms – indulgences, for instance, were abolished – but it made no concessions to Protestant faith. By the time that the Council had finished its debates in 1563, the lines of division were clearly drawn.

Catholicism was now on the counter offensive. As in the past, monasticism provided the papacy with its front line troops. In 1540, Ignatius Loyola, who had been a fellow student in Paris with John Calvin, established the Society of Jesus, or Jesuits. Members were bound to total loyalty to the Pope, and this provided the reforming papacy with a means of circumventing special interests within the church. Jesuits became particularly prominent in education and in missionary work.

Spain and the Netherlands

The Expulsions

Even without Charles' eastern lands, Philip II's Spain remained the dominant power in Europe. He controlled southern Italy and Sicily and succeeded in conquering Portugal. Spain's European power was now underpinned by the revenues of a two huge overseas empires.

The nation's weakness was not clearly evident at the time. When the Moors were finally defeated, Muslims and Jews had been promised security within the Christian state. The presence of infidels, however, proved too much for Catholic rulers, still driven by the intolerance of the Inquisition. Moors, Jews, and converted Moors, the Moriscos, were all driven out of the country. These, however, were the very trades-people and skilled craftsmen on whom the economy of the nation rested. As a result, Spain became heavily dependent on imported goods, particularly from the prosperous northern Netherlands. On occasions the Panama fleet had to be diverted and sailed direct to unload its treasure in the Netherlands.

The Spanish Netherlands

The old Burgundian lands covered both of the modern states of Belgium and Holland. The greatest centres of prosperity, with Antwerp outstanding, lay in the south. The northern part, mostly consisting of land drained from the Rhine delta, contained the finest farmland in Europe, but, even with intensive agriculture, it could not feed the growing towns. Calvinist Protestantism had won adherents both in the north and in the south.

Charles V was born in the Netherlands, and during his reign the two religions coexisted with reasonable tolerance. The accession of Spanish born Philip II, however, brought change. As king, he was determined to bring the old Burgundian noble families under his control, and, as a faithful son of the church, he meant to stamp out heresy in his land. The Spanish Duke of Alva was sent with an army to bring the area under control.

Dutch Independence

In 1572, William 'the Silent', Prince of Orange led the People of the Netherlands in revolt. As Spanish armies established control of the south, many Protestants moved north behind the protection of the dykes, and the religious division between the Catholic south and the Protestant north was established. In 1581 the followers of William of Orange declared their independence from Spain. No matter how bitter the fighting, the trade between Spain and her rebellious provinces never ceased. Philip was in no position to cut off this channel of supplies for his people and the Dutch were happy to drain the enemy of wealth. William was murdered on Philip's orders in 1584, but the struggle continued until Spain made a truce in 1609. Almost forty years would pass before Spain finally recognized the independence of the Dutch people, but in practice Holland had established its independence from its traditional ruling house.

The Dutch Republic

The new nation was unique in that power was based on trade, rather than on inherited land. A successful Dutchman did not plan for the day when he would put aside the cares of trade and live as a gentleman – his objective was to hand a thriving business to his heirs. The people lived by a strict work ethic, and made the most of the limited resources of their small land.

National wealth was founded on north-south trade, carrying products such as grain, timber and iron from the Baltic to the overpopulated Mediterranean lands. Dutch flyboats, little more than floating holds, plied the oceans. 'Norway was their forest, the banks of the Rhine and the Dordogne their vineyard; Spain and Ireland grazed their sheep; India and Arabia were their gardens and the sea their highway.' Scholars also provided vital information for the sailors and, in doing so, laid the foundation of modern geography.

The Decline of Spain

The loss of the Netherlands was the clearest marker of Spain's fall from the position of being Europe's dominant power. In 1588 a Spanish naval armada was also defeated by the English fleet. In 1640 Portugal re-established her independence under the house of Breganza. The nation could have overcome military reverse; the basic problem was that Philip II and his successors concentrated on military and colonial affairs at the expense of the economy, which had been shattered by the mass expulsions.

The French Wars of Religion

The French Monarchy

In the middle of the sixteenth century, French royal power stood at a low ebb. Financial stringency led to offices being sold to the highest bidder, and, partly as a result, the size and independence of the aristocracy was ever increasing. Calvinism was strong in Brittany and Normandy, and growing in power further south on the Atlantic coast and in Languedoc. Its strength was based on craftsmen and some poorer nobles, followed by a growing number of peasants. By 1562 there were over fifteen hundred 'Huguenot' congregations, many led by Geneva-trained pastors. The Catholics themselves were divided into two parties – the moderates, led by the Regent, Catherine de' Medici, who at first planned to keep the peace by giving a measure of toleration to the Protestants, and an extreme Catholic party, who wanted to see heresy stamped out.

The Wars

Fighting broke out after extremist Catholics massacred a Huguenot congregation at Vassy in 1562. The ensuing wars were fought with great ferocity on both sides. In 1572 three thousand Huguenots were massacred in Paris on St Bartholomew's Day, and in 1588 the king, Henry III, was ejected from his own capital by extreme Catholics. In 1584 the Huguenot Henry of Navarre had become heir to the throne. He succeeded in bringing the war to an end by turning Catholic and reaching an agreement with his former Protestant followers in the Edict of Nantes. This left the Huguenots with freedom of worship in large areas of the country, as well as certain fortified cities. These now effectively lay outside royal control.

Germany

The Empire after Charles V

Emperor Charles V's brother Ferdinand saw himself as a faithful Catholic and soldier of the Counter Reformation. His own lands and the south of Germany remained Catholic. The Protestant forces set against him were divided. In the north were the Lutheran powers of Denmark, Saxony and Brandenburg. The Calvinist stronghold lay to the west around the Rhine. Ferdinand dreamed of winning back the whole of Germany to Catholicism, while at the same time bringing it once again under imperial rule.

Ferdinand was unable to achieve his ambition because his empire was exposed on its eastern flank. In the south, the Ottoman Empire reached the peak of its power under Suleiman 1, and even threatened Vienna itself. In the north, Sweden was establishing control of the Baltic Sea while Poland and Russia both pressed on German land.

The Thirty Years' War

In the early seventeenth century, the religious divisions became more sharply fixed. In 1608–1609 the Catholic League and the Calvinist Union were set up as rival military blocks. The first of a series of wars broke out in 1618, when the Calvinist Elector Palatine was elected King of Bohemia. The Catholic armies, led by virtually independent war lords, won early successes, but this rallied the Lutheran armies to the Protestant cause. The Protestant champion turned out to be Gustavus Adolphus, King of Sweden, who won a series of battles before he was killed at Lützen in 1632.

By this time the religious battle lines were becoming blurred. Catholic France, under Cardinal Richelieu, was prepared to fund Protestant armies and even to intervene directly to prolong the war and so prevent a re-emergence of imperial power in Germany. This brought in Catholic and Hapsburg Spain on the imperial side.

The war was a disaster for the people of Germany. Roaming armies stripped the countryside of food; the devastation caused by the imperial sack of Magdeburg in 1629 rivalled that of a Mongol army. When the war limped to a close in 1648, the countryside was impoverished and depopulated. Ferdinand's ideal of a Catholic Germany, united under the empire, was destroyed. Protestantism was unassailable in the north, and the effective power of the emperor in the German-speaking lands was henceforth limited to his Austrian heartland. In the Treaties of Westphalia the Emperor had to accept the independence of Switzerland – a reality since the end of the fifteenth century – and the King of Spain that of the Netherlands. France and Spain both made achieved territorial gains in German lands. Most significant for the future, the new power of Brandenburg had emerged in the north.

Brandenburg-Prussia

In 1640, 'The Great Elector' Frederick William of the House of Hohenzollern, inherited Brandenburg and the eastern territory of Prussia. A man of great energy, he set about creating a well-run, modern state. His twin tools were an efficient civil service and a highly disciplined army, which served as a model for later German armies. The Great Elector's work was consolidated a century later by Frederick II 'the Great'. He had no vision of a united Germany, but he ruthlessly expanded his family lands at the expense of the Empire.

The Hegemony of France

Richelieu

Henry IV was assassinated in 1610 by a Catholic fanatic, leaving a country at peace, but with many problems. The Huguenots were a state within a state; the nobles were over powerful and contributed little to the national life; the peasants were desperately poor and over-taxed.

In 1624 Henry's son and successor, Louis XIII, appointed Cardinal Richelieu as head of the royal council. For eighteen years, Richelieu worked single-mindedly to establish royal power within the nation. He had no wish to persecute the Protestants, but he destroyed the independent Huguenot fortresses, including La Rochelle and Montauban. He made examples at a high level to bring the nobles under his control. Regional government was delegated to directly appointed intendants, who exercised the complete range of royal power.

Richelieu's foreign policy was directed at limiting the power of Spain and improving national security by achieving 'natural frontiers' at the Rhine and the Alps. For this, he was prepared to ally with Protestants and to prolong the misery of the Thirty Years' War (1618–48).

Richelieu represented the apotheosis of the Machiavellian ideal; his policy was driven by a cold analysis of *raison d'etat*. He did not, however, recognize that some improvement in the lot of the poor was essential if the state was to be securely based. Shortly after Richelieu and his royal master died in 1642–43, there was a series of popular uprisings across the country, which were known as the Frondes.

Louis XIV

The young king who succeeded was to rule the country until 1715. His domestic and foreign policy was a continuation of that laid down by Richelieu. All real power lay in the hands of non-noble ministers and the intendants, while the nobles were emasculated by being drawn into the glittering court of Versailles.

Unlike Richelieu, however, Louis determined that he would not rule over heretics. He revoked the Edict of Nantes, facing Protestants with the choice of conversion or expulsion. Like Isabella of Castile, he was hereby driving a productive group out of the nation. Economic conditions did improve, but the poor continued to suffer harshly enforced penal taxation.

Much tax revenue was spent on foreign wars. As France had organized leagues to limit the power of Spain, so now others united to contain France. The driving force in the anti-French Grand Alliance was William of Orange, Stadholder of the Netherlands. His power strengthened when, in 1688 he also became king of England as William III. The War of the Grand Alliance (1689–97) was followed by the War of the Spanish Succession (1701–14), which sought to prevent Louis from unifying the crowns of Fence and Spain by dynastic succession.

Eighteenth-century France

In 1715 France was clearly the leading power in Europe. Major losses of overseas territory to England in India and North America during the Seven Years' War (1756–73) did not appear as significant at the time as they were later to become. Financial weakness, however, underlay the pageantry of the France monarchy. The huge noble class – estimated at up to a quarter of a million strong – had lost political power but not financial and legal privilege. The state sank ever more deeply into debt, but had no means of tapping the huge reserves of noble wealth. Here lay the seeds of revolution.

England

Sea Power

When Roman soldiers were posted to Britain, they considered that they were being consigned to the edge of the civilized world. Through medieval times, the British Isles remained on the periphery of the known world. The discovery of America moved the centre of gravity away from the Mediterranean towards the Atlantic Ocean. Geography therefore now favoured England.

As an island nation, the English were perforce a seafaring people. By 1500, however, this seafaring tradition had not been converted into naval power. The defeat of the Spanish Armada in 1588 proved to be a turning point. The battle was won by strategy rather than by fighting force, but the Elizabethan sea dogs created a national myth that would survive into modern times. Governments, reluctant to involve troops in European land battles, laid the greatest stress on building up naval power and securing naval supplies. The navy provided protection for the island, maintained links with overseas colonies, and secured trade routes against competition.

Monarchy and Parliament

The Tudor monarchs, Henry VIII and his daughter Elizabeth, dominated sixteenth-century English politics. The English nobility were few in number, and were generally content to concentrate their efforts on field sports and the efficient management of their estates. While parliamentary government was withering on the continent, in England the old institutions remained robust. Henry found it convenient to use the

House of Commons as his ally against the Church, and Elizabeth was able to manage parliament, even if sometimes with difficulty, both as a source of revenue and as a channel of government.

When Elizabeth died in 1603, the succession passed to the Scots House of Stuart, which, through family and cultural ties, was more influenced by the French model. Very early, James VI of Scotland and I of England became involved in disputes with both the legal and parliamentary establishment. James proclaimed the divine right of kings, which, he claimed, gave the king the power to appoint and dismiss judges and to raise taxes. Jurists recovered documents such as Magna Carta from obscurity to defend ancient privileges against the new royal pretensions. Implicit in their arguments lay the notion that royal power was derived from the consent of the people – however the people might be defined. The conflict was made more acute by the fact that personality did not match pretension. The Tudors had maintained authority through the force of their personalities, rather than through modern concepts of kingship. James was intelligent but personally unimpressive; his son Charles I was an inadequate recluse.

The Civil War

Charles I soon found himself in direct confrontation with parliament. In 1628 parliament presented a Petition of Right against the use of arbitrary royal power; in 1629 Charles dissolved parliament and began eleven years of direct rule. Many aspects of royal government were unpopular to influential subjects. An attempt was made to impose 'high church' worship, not only on England but also on Calvinist Scotland. An increasing number of cases were heard in royal prerogative courts, rather than in the courts of common law. Direct taxes, such as ship money, were levied without parliamentary approval. It seemed to many as though Charles would soon follow Richelieu's example and centralize all government.

The outbreak of war in Scotland brought financial disaster and Charles was forced to recall parliament in 1640. A struggle for power led to the outbreak of war in 1642. Historians have long argued the economic, religious and social issues that lay behind the conflict; certainly it was very different in nature from the violent upheavals that would later shake France and Russia. Parliamentary power was based in the rich south east, while the king's was centred in the poorer north and west. The parliamentary victory was due both to this difference in resources, and to the leadership of Oliver Cromwell, who emerged as the outstanding general in the conflict. He kept his New Model Army under such firm control that it could march across countryside and leave fields and property as they had been before the army passed.

The Commonwealth

The parliamentary broke into factions after the defeat of the king. In 1648 one faction seized power, with army support and staged the trial of Charles I. The execution of the king in 1649 provoked a shocked response across Europe. No action could have expressed the rejection of divine kingship more vividly. In 1653, Cromwell staged a military coup and assumed power as Lord Protector. Cromwell died in 1658, and a brief attempt was made to continue the protectorate under his son. This failed, however, and in 1660 the army again was responsible for bringing Charles II back to London.

The Glorious Revolution

The saga of the conflict between the Stuarts and their parliaments was not, however, over. Charles was mistrusted, both for his French sympathies and for his leaning towards Catholicism, but he still depended on parliament for revenue. In 1685 he was succeeded by his Catholic brother, James II. Three years later James was forced to leave the country, to be replaced by his Protestant daughter, Mary and her husband, the Dutch William of Orange, who exercised the practical power. William was more interested in securing the English alliance against France, than he was in pursuing power struggles with the English parliament. He therefore accepted laws that established that the king would henceforth require parliamentary consent to raise money and keep a standing army in peace time. It was also agreed that he could not alter or suspend any act of parliament.

In 1714 the English throne passed to the German house of Hanover. Since the new king could not speak English, day to day government passed to a prime minister and a cabinet, drawn from the majority party in the House of Commons. Political power had now finally passed from the monarchy to the property owning classes, who were represented in parliament. In the century that followed, parliament largely used its power to improve the position of the landowning class, often at the expense of the poor. English politics had, however, run against the European tide, which favoured greater centralization in the hands of the monarch.

The Act of Union

Throughout history, there had been strife between England and her smaller, poorer northern neighbour, Scotland. The union of the crowns in 1603 did not put an end to this. In 1707, however, the two countries became formally united in the Act of Union. Two clan uprisings followed in 1715 and 1745, in favour of the exiled Stuarts, but these were suppressed. Scots engineers, doctors and scholars were shortly after to make a major contribution to the great surge in national prosperity of the united Great Britain.

Russia

Boyars and Serfs

Across the continent the Russian state was following a very different pattern of development. The noble boyars held their land from the Tsar in return for defined services. Since Russia had no law of primogeniture, this class was getting ever larger, and most of its members poorer, as estates were split one generation after another. The mass of the people remained in the medieval condition of serfdom. Families were owned by their masters, had no right to move of their own free will and had no redress except in their masters' court.

The relationship of Tsar and boyars was often marked by bloody conflict. Ivan IV 'The Terrible' allied himself with the merchant class and the common people in an attempt to break noble power. He achieved many real reforms before mental disorder led him, in the latter years of his reign, to behaviour that anticipated that of Joseph Stalin in the twentieth century.

National Objectives

Russian development was hindered by the lack of a warm weather outlet to the ocean. The port of Archangel was ice-bound in winter, and all year the journey round northern Scandinavia was long and dangerous. The port of Rostov in the south was of little use as long as the Ottomans controlled the mouth of the Sea of Azov and the Dardanelles. National policy therefore became directed at winning a port on the Baltic Sea. This brought Russia into conflict with the advanced military state of Sweden, which regarded the Baltic as a Swedish lake.

The Russian tsar could mobilize huge armies, by raising levies, but there was no adequate support structure. Forces were sent to war with the vague hope that they would be able to live off the land. Often countless thousands of soldiers starved, and those who did manage to survive were in no condition to fight the world's most efficient army.

Peter the Great

Peter succeeded to the throne in 1682 at the age of ten, and suffered huge indignities from guards and boyars while still a child. Once a man, he announced his intention to bring his nation up to date and orientate it towards the West. A man of little education but enormous energy, he immersed himself in every detail of western science and technology. In a famous visit to the west he was equally at home working in disguise as a dock worker in Holland and meeting with scientists in England. His methods of enforcement were effective, if sometimes eccentric.

The vindication of Peter's work came in 1709 when his army won a decisive victory over the Swedish army under Charles XII at Poltava. Russia had won its outlet to the Baltic Sea, and here Peter decided to build his capital of St Petersburg.

Peter's great failure was that, like Louis XIV in France, he failed to do anything to improve the lot of the Russian poor. Someone had to pay for wars against Turkey and Sweden, for the modern weapons, for new ships and for the fine capital city. The poor were taxed and taxed again until they were left with the barest minimum necessary to keep themselves and their families alive. It is a measure of the depth of the misery and the capacity of the Russian people to absorb suffering that revolution did not erupt in violence for another 200 years.

The Western Mind

The Renaissance

Italy

The word *renaissance* was coined in the nineteenth century to describe the rebirth in Italy of the classical ideal in art, architecture and letters. The 'Middle Ages' was looked upon as a dark period before the great transformation of the fifteenth and early sixteenth centuries. Recent study has shown that the picture was more complicated; classicism remained strong throughout the Middle Ages, and there was more cross fertilization between Europe north and south of the Alps than had been assumed.

Any gallery visitor can, however, see the astonishing change that happened in visual perception within a comparatively few years. Across northern Italy artists experimented with new forms. In the words of the art historian, Giorgio Vasari, Giotto 'restored the art of design'. In Umbria, Piero della Francesca used mathematics to work out laws of perspective, well beyond any classical achievement. In Florence, Michelangelo combined an analytical eye with his huge talent to create a new vision of the human – or at least male – form. Even when painters and sculptors continued to work on church commissions, they now used live models to give a new sense of naturalism.

There was a keen awareness among the artistic community that they were living in an exciting new age. The Medici and other patrons commissioned works with secular themes, often drawn from Greek mythology. Artists were no longer faceless craftsmen who had produced so many medieval treasures. Art had found a new self-consciousness.

The same, secular driven, innovation was reflected in music and literature. There was a passionate interest in all aspects of antiquity. Some sculptors even buried their own work and dug it up again, claiming it as a classical discovery. Old manuscripts were found in monastic libraries or brought from the east and studied with a new intensity. Enthusiasm for antiquity did not preclude Christian belief; rather the classical tradition was seen as one element in divine revelation, so producing a syncretism that alarmed conservative churchmen.

By the mid-sixteenth century the Italian renaissance was losing its impetus. The first unique burst of innovation could not be maintained. The Counter Reformation church now demanded a more orthodox treatment of subject matter, both in literature and in painting. Much great work continued to be done, particularly in the Veneto. Paladio used Roman models in creating the architectural style that would bear his name, while Titian and his contemporaries were laying the foundations of what would become the baroque style. Generations of artists and patrons continued to travel to Italy to absorb the culture both of its classical past and of the present.

The Northern Renaissance

Some of the great painters of the Flemish school crossed the Alps and were much admired by Renaissance artists. Perhaps because they were not surrounded by antiquities in their home environment, however, they never made the sharp break with the gothic. Italian styles took many years to become established north of the Alps.

Northern Europe's unique contribution came in the field of scholarship and literature. Here writers were free from the restrictions of the Counter Reformation and fear of the Inquisition. Protestants wanted to make the Bible available to all. The translations of the scriptures by Martin Luther and William Tyndale were immensely influential in formalizing the written forms of German and English respectively. Traditional interpretations of the Bible were challenged when Erasmus of Rotterdam produced a version of the New Testament in the original Greek. Latin was now ceasing to be the universal language of scholarship. While a return to the vernacular liberated learning from the cloisters of the church, it also fractured the international culture, which had reached its peak in the twelfth century.

A strong secular tradition now flourished in England. Chaucer had already written for the newly educated merchant class. In 1510 John Colet, Dean of St Paul's Cathedral and close friend of Erasmus, made a gesture to the secularization of learning when he closed his cathedral school and refounded it under the control of a trading guild. The combination of Tyndale's language and renaissance scholarship had created a uniquely favourable environment when in 1585 an actor called William Shakespeare left his native Stratford to chance his fortune in London.

The great flowering of French literature came in the seventeenth century. Corneille and Racine were still in essence renaissance writers, handling classical themes with a paladian sense of form and style.

Printing

Most importantly, the re-invention of printing by movable type provided the means of dissemination of both religious and secular literature. Whether the innovation be credited to Johannes Guttenberg of Mainz or Lourens Coster of Haarlem, the technique provided the means of dissemination of the works of any author. Books became cheaper as print runs grew longer. In the following centuries print was used to promote colonies, to circulate scurrilous pamphlets to produce works on magic – as well as to disseminate works of scholarship, religion and literature. In 1702 *The Courant*, the world's first daily newspaper, was published in London. Soon afterwards works of popular fiction began to come off the presses. Print had become an integral part of Western life.

The Advancement of Science

The Copernican Revolution

In Hellenistic times the idea had been posited that the earth rotated round the sun, but this had not won general acceptance and in the sixteenth century it was still generally accepted that the heavenly bodies rotated around a stationary earth. In 1543, however, the Polish scholar Copernicus published a book arguing the theory of heliocentric astronomy.

Copernicus' theory received little attention. During this time, however, Dutch craftsmen were experimenting with glass lenses. They made spectacles and also telescopes for use at sea. One of these telescopes fell into the hands of the Italian teacher, Galileo Galilei, and he turned the instrument towards the skies. By studying sun spots, the phases of Venus and the rings of Jupiter, he provided clear proof that Copernicus had been correct.

Galileo delayed publishing his findings because he recognized that they must arouse a storm of controversy. Authority, both of the Bible and of ancient authors clearly supported a geocentric universe, and the church still held to authority as the arbiter of truth. He published his findings in 1632, but, faced with the terror of the Inquisition, he recanted in 1633.

Descartes – the Turning Point

Tradition states that, after formally accepting that the earth remained stationary, Galileo muttered 'it goes on moving'. Certainly the scientific impetus continued. In 1637 the French philosopher Descartes published *Discours de la Méthode*, which laid down what has become known as the Cartesian method. He argued that the experimental scientific process was the arbiter of truth. The pursuit of truth now involved breaking down knowledge into ever smaller areas of study. Medicine, for instance, became concerned with analysing the symptoms of disease in minute detail – arguably at the expense of a more integrated approach to the healing process.

In his dictum, *cogito ergo sum*, Descartes proclaimed the individualism that was to be the hallmark of modern European society. Western man had at last emerged from the shadow of past authorities, be they religious or classical. Personally a devout Catholic, Descartes rejected authority as an arbiter of faith and proclaimed that it had to be discovered through the human intellect. This was recognized as a fundamental challenge to the church, and Louis XIV personally ensured that Descartes was denied Christian burial.

Northern Europe

The condemnation of both Galileo and Descartes, and continued activities of the Inquisition placed scientists who lived in Catholic countries in an invidious position. In Protestant countries, scientists might meet hostility from those who defended religious authority, but they did not face persecution. The impetus for scientific innovation therefore passed to Northern Europe.

The first protestant scientist was the German, Kepler, who provided information on the movements of planets. Dutch scientists, continuing their work with lenses, developed the microscope. This opened up whole new areas of study in such areas as the biological sciences. In England the cause of experimental science was argued by the Lord Chancellor, Francis Bacon, who had early visions of its potential. In 1619, William Harvey demonstrated the mechanism of the circulation of the blood.

The advances in navigation, first in Holland, and then in France and, above all, in England, drove forward skills in cartography and geographical study. Progress in astronomy and in the construction of clocks were spin-offs from this navigational programme. Landsmen could now own clocks and watches that told the time with great accuracy. People began to organize their lives around them, and to treat the hours and minutes of the day with a new respect.

The revolution started by Copernicus was completed by Isaac Newton, who published his *Principia Mathematica* in 1687. While Galileo argued the structure of the universe, Newton demonstrated the gravitational mechanism by which it worked. In the words of the poet Alexander Pope;

Nature and nature's laws lay hid in night:

God said, 'Let Newton be!' and all was light.

Until Newton's time, humans were uncomprehending playthings of fate or divine providence. Now they began to understand that the everyday events of life were driven by a structure of causation. Later generations of scientists have maintained the process. Mendel worked out the structure of genetic inheritance, Darwin illustrated the mechanism evolution, Pasteur demonstrated the causes of disease, Crick and Watson unravelled the DNA code. These and many other insights make up the intellectual baggage of Western man.

Enlightenment to Romanticism

The Philosophes

The new enlightenment was to find its home in France, but the pattern of thinking owed much to seventeenth-century British writers, notably John Locke, who published his *Essay Concerning Human Understanding* in 1690. Locke said that many religious issues were beyond human knowledge, and he argued for tolerance and reliance on reason and reasonableness. His work reflected a wide change of mood, signalling the end of two centuries of religious strife; never again would the battle lines of Europe's terrible wars be drawn along religious lines.

The scientific advances of the seventeenth century encouraged philosophers of the following century to see the world as an ordered machine, much like one of the new clocks. There was an optimistic view that the universe was driven by a well-oiled logic, and, if people could only behave in a reasonable manner, the world's problems could be readily overcome. Past religious passions now appeared irrelevant. Many thinkers no longer saw God as an imminent cause of good or evil, but as a great watchmaker, an ultimate mover, who no longer had immediate relevance to life. The poet Pope, himself a Catholic, again provided the aphorism of the age with the couplet;

Know then thyself; presume not God to scan;

The proper study of mankind is man.

The dominant personality among the *philosophes* was the Frenchman, Voltaire. He was a satirist, rather than an original thinker, and he turned his barbed pen on anything that he saw as repressive or pretentious. Voltaire had problems with the French authorities, but he and his circle sewed seeds of scepticism about the old order, which would have immense repercussions in the later years of the century.

Evangelicalism

The first reaction against the intellectual emphasis of the age came with a religious revival that developed in parallel in England and her North American colonies, both within and outside the Church of England. John Wesley set the emotional tone of the movement, sharply in contrast with the language of the *philosophes*, when he described how he 'felt his heart strangely warmed'. This new Protestantism appealed primarily not to authority, but to the conversion experience. Until then, the Protestant churches had left missionary work almost entirely to the Catholic orders, but, by the end of the century, the worldwide tide of Protestant missions was beginning to flow, with incalculable, if often ambiguous, effects on non-European cultures.

Romanticism

If John Wesley represented the religious, Swiss-born philosopher, Jean Jacques Rousseau, led the secular reaction against Cartesian intellectualism. He proclaimed that man was pure when in the simple state, be that the uncorrupted form of a noble savage, or a new born child. The quest for goodness therefore involved a return to nature. Rousseau, more than any other person, taught people to look on their environment as a place of beauty. Since the time of Hannibal, travellers had crossed the Alps, without pausing to recognize them as anything other than a barrier on the road to Italy. Now, as if overnight, Rousseau's Swiss mountains were discovered as majestic things of beauty.

As romanticism emphasized the emotions above the intellect, so it elevated the creative artist, as the person most able to express those emotions. The great milestones of the movement, such as Wordsworth and Coleridge's *Lyrical Ballads*, Beethoven's *Eroica Symphony*, the late paintings of Turner, explored new forms and emotions. This could lead to excess, but it also opened the way to the achievements, such as those of French impressionist painters and the great romantic composers.

Social Reform

At about the same time, first clearly surfacing in the 1770s, a transformation began to occur in attitudes to social issues. For centuries, Europeans had been shipping Africans to slavery with no apparent compunction. Now powerful antislavery movements made themselves heard in France, Denmark, England and other countries. Movements for the reform of vicious penal systems, the abolition of the 'hanging codes' and for the humane treatment of the insane can be dated to the same time. Educational reform also became a cause for the future.

Credit for this new mood of social reform has been given to the pen of Voltaire, the preaching of Wesley and the ideals of Rousseau. All played their part. In education, for instance, evangelical passion to bring truth to the poor led directly to the opening of ragged schools, while Rousseau was laying the foundations for the quite separate development of child-centred learning, which was carried forward by the Swiss educator, Pestalozzi. The cause of reform was uniquely in the air, and the traditional political structures were ill equipped to contain it. Europe was ready for the cataclysm of the French Revolution.

Revolution

The French Revolution

The Estates General

In 1776 the British government was faced with a major revolution in its American colonies King Louis XVI of France, recognizing this as an opportunity of regaining some of the ground lost in the Seven Years War, involved France in the conflict. In military terms the intervention was successful; in financial terms it was a disaster. The French government, always in financial straits, was now unable to function. The shortfall could no longer be met by the time honoured device of increasing taxes on the poor, but those able to pay could only be taxed with their own consent. Members of the aristocracy recognized an opportunity of winning concessions from the monarchy in return for money, and they insisted that Louis should recall the French parliament, the *Estates General*, which had not met for 150 years.

The body met in three separate houses – aristocracy, clergy and the third estate. This last house represented the property owning middle classes and was largely made up of professional men. They had no vision of themselves as revolutionaries, but they were influenced by the ideas of the *philosophes* and of the American Declaration of Independence. Louis anticipated doing his business with the other two houses before disbanding the body, but the Third Estate had equal representation with the other two, and could count on considerable support in the House of Clergy. In the summer of 1789 the Third Estate declared that it constituted a National Assembly. Louis gave way before its demands and the body set about a huge programme of constitutional, administrative and social reform.

Popular Unrest

Since the time of the Frondes, French kings had been acutely aware of the dangers of uprisings among the poor, who remained unrepresented in the National Assembly. There was unrest in many parts of the countryside, where chateaux were attacked and hated rent books burned. The most immediate danger, however, came from the poor of Paris, who found themselves caught in a spiral of inflation, most crucially in the price of bread. By 14 July, it was estimated that only three days' supply remained in the storehouses of the capital.

The mob possessed armaments, but little ammunition. This lay under close guard in the royal castle of the Bastille. On 14 July the mob stormed the Bastille, leaving Louis quite helpless. He could not use his army because the loyalty of rank and file soldiers was in doubt. Many of the aristocracy were now fleeing France and in June 1791 Louis and his family made their bid to escape. They were captured and brought back as prisoners to the capital. The Assembly maintained the King as a figurehead until he signed the new Constitution in September. The body disbanded itself to make way for the new Legislative Assembly.

War and the Terror

Since the National Assembly had barred any of their number from seeking re-election, the new body was made up of inexperienced men. The dominant figures were Danton, who surrounded himself with members from the Gironde, in southern France, and the little lawyer Robespierre, whose power was based on the Jacobin Club. Protagonists of the new order now felt under siege. The King could still serve as a focal point for a royalist counter-revolution, and both Austria and Prussia were issuing threats. Robespierre argued that peace should be preserved, but Danton believed that the nation could only be united by war. He urged his fellow countrymen to 'dare and dare and dare again', and Frenchmen responded to his cry that the *patrie* was in danger. In April 1792, France declared war on Austria, and Prussia came in on the side of Austria. Early news from the war was disastrous, and the capital was gripped in a fever. On 30 July a contingent marched into the capital, singing the song that would become the national anthem. They demanded that Louis should be dethroned and a republic proclaimed. The men of Marseilles were soon joined by a huge citizen army that, chanting the *Marseillaise*, threw itself on and routed mercenary enemy soldiers at Valmy on 20 September. Two days later, France was declared a republic. Louis was placed on trial in December and executed on 21 January 1793.

The citizens' army swept across the Netherlands and at last achieved the 'natural frontiers' that had been beyond the reach of the armies of Louis XIV. The victors proclaimed liberty and equality for the poor of all lands, but in practice all too often they laid new tax burdens on those same poor to pay the cost of war.

In February 1793 France faced a coalition of Britain, Austria, Prussia, Holland, Spain, Sardinia and Italian states. Action taken against the Catholic church also provoked civil war in the conservative regions of the Vendée and Brittany. Effective power now passed from the Assembly to a Committee of Public Safety. In June, Danton's Gironde fell to Robespierre's Jacobins, and the period known as the Reign of Terror began. Among the victims were successive waves of politicians, including both Danton and his Girondins, and Robespierre and the Jacobins. As a result, power passed to a new generation of second rate men, who could not command the respect of the nation.

Meanwhile, the French citizen army, now reinforced by the first use of conscription in modern times, was more than holding its own in the war. Britain, while formidable at sea, was poorly equipped for a land war and the old enemies, Prussia and Austria, failed to coordinate their effort. The French armies, now led by a new generation of generals, remained firmly entrenched on the Rhine.

The Empire

The rise of Napoleon

In May 1798 a French army, led by the Corsican Napoleon Bonaparte, was sent to invade Egypt in an attempt to cut British trade routes. Land victories were made worthless when the British fleet, commanded by Admiral Nelson, destroyed the French supply fleet, and so cut the army off from Europe. In August 1899 Napoleon abandoned his army and returned to France to challenge the discredited leaders of the nation. His gambler's throw succeeded and on 9 November he staged a coup d'etat and assumed the title of First Consul. He set about centralizing power in his own hands; in 1802 he became consul for life, and in 1804, he followed the example of Charlemagne by crowning himself as Emperor Napoleon I. Any dismay at this negation of the ideals of the revolution was overwhelmed by the relief of ordinary Frenchmen at the return of ordered and firm government.

Imperial Government

Napoleon had a genius for administration. After an initial purge of remaining Jacobins, he set about healing old divisions and reuniting the country. He recognized that the continuing civil war in the Vendée could not be brought to an end unless the state came to terms with the Catholic church, so the old religion was restored to its position as the national faith. He set about recruiting the ablest men into government, regardless of whether they held republican or royalist sympathies. Most enduringly, he personally supervised a detailed revision of the whole of the French legal system into the *Code Napoleon*. Had Napoleon been content to hold the Rhine frontier and bring sound administration to France, his rule could have been outstandingly successful. But he was by instinct a general and the symbolic identification with Charlemagne at his coronation illustrated his determination to build the greatest empire that the world had seen. 'I am destined to change the face of the world. ' he declared. But Napoleon, like Louis XVI, discovered that wars could only be fought at a financial cost, which had to be passed on in taxes to the ordinary people of France and the conquered countries.

The Napoleonic Wars

The great struggles of previous centuries had achieved little more than change the line of a frontier here and there. In the three years from 1805, Napoleon completely redrew the map of Europe. He owed his success to the army that he had inherited from the revolution. Opposing generals recognized that the citizens' armies of France were carried forward on a tide of national energy, which had been released by the revolution. Napoleon added to this a military professionalism, identified with the magnificent Imperial Guard. The surge of victories carried the army across Europe as far as Bohemia, north into Scandinavia and south into Italy and Spain. Ancient rulers were replaced by members of the Bonaparte family or generals from the army. Even then, however, Britain, Spain and Russia remained as weak points remained in the French Continental System.

Giving priority to the invasion of Britain, Napoleon gathered barges at the channel ports. Any hope of carrying out this operation, however, ended in 1805 when the French fleet was destroyed at the Battle of Trafalgar. Britain therefore remained an implacable foe across the Channel.

The victorious French army in Spain found itself unable to overcome a fierce guerilla resistance that made full use of the broken terrain. The British despatched a force under the general who would later become the Duke of Wellington. In August 1812, after a relentless campaign, Wellington led his army into Madrid.

As Madrid fell, Napoleon was on the other side of Europe, leading 450,000 men on his disastrous campaign against Russia. He had already heavily defeated the Russian army and he believed that serfs would flock to join him once they heard that he had proclaimed their emancipation. He defeated the Russian army again at Borodino and marched on across the scorched countryside to occupy Moscow. But, when the Russians burned their own capital city around his army, and winter began to set in, he was forced to order the terrible retreat. In the end, only a tenth of his great army survived the ordeal. The Imperial Guard was reduced to some 400 men; 80,000 horses had died, leaving the emperor with no effective cavalry to put in the field.

Defeats in Spain and Russia shattered the myth of invincibility and by 1814 Napoleon had lost everything. Paris fell on 30 March, and he abdicated his imperial crown on 11 April. In France, however, loyalty to the deposed emperor remained strong, and, when he escaped from exile in 1815, men flocked to join his army. The hundred days' adventure ended when he was defeated by the combined British and Prussian armies Waterloo on 18 June.

Napoleon passed the remainder of his life in well-guarded exile, but the Napoleonic legend lived on. As French power declined, people remembered that it was the Little Corporal who had led them to glory.

Reaction and Revolution

The Return of the Old Order

After the defeat of Napoleon, members of the old ruling houses moved back into their palaces. The statesmen met in Vienna to reorganize the continent. The treaty took little account of nationalist aspirations. Poland was awarded to Russia; Venice and Lombardy to Austria; the Rhineland was taken from France and given to Prussia; the southern Netherlands were incorporated into Holland; Norway was made a part of Sweden.

The Austrian Prince Metternich was the main architect of this restoration of the old order. He fully recognized the huge changes in political consciousness brought about by the French Revolution, but he believed that these had to be suppressed, and that structures should return to return to their dynastic roots. He opposed all representative institutions, and established the Holy League as a coalition of powers dedicated to suppress ideas of liberty and nationalism, wherever they might show themselves. Of the major powers, only Britain – itself, however imperfectly, a representative government – stood apart to uphold a more liberal tradition.

The policy of intervention was successfully invoked when the Spanish people rose in rebellion in 1820. Austria also put down rebellion in her Italian possessions. Metternich was wise enough to see himself as the defender of a dying way of life. In 1821 the people of Greece rose against their Turkish masters. True to his principles, Metternich gave Austrian support to the Ottoman Turks, but the rebels won backing from Russia and Britain and achieved their independence in 1829.

Also in 1830 the people of Paris rose again and replaced the conservative king with his more liberal cousin, Louis Philippe and revolutions broke out in Poland and across Germany. In the same year, the Catholic Belgians rebelled against their Dutch masters. The conservative powers threatened to intervene, but Britain, in a gesture that would be called in eighty-four years later, guaranteed Belgian independence.

The Year of Revolutions

The unrest of 1830 was a prelude to much greater upheavals of 1848. In January, rebellion broke out in Sicily. In February the people of Paris drove Louis Philippe, now a figure of fun, into exile. In March, Venice, Parma, Milan and Sardinia all rose against Austria. As the year progressed, there was revolution in Poland and Hungary. Smaller German princes fell, most never to return. Uprisings in Berlin and Vienna even brought the powerful Prussian and Austrian states to the point of collapse, and the elderly Metternich had to follow Louis Philippe into exile.

The Hughes Capet French monarchy was finished for ever, and, after a period of civil war the French people turned again to the magic name of Napoleon, in the person of his nephew, Louis Napoleon. He followed family tradition by staging a coup d'état and assuming the title of Emperor Napoleon III. Across the rest of Europe, the ruling houses re-established control over their dominions.

New Nations

The Unification of Italy

A decade later, Camillo Cavour, a statesman in the Italian kingdom of Savoy, set about achieving by, political means, what had been beyond the powers of the revolutionaries. In 1858 he met with Napoleon III to discuss how Austrian rule might be ended and Italy unified under his King, Victor Emmanuel of Savoy. In 1859 French armies inflicted heavy defeats on the Austrians at Magenta and Solferino. In 1860, the popular soldier Garibaldi led 'the thousand' against the rulers of Sicily and Naples. He handed these territories over to Victor Emmanuel. For a time, Austria held on to Venice but the city fell in 1866. Finally the Papal States were brought into a united Italy in 1870. The political task was complete, but the new country faced formidable problems of poverty, and large numbers, particularly from the south, emigrated to find a better life.

The Unification of Germany

In 1862 Otto von Bismark, a nobleman of Junker descent, became Prime Minister of Prussia. His first speech was ominous for the future of European peace. 'The great issues of our day cannot be solved by speeches and majority votes – but by blood and iron.' The German-speaking people were already showing a formidable potential, but to achieve it all they had to be united into a nation state. Only Austria or Prussia could be the focus of such a state. Bismark determined that it should be Prussia.

In 1864 the two powers collaborated to annex the German-speaking lands of Schleswig and Holstein from Denmark. Then, two years later, Prussia went to war with Austria. On 3 July 1866 the Hapsburg army was devastatingly defeated at Sadowa. The Hapsburg monarchy retained Austria, but Germany was now effectively united. In 1870 Germany went to war with France, and the Napoleonic legend was laid forever on the field of Sedan.

As Bismark's army occupied Paris, there could no longer be any doubt that Germany was the dominant power in continental Europe. The violent methods by which this had been achieved were no innovation in European politics. The new state was based on admirable organization. German cities were models of organization and sanitary efficiency. A state school place was provided for every child, and illiteracy rates became the lowest in the world. The poor, who until that time had emigrated in large numbers, now showed their confidence in the government of their country by staying at home, and by playing their part in constructing the impressive industrial base of the new nation.

A Changing World

The Infrastructure of Change

Population

The population of Europe had been growing relentlessly since the time of the Black Death. Demographers have argued why, for instance, the increase was particularly pronounced in the sixteenth century. It appears as though women started marrying younger, and therefore having a longer child bearing life. But this leaves unanswered the question why such a social change should have occurred. The eighteenth century again saw a steady increase across western Europe, which predated major medical advances of the following century. A modest alleviation of the harsh conditions of rural life, the improvement of the housing stock, and some advances in public health may all have contributed to a reduction in the death rate.

Rulers generally welcomed a rising population; it provided an larger manpower pool for the military, and increased the tax base of the nation. In 1798, however, an English clergyman, called Thomas Malthus, published his *Essay on Population*. The world, he argued, possesses limited resources. As population grows, so the most vulnerable – the poor – must inevitably experience disaster and hunger. Malthus' work was influential, but his warnings were not, in the short term, authenticated by events. The reason for this was that, at the same time that the population was increasing, Europe was experiencing a green revolution, which greatly increased the amount of food.available to meet the growing demand.

The Second Agricultural Revolution

The first great change in farming practice came with the introduction of settled agriculture at the beginning of historical times. Even in Babylonian cities, farming families had to produce a surplus to feed craftsmen, priests and warriors. By the beginning of the eighteenth century, little had changed. It is estimated that in England eight out of ten people still lived in the countryside and that, on average, one farming family had to keep one other family from the produce of its land. People still ate bread baked from their own wheat and drank beer brewed from their own barley. Animals, except for breeding stock were still slaughtered and salted down for the winter.

Once again, change originated in small, highly urbanized, seventeenth century Holland. Dutch farms had to be more efficient than those of their larger neighbours, and major improvements were pioneered, particularly in the development of root vegetables, largely for animal winter feed, and in high yield artificial grasses, such as alfalfa and lucerne.

In the eighteenth century, the English gentry, unlike their neighbours in France, lived on their estates and it became fashionable to take an interest in farming. George III set the tone by contributing articles to a farming journal. Some began to introduce the Dutch innovations on their estates. New crops and methods of rotation were introduced and selective breeding produced remarkable improvements in the quality of livestock.

These improvements could not be introduced without radical changes in the organization of the countryside. Improved agriculture could not be successfully introduced in the old communal fields, so enclosures, which had been taking place for two centuries, were given a new impetus. In the change from peasant holdings to larger farms, worked by landless labourers, many lost land and ancient rights. The production of food, however, became a much more efficient process. By the late eighteenth century, British farmers were in a position to support a huge increase in the nation's urban population.

Financial and Human Resources

Any major economic expansion needs to be built on a sound financial base. Britain's growing international trade brought prosperity, and her island position meant that wealth did not have to be dissipated on the maintenance of a large standing army. By the standards of the time, she also had a sophisticated and well-capitalized banking industry.

It is harder to establish a link between the skills required for technological advance and the social and educational structure of the day. Few of the innovators of the new age came from the conventional academic background, which had produced Isaac Newton; they were more typically self-taught, or the products of Scottish or dissenting education.

Economic Theory

In 1776 Adam Smith published *The Wealth of Nations*, which laid the basis of modern economics. He argued the benefits of competition in a free economy, against both state control and the abuses of monopoly powers. His arguments were influential both in government and business circles, initially in Britain and later in the United States and elsewhere.

The First Industrial Revolution

Iron and Coal

Since the time of the Hittites, iron working had been centred on the great forests. The charcoal used in the smelting process consumed large quantities of timber, which was also vital for building and naval supplies. Over the centuries, the forests receded to the more remote areas. By the end of the seventeenth century, Britain faced something of a crisis. In the fourteenth century, German craftsmen of the Rhineland had learnt how to make cast iron, so that the metal could now be used to make a wider range of products, but there was an acute shortage of the wood needed to drive the blast furnaces.

Early in the eighteenth century, the Darby family of Shropshire finally solved the problem of how iron could be smelted from coal. As this technique became widely known, industry moved from the forests to the great coal fields that lie across Europe in a band from mid-Russia to Wales. Surface coal was soon exhausted and deep mines were sunk to exploit the seams. Iron goods could now be produced in bulk.

Steam Power

As early as Hellenistic times, it had been recognized in theory that steam could be used to drive an engine, but the technological basis was lacking. The need for pumps to drain the new deep mines made progress all the more essential. The Scottish engineer, James Watt made the essential breakthrough when he separated the cylinder from the condenser. As a result, industry could now be liberated, not only from the forests, but also from the banks of fast flowing rivers.

Water Transport

Before the eighteenth century, land transport was rudimentary over most of Europe. Once again, the Dutch had pioneered the use of the canals, which drained their country for transporting loads. The French government also constructed the magnificent Canal du Midi, designed to prevent goods having to be carried around the coast of Spain. France also had a high quality road network, built by forced labour, but these, like those of the Romans, were built for military use.

In 1861 the Duke of Bridgwater opened a canal that linked his coal mine at Worsley with the growing town of Manchester. The potential for improved communications to lubricate economic growth was illustrated when the price of coal in Manchester fell immediately by a half. The great revolution occurred, however, when steam power was applied to locomotion. Here the initiative was taken in the United States, where inland waterways provided the essential communication links for the new nation. In 1807, Robert Fulton sailed *The Steamboat* from New York to Albany in 32 hours – a journey that had previously taken four days. Two years later, steam power was applied to ocean navigation.

Railways

The world's first commercial railway was opened in Britain in 1825, between Stockton and Darlington. Huge sums of money were invested in railway building in many nations, but, despite massive construction programmes, especially in the United States and Germany, Britain retained her initial advantage. The age of cheap and rapid communication brought important social, as well as economic, change as the structure of society began to reflect the new mobility.

Cotton and the Factory System

There had long been a market for fine fabrics in western Europe. By the early eighteenth century a substantial silk industry had grown up in France, which reduced dependence on imports. At this time, cotton was still a luxury fabric, and ready woven cloth was imported from India. Entrepreneurs then began to import raw cotton, which was put out for manufacture to domestic workers. Whole families worked immensely long hours at carding, spinning and weaving to earn a modest subsistence. The early machines were invented by enterprising craftsmen to help boost domestic output.

The first large spinning factory was built by Richard Arkwright at Cromford, near Derby in 1771. By the early nineteenth century all the stages of cotton cloth production had been brought within the factory system. Britain, backed by her huge merchant marine, had established a dominant position in the world supply of textiles. One machine, tended by a woman or a girl, could now do the work of many domestic workers, and traditional producers, from Britain itself to India, lost their livelihood.

Despite being a closely guarded secret, the new technology was bound to become known. The United States was already showing itself a fertile ground for industrial development and a substantial industry grew up in New England.

Urban Growth

The population of Europe continued to grow rapidly throughout the nineteenth century, but the increase was now concentrated in the urban centres. In the nineteenth century, the population of London increased from about 900,000 to some 4.7 million, that of Paris from 600,000 to 3.6 million; small country towns turned into conurbations. This growth in Europe was matched by comparable expansion of New York and the Midwestern cities of the United States.

The urban centres grew faster than their service infrastructure, and so the industrial revolution became identified with slum housing, malnutrition and cholera, on a scale that remains common in the burgeoning cities of modern developing countries. For most of the workers, however, the change from rural to urban poverty was not the disaster that has often been painted. The poor had always lived on the edge of subsistence; there were indeed reverses, as during the 'hungry forties', but the overall tendency was towards an improvement in living standards. Pasteur's discovery of the germ causation of disease stimulated major sewage and other sanitation projects in the second half of the century.

The Second Industrial Revolution

The Decline of Britain

Visitors to the Great Exhibition, which was held in London in 1851, would not have readily recognized that the age of British industrial supremacy was already nearing its end. Britain possessed half of the world's mileage of railway lines, and half of its merchant marine. Five years later, the British inventor, Henry Bessemer would present his Convertor, which made possible the mass production of steel. The nation's lead still appeared unassailable.

In hindsight it is, however, possible to recognize the signs of decay. Too much investment lay in the industries of the first industrial revolution, which were vulnerable to competition from low cost countries; the educational system, both for the rich and poor was ill equipped to train in the more technical skills needed to meet the ever growing complexities of industry; British industry was already at times failing to capitalize on the skills of the inventors.

Germany and the United States

In the second half of the century two powers demonstrated great economic potential. German military expenditure funded the expansion of the mighty firm of Alfred Krupp, which was soon competing with British companies for the supply of railway and shipyard equipment. The electric dynamo was invented simultaneously in Britain and Germany, but the German firm of Siemens reaped the benefits. In 1885 Carl Benz produced the first working automobile using the internal combustion engine, so initiating the greatest transport revolution in the world's history.

The United States was also showing both creativity and economic power. Inventive geniuses, like Bell and Edison, found that the young nation, with its growing market base, provided an ideal environment for the exploitation of new technology. The telegraph, the telephone, the domestic sewing machine, mechanized agricultural machines, the safety lift, air conditioning, the electric light, the phonograph, the cine camera and the aeroplane were all American contributions to the more sophisticated second phase of industrialization. Andrew Carnegie and Henry Ford also showed the American capacity to build great operations on the inventions of others.

Capital and Labour

Trades Unions

Throughout history, there had always been a sharp divide between the rich and the poor, but the working people within the new factory system became acutely aware of the polarization between those who owned the means of production and their employees. By gathering workers together in large units of production, the owners made it practicable for them to organize in defence of their living conditions.

Robert Owen, a working man turned successful cotton master, attempted to establish a model industrial society at New Lanark, Scotland; he introduced schools and all kinds of leisure activities for the working people, and still was able to show a profit for the mill. He became dissatisfied with this paternalistic approach and set up a cooperative venture in New Harmony in America. This proved less successful, and he returned to Britain, where he founded the ambitious Grand National Consolidated Trades Union. This was a bid to harness the power of the working people, so that they could control the industries in which they worked. Owen's union failed, as did most of the early attempts to organize labour. Unskilled workers, faced by organized management, lacked credible bargaining power. Over much of Europe, they were further weakened by being divided between opposing Christian and socialist unions.

The battle between capital and labour could be seen in its rawest state in the United States. The owners mobilized city and state authorities and hired private armies to break strikes. Also there were as yet no antitrust laws to prevent employers from combining to achieve their objectives. The workers responded by organizing themselves into violent secret societies, like the Molly Macguires of the Pennsylvania coal mines. At Andrew Carnegie's Homestead works at Pittsburgh in 1892, the two sides confronted each other in pitched battle.

At Homestead, as elsewhere, management emerged victorious because there was always unskilled 'blackleg' labour on hand to fill the jobs of those who went on strike. At the end of the century, however, there emerged a new generation of union leaders who recognized that progress could best be made by organizing the skilled labour that was now vital for the more sophisticated industries. In The United States, in 1886, Samuel Gompers organized these skilled trades into the more successful American Federation of Labour. In the years that followed, the rights of organized labour were increasingly recognized by the legal systems of the industrialized nations.

Socialism

During the time that Robert Owen was experimenting with new structures, continental thinkers were beginning to challenge the laissez-faire theories of Adam Smith. Most influential was the French nobleman, Claude de Saint-Simon, often looked on as the founder of socialism, who published his critique of the new industrial age in the 1820s. He argued for the replacement of the existing ruling elite by a 'meritocracy', which would manage the economy for the general good of the population, rather than for individual gain.

Saint-Simon's ideas gained ground in France. In 1848 Paris experienced two distinct revolutions. The first unseated the king; the second was a bloody confrontation between workers, proclaiming the new socialists ideas, and the bourgeoisie, who defended traditional property rights.

Communism

Karl Marx watched the destruction of the Paris workers in 1848 with distress but without surprise. He had been associated with the revolutionary movement in his native Germany before being forced into exile. He believed that history showed two struggles. The first, as in all earlier revolutions, had been between the feudal authorities and the bourgeoisie. The second, in his own day, lay between the bourgeoisie and the proletariat.

Marx held that the value of goods lay in the labour that had been expended in its production, and the interests of the proletariat lay in winning a fair return for that labour. That was in conflict with the interests of the owners, or bourgeoisie, who were dedicated to achieving a profit on the product. Within a capitalist society the proletariat was therefore alienated from the production process, and both sides were inevitably locked in class war. The objective for the proletariat was to win control of the machinery of government by revolution, and then to use the new communist state to control the 'commanding heights of the economy' – land, transport, factories and banks.

Marx and his friends tried to gather the revolutionary movement into the unity without which he believed it could never be effective. In 1864 the First International meeting of the Communist party was held in London, with delegations from France, Germany, Italy, Switzerland and Poland, as well as Britain. The party, however, quickly showed its capacity for splitting into factions. When, by the beginning of the next century, none of the great industrial nations had fallen, many thought that the communist challenge had passed away. It was not anticipated that the revolution would come in Russia, which, under Marx's definition, still lay within the feudal stage of development.

Change and Society

Education

The movement for educational reform can be traced to the late eighteenth century, but another century had to pass before change affected the lives of working people. In Germany and the United States, and later in Japan, politicians recognized that, if a nation were to remain competitive in the new world, it needed an educated labour force. All across the industrial world there was a huge increase, not only in basic education but in the provision of higher education. Literacy and numeracy were at last seen as functional skills, rather than as the prerogative of a privileged élite.

The Women's Movement

Before the middle of the nineteenth century individual voices had been raised to protest against the subjugation of women in western society, but the origin of a formal movement can be placed in 1848, the year of revolutions. In that year a group of women, with men supporters, met at Seneca Falls in New York State and laid out a programme that was to be the blueprint for the women's movement. The resolutions demanded voting rights, equality before the law, the right to hold property, justice in marriage, equal opportunity in education, free access to jobs and an end to the pervasive double standard in morality. The political struggle became identified with the names of Susan Anthony in the USA and later with the Pankhurst family in Britain. Many advances were made, particularly in educational provision, but the radical change came with the First World War. Women who undertook a wide range of men's work could no longer be denied basic rights.

Leisure

Towards the end of the century working hours began to be reduced and, perhaps for the first time in history, the less privileged found themselves with time for leisure activities. Virtually all the major sports that are popular across the world today were codified during these decades, and this happened mainly in Britain, where the industrial achievements brought the earliest benefits. By the beginning of the twentieth century, the bicycle and the railway excursion were giving urban dwellers a new sense of freedom. Many problems remained, but those who lived in the industrial societies experienced a genuine improvement in the quality of life. This improvement made the programmes of the revolutionaries less attractive than Karl Marx and his followers had anticipated.

America

The Birth of the United States

The Causes of Conflict

When the Seven Years' War ended in 1763 it appeared that Britain had achieved her aims in the New World. The French colonies in Canada had fallen under British rule and the stranglehold on the Thirteen Colonies by French forts on the Ohio River had been broken. Very shortly, however, it became clear that strains were building up in the relationships between the American colonists and the mother country.

Under the mercantilist system, it was taken for granted that the colonies existed for the benefit of the other country. As American economies strengthened, however, they began to generate their own momentum. Slaving ships from New England, for instance, now competed directly with those from Bristol on the Guinea Coast.

The American colonists had already developed the westward momentum, which remains a feature of the nation today. Pioneers were penetrating into the rich lands to the west of the Appalachians. Britain, as the colonizing power, was responsible for security, and the London government therefore had to decide whether to expand budgets to provide protection to these pioneers. To the annoyance of many colonists, a decision was taken that a limit should be drawn along the ridge of the Appalachians. The government further decided that the American colonies should be taxed to help pay security costs. When the traditional colonial assemblies refused to vote the funds, the British government decided to establish the principle of its right to impose direct taxation. The Stamp Act, the Sugar Act and the duty on tea were all stages in the deteriorating relationships. None were in themselves onerous, but they created genuine anxiety. Sugar molasses, for instance, was turned into rum, which was the staple of the slave trade. Any tax could be used to make American ships uncompetitive with their British rivals.

Independence

Tension centred on the largest city and trading port of Boston, where fighting started in 1775. In the following year representatives from the Thirteen colonies, now to become states, met in Philadelphia to declare themselves independent. The famous and highly influential Declaration of Independence, drafted by Thomas Jefferson, justified the act of rebellion in terms that drew from Locke and the *philosophes*. It declared that government derives from the consent of the governed and the misgovernment, listed in detail, broke that tie of consent.

The colonists faced serious problems in organizing themselves to fight a major European power; there was little natural unity, and money to fund the conflict proved as hard to raise as it had been under British rule. American success was largely the result of the outstanding leadership qualities of George Washington and the ability of the colonists to adapt to a guerilla style of warfare, well suited to the heavily forested terrain. In 1781, the British army surrendered at Yorktown and two years later, Britain accepted defeat.

The Constitution

It was not immediately clear, however, whether one or thirteen new nations had emerged from the conflict. Many of Washington's army remained unpaid and no mechanism existed for a central government to raise money from the states. The Constitutional Convention of 1787 was faced with serious division between the interests of large and of small states, and between those who wanted to see a strong central government and those who preferred to see real power continue to lie with the individual states. The final document, which was ratified in 1788, steered a compromise course between the interests. The Executive, Legislature and Judiciary all had their own spheres of responsibility, and acted as a control on one another by a complex structure of checks and balances.

Canada

The successful rebellion by the American colonies left the British government reluctant to expend further effort and resources on colonization. Many loyalists from the south had moved north, and the division between the French and English population remained deep. The colonies covered much sparsely populated territory and communications remained poor. The people were united only in a common hostility to any threat of annexation by the more powerful neighbour to the south.

In the first half of the nineteenth century, progress was made towards the establishment of a confederacy. In 1867, The British North America Act brought together four provinces into a federal Dominion of Canada. To protect minority French interests, language and education remained provincial concerns and other provinces joined the federation in subsequent years. In 1885, the last rivet was driven into the Canadian Pacific Line, bringing together east and west and opening up the prairies for agricultural development.

Latin America

To the south, the countries of Latin America remained under the colonial control of Spain and Portugal. The successful rebellion of the British colonies was shortly followed by the collapse of the old monarchies in the face of Napoleon's army. Links with the old countries were cut during the European wars, and this generated an outburst of nationalist fervour.

Spain fought a series of devastating wars to recover control of her American empire. In 1810, the Mexican priest Manuel Hidalgo y Costilla led the poor in a rising, but independence was not finally won until 1821. Power then passed, not to the poor, but to the wealthy classes of Spanish descent. Rulers like Santa Anna treated the country as a personal *hacienda*, and the situation of the poor became, if anything, worse than it had been in colonial days.

In 1811 Venezuela declared its independence under the Francisco de Miranda and his lieutenant Simon Bolivar. Bolivar had travelled in Europe and was particularly influenced by the writings of Voltaire, and he now saw himself as the George Washington who would bring unity to the Spanish-speaking countries of South America. He won a series of victories against Spain, and independence seemed assured, provided the conservative European powers did not follow Metternich's plan and intervene to uphold the old order. This was prevented by American President Monroe, who warned off any intervention by proclaiming his doctrine of 'hands off America'.

Bolivar seemed on the verge of creating a United Republic of Columbia, which could be a comparable power to the USA. He was, however, unable to hold the new country together, and one part of the country after another broke off to form new nations. As in Mexico, the privileged classes preserved power for themselves. The European nations competed to invest, particularly in Argentina, and there was a steady stream of immigration from the Old World, but the old inequalities remained, and the economies of many of the new Latin American countries became dangerously dependent on single primary products.

The path to independence was smoother in Brazil. The Portuguese royal family decided not to defend its rights, and in 1822 the country was declared an independent empire by consent. Here, too, old social inequalities remained and, as late as 1888, Brazil was the last American country to abolish the Atlantic slave trade.

Slavery and the Civil War

King Cotton

Dr Samuel Johnson spoke for many when he poured scorn on American ideals of liberty, which were denied to the black slave population. The continuance of the institution was one of the issues discussed in the Constitutional Convention. There were three broad points of view. Opponents of slavery wished to see the institution outlawed in the new nation; representatives of the southern states would not contemplate joining a union that deprived them of their property; moderates, like Washington himself, opposed slavery, but they believed that they could let history take its course. Slavery, they argued, was outdated and it would wither away of its own accord. Events proved them wrong.

The new English cotton mills created an insatiable demand for raw cotton. The native short staple cotton was an uneconomic crop until in 1793 Eli Whitney invented a gin, which enabled it to be cleaned in large quantities. In the decades that followed huge areas of the south was given over to cotton cultivation. This created a demand for slaves. The Atlantic slave trade was declared illegal, but many were smuggled into the country; others were 'sold down the river' by plantation owners from the more northerly slave states.

This resurgence of slavery led to widespread unrest. Slave risings broke out and an increasing number of slaves used the freedom road to escape north. White and black activists combined in a highly organized antislavery movement. Anger rose when in 1850 Congress passed the Fugitive Slave Law, which gave southern owners the right to pursue their property into the free northern states.

Slave and Free States

The House of Representatives, elected by population, was dominated by the free states. The Senate was more finely balanced. As new states were added to the Union, the balance was maintained. California and Oregon tilted the balance towards the free states. 'Bleeding' Kansas, a fierce bone of contention, fell to the slave party. When, in 1860, a republican from Illinois called Abraham Lincoln was elected president, the slave states felt that the political balance had swung irretrievably against them. In March 1861 eleven southern states declared their secession from the Union and the following month they attacked the federal Fort Sumter.

The Civil War

Over six hundred thousand men died in the four years of war that followed. The southern armies were highly motivated and generally well commanded, but they were bound to lose a long war of attrition. The industrial north had a larger population, more industrial production and more miles of railway. This was the first major war in history fought with armaments that were the products of the industrial revolution, and great battles, like Antietam and Gettysburg presaged the terrible loss of life at Verdun and on the Somme half a century later. When the war ended in April 1865, the south lay devastated. Lincoln was assassinated five days later.

Civil Rights

The war had been fought over the right of the south to secede from the Union. Slavery was abolished in the process. Lincoln's emancipation decree was given the force of law by the Thirteenth Amendment of 1865, and further amendments wrote civil rights into the constitution. In the years of reconstruction, black legislators took their seats, and it appeared as though political and social equality might be close. Gradually, however, by a process of manipulation and terrorization, the white supremacists regained control of the southern states. The liberal fervour of the antislavery years was now spent, and the Supreme Court proved unwilling to uphold even the most clearly defined constitutional rights. Disillusioned, many blacks migrated to the booming industrial cities of the north, where they encountered new forms of discrimination.

The situation only began to improve with the great Civil Rights movement of the 1960s, when Dr Martin Luther King provided a rallying point for his people's aspirations and liberal white sympathizers were again mobilized, as they had been a century before in the antislavery campaign.

The Westward Movement

Thomas Jefferson

Of all the founding fathers, Jefferson had the clearest vision that the new nation could become a great power and that this had to be based on an exploitation of the great potential of the continent. He was the architect of the system whereby new states could be added to the Union. By 1803 Napoleon had decided that the Mississippi lands of Louisiana, which remained French, were of no value, and Jefferson, now president, negotiated to buy them for $15,000,000 – and so doubled the land area of the United States. In 1804 he sent out an expedition led by Lewis and Clark to cross the continent and report back on its potential.

Jefferson's vision of the west as the land of opportunity gradually captured the American imagination. It was argued that the American people – by which was meant the white American people – had a 'manifest destiny' to possess the continent from the Atlantic to the Pacific Oceans.

The Dispossession of the Indian People

During the early years of the nineteenth century, Americans of European origin were pushing into traditional Indian territory beyond the Appalachians. Every expedient was used, from purchase to forced expulsion, to drive the Indian people back into the western grasslands, which remained unattractive to white settlement.

The nomadic buffalo culture of the plains Indians was based on horses originally acquired form the southern Spanish settlements, and it was therefore a comparatively recent development. In the middle of the century, migrants were attracted, not to the featureless plains with their extremes of climate, but to the far west. For a brief period, wagon trains and nomadic Indians were able to coexist. By the 1870s, however the white men began to move into these last hunting grounds. The buffalo were hunted to deprive the Indian people of their livelihood and provide food for railway construction workers; then the railway link with the eastern markets made the grasslands attractive for cattle farming. Finally new agricultural machinery and irrigation techniques made large scale wheat farming economic. With the buffalo herds destroyed and their whole way of life undermined, the surviving Indian people were driven back into ever more arid and infertile reservations.

Oregon Country

Lewis and Clark reported on fertile land on the Pacific coast around the mouth of the Columbia River. Many Americans were prepared to go to war with Britain over British Columbia, but agreement was reached on the 49th parallel boundary. This left ample scope for colonization in the north west. The wagon trains that followed the Oregon trail brought farming families into this attractive region.

The Southwest

The new Mexican state claimed the whole of the southwest, from Texas to California and as far north as Utah and southern Wyoming. Spanish settlement had been based on missions, which were often widely dispersed, and the non-Indian population of the region remained low. Between 1836 and 1847 the United States and Mexico were in an intermittent state of war, which ended with the capture of Mexico City and defeat for Mexico. Under the treaty, the United States won the whole of the southwest. Existing property rights of the Spanish speaking people were, in theory, protected, but, in practice, they had no protection against the newly arrived 'Anglos', who controlled the courts.

Shortly before the treaty was signed, gold was discovered at Sutter's Mill in Northern California. This set off the Gold Rush, which brought fortune hunters flocking to California from the east, and, indeed, from many parts of the world. The influx of population in turn created a farming boom and California was rap idly converted from a thinly populated region, largely consisting of mountains and desert, to the world's most rapidly expanding economy.

Immigration

From Europe

Any measurement of the population rise of Europe from the middle of the eighteenth to the end of the nineteenth centuries should properly include, not only statistics on those countries themselves, but also of the millions who emigrated to destinations in many parts of the world – as well as their descendants. Figures cannot be collated, but people of European stock took over great areas of the world, often at the expense of the indigenous population.

In order to overcome human reluctance to disrupt living patterns, there needs to be a 'push factor' propelling people from their homes, and a 'pull factor' drawing them to a new environment. As in the early years of colonization, the growing wealth of the United States drew economic, political and religious refugees from Europe. The British still came. Many of the Mormons who pulled their handcarts across the plains to Utah originated from among the cotton mills of Lancashire. The depopulation of the Scottish glens provided a new stream, although most preferred to go to Canada. The Catholic Irish, angered by English protestant rule and by unjust land laws had long been ready recruits; the disastrous potato famine of 1845–46, which is estimated to have claimed the lives of a million people, turned the stream into a flood.

People now came from new countries of origin. Norwegian families, long accustomed to extremes of climate, left their marginal fiord farms to farm in the harsh environment of Wisconsin and the Dakotas. Germans fled from the political and social upheavals of their country. Peasants from southern Italy, condemned to live on the brink of subsistence under rapacious landlords, took the boat to America. Towards the end of the century, people were coming from further east. Russian Jews fled the pogroms; Poles fled Russian oppression. All funnelled through Ellis Island to emerge, often penniless, and speaking no English, onto the streets of New York. They worked as they could, in clothing sweatshops, on construction, in domestic service. Each new national group faced discrimination as those who were settled in jobs and homes tried to protect their position from the work-hungry newcomers.

The New Immigration. The capture of the south west brought a significant Spanish speaking population within the United States. Civil war in Mexico and an increasing divergency of the standards of living brought an increasing number of immigrants across the border. Most came as migrant workers, following the crops into California and far beyond. In good times, they were welcomed as cheap labour, but in times of depression they proved easy targets for discrimination. In the twentieth century immigrants from Puerto Rico and other Caribbean islands have also increased the Hispanic population of the eastern side of the country.

Asian immigration began when Chinese labourers were recruited to work in the 1849 Gold Rush. Distinctive in those early days in their 'queues' and national clothing, they found themselves at the bottom of the immigrant 'heap', increasingly shut out from desirable employment and property ownership by Chinese Exclusion Acts. They, like subsequent Asian immigrants, preserved a respect for education, which enabled them to improve their status rapidly when the legal discrimination was brought to an end.

The United States Abroad

The Continent

The Monroe Doctrine was originally proclaimed to protect emerging Latin nations seeking to establish independence from European colonial powers. In the later years of the century it was used to promote the continent as a sphere of US interest.

One major thrust lay through the Caribbean towards South America. In 1903 effective control over the Isthmus of Panama was wrested from Columbia and the Panama Canal linking the two oceans was opened in 1914. War with Spain in 1898 also ended with the acquisition of Puerto Rico and Cuba.

American interests also led expansion across the Pacific. Alaska was purchased from Russia in 1867, providing the westward bridge of the Aleutian Islands. Midway Island was won in the same year, followed by Samoa and the Hawaiian group. The war with Spain finally brought Guam and the Philippines within the American empire.

Although the United States was no longer a new country, the need to absorb waves of immigrants fostered an introversion and at times an aggressive nationalism. Many American statesmen, wishing to distance their country from what they saw as the destructive quarrels of the old world, proclaimed a policy of isolationism. The history of the twentieth century was to show that the world's greatest power could not successfully stand back from international events.

The Age of Imperialism

India

The East India Company

The battles in the eighteenth century between rival trading companies were fought, not to win territory, but to establish trading advantage. In 1757, however, the British East India Company's army in Bengal first captured the French trading station and then defeated the Nawab's army at Plassey. The company then found itself, by default, the inheritor of Mogul power. Now irretrievably involved in politics, it gradually extended its control over large areas of the subcontinent.

Company officials never lost sight of the fact that their objective was to turn in a profit. As the company extended its control over all internal as well as external trade, the standard of living of many Indians declined. Company officials took the opportunity of amassing private fortunes, often by corrupt means. In the days before steam ships and the opening of the Suez Canal, India was far distant from home. Men travelled out as bachelors and many took local women and lived much as Indian princes.

After the American revolution, the British government was reluctant to become involved in further colonial expansion. To bring the Company under control, however, it assumed dual control of the Indian possessions in 1784. The writings of Adam Smith had discredited the old mercantilist ideas, which had been the justification for early colonization. In line with prevailing doctrines of free trade, the company therefore lost its monopoly trading rights and was reduced to an administrative organization.

Modernization

The evangelical fervour of the age brought Protestant missionaries of many denominations to the subcontinent. Most had a simple desire to replace the traditional religions of Hinduism and Islam. They started schools that offered western education and encouraged converts to adopt western dress and habits. These missionaries looked to the Christian rulers for protection and active encouragement.

The new generation of administrators was less directly motivated by the profit motive and more by a desire to bring the benefits of modern life to the people of India. Many had a genuine, albeit paternalistic, respect for Indian culture, and they resisted the missionaries' attempt to overturn traditional ways. These administrators did, however, believe in reform. Laws, based on western practice, were introduced to stamp out traditional practices, such as the burning of widows and the killing of infant girls. The products of the industrial revolution, such as the electric telegraph and railways were also enthusiastically introduced.

The Mutiny

The modernization programme inevitably created tension. Railways, for instance, were looked upon as a threat to the caste system. There was also powerful resentment against British acquisition of new land, particularly in the northern province of Oudh. The introduction of a new form of greased cartridge was the immediate cause of the Indian Mutiny of 1857. This was as much a traditionalist reaction against modernization as it was a rebellion against the ever expanding foreign rule. Many educated Indians, like the operators of the Delhi telegraph, died at the hands of the mutineers. The mutiny was put down with as much ferocity as it had been waged. The British parliament at last accepted direct responsibility for government. In 1877 Queen Victoria was proclaimed Empress of India and her rule over the subcontinent became the symbol of British power. The true age of imperialism had begun.

The Raj

The new rulers determined that mistakes that had led to the mutiny should not be repeated. They therefore took care to respect the rights of the traditional ruling class. When early representative institutions were introduced, this ruling class was called upon to represent the Indian people. The aspirations of the rising intelligentsia were therefore overlooked. Indeed, the contempt for the educated 'westernized native', which was to be characteristic of British imperialism, was first shown in India. The first meeting of the Indian National Congress was held in Bombay in 1885, but a further twenty years would pass before independence appeared on the Congress agenda.

Throughout history, India, like China, had shown a capacity to absorb its conquerors; the British alone resisted assimilation. The new rulers of the Indian Civil Service were drawn from the elite and many acquired a knowledge of Indian language and customs, but, in the wake of the Mutiny, a barrier existed between the two races that could not be crossed. Fast and comfortable steam ships now linked Europe and India, and the journey time was much reduced when the Suez Canal opened in 1869. Administrators and traders increasingly kept their roots in Britain, while serving tours of duty overseas. Also men were now joined in India by their womenfolk. Few of these *memsahibs* had work that brought them into contact with Indian people, so their cultural values were never seriously challenged.

In the second half of the century new concepts of racial superiority were fashionable, particularly in northern Europe. Europeans had long treated other races as inferior, but they had not theorized about it. Now concepts of racial superiority were becoming fashionable, partly based on popular Darwinianism. The European rulers of India, as of other colonized people, were therefore ill equipped to understand the nationalist aspirations when they did come to the surface.

China

The Manchu Empire

In the middle of the seventeenth century, invaders from Manchuria overthrew the Ming emperor and established the foreign Manchu (Ch'ing) Dynasty. Following the ancient pattern, the early rulers were able men, who established a working relationship with the mandarin administrators, and for more than a century the land experienced one of its more prosperous periods.

By the end of the eighteenth century, however, problems were growing. It is estimated that the population trebled, from 100 to 300 million between 1650 and 1800, and it would reach 420 million by 1850. In China, Malthus' forecasts on the effects of population growth proved accurate. All available land was already under cultivation, so production could not match increased demand. The situation became disastrous in the terrible northern famine of 1887–89, when some ten million people starved to death. As social problems became worse, so the quality of imperial government deteriorated into corruption and mismanagement. Resentment boiled and people remembered that the Manchu were a foreign race.

In 1786 rebellion broke out in Shantung, and this was followed in 1795 by the White Lotus Uprising on the borders of Szechwan and Shensi. These were the preludes of a century of peasant unrest on a scale far beyond anything experienced in human history before that time. It is estimated, for instance, that more people died in the T'ai-p'ing Rebellion of 1850–64 than in the whole of the First World War, while huge Islamic risings of the north and southwest left wide areas of the country devastated. The Manchu Dynasty, however, managed to cling to power through all these upheavals.

China and the West

Since the earliest times, China had always had a favourable balance of trade with Europe. There was a demand in the West of porcelain and silks, but, apart from a few clocks and toys, Europe had little to offer in return. Towards the end of the eighteenth century the balance took a turn for the worse. There was a fashion in Europe for Chinoiserie, reflected in some of the art of the period. More important, tea became the staple drink of many Europeans. This could only be bought by a steady drain of bullion.

Western merchants were convinced a huge Chinese market, was waiting to be opened up, but contact was strictly controlled through a few merchants in Canton. Attempts to open the market ended in frustration. In 1793 George III of Britain sent an emissary to the Manchu court with gifts. The Emperor thanked King George for his 'submissive loyalty in sending this tribute mission' from 'the lonely remoteness of your island, cut off from the world by intervening wastes of sea', but the mission achieved nothing of substance.

The Opium Wars

In the early years of the nineteenth century British traders found that the drug opium could right the adverse balance of trade. A great deal of Indian farmland was placed under the crop and the flow of bullion into China was quickly reversed. Apart from the direct damage done by the opium, the Chinese government found that the drain of wealth quickly created financial crisis. The opium trade was a breach of Chinese law, and in 1839 a large quantity was destroyed. In the following First Opium War the Chinese forces proved ill equipped to fight a modern war, and they were defeated. In 1842, China was forcedly opened up to foreign trade and missions, and Britain won control of the trading outpost of Hong Kong.

Thirteen years later, the British Prime Minister, Lord Palmerston, decided to assert British authority once again. His declared policy that half-civilized governments such as those of China 'all need a dressing every eight or ten years to keep them in order' made him popular at home. He was prepared to defend British citizens against the valid operation of foreign law and in 1856 he defied parliament to take Britain, with French help, to war with China again. The imperial army was weakened by the T'ai-p'ing Rebellion and in 1860 the allied army marched into Peking and burned the Imperial palace.

European Influence and Reaction

Although China herself remained nominally independent, her influence in Asia was much reduced. Russia used the British and French invasion as a cover for occupying the northern Amur river, so winning the Pacific outlet of Valdivostok; Britain won Burma, against fierce local opposition; France defeated Chinese armies to win Indo-China; Korea won its independence, later to fall to Japan; Japan conquered Taiwan, even the United States closed in by conquering the Philippines, again in the face of fierce nationalist resistance. Within China itself, the European powers jockeyed for privileges. Even more threateningly, the country was now open to western missionaries who, along with the Christian gospel, brought cultural assumptions profoundly at odds with traditional Confucian values.

The End of the Manchu Empire

By the last years of the century the ancient civilization was beginning to collapse. In 1898 the young emperor and his advisers decided that China must follow the Japanese example and adopt western ways. The experiment was short lived as the dowager Empress led the faction of reaction. She imprisoned the emperor and gave support to the xenophobic Boxers, who were attacking mission stations and other western interests across the country, and the embassy area of Peking was besieged. The western powers replied by sending a combined army to relieve the city. Still the Manchu rulers clung to power, but they were threatened from two directions. The army war lords were now unreliable, and outside the country, young foreign educated men plotted to overthrow the dynasty. In 1911–12 the two combined to bring down the Manchu Dynasty. The foreign educated Sun Yat-sen became president, but one year later he gave way to one of the military commanders.

Japan

The Shogunate

In 1603, at a time when the imperial family had lost effective power, the military leader, or Shogun, Tokugawa Ieyasu established power over the whole of Japan. In the centuries that followed, the Tokugawa shogunate closed Japan off from the outside world. The Japanese were prohibited from travelling abroad, Jesuit missionaries were expelled and their converts persecuted; only a few Dutch traders were allowed to operate from the city of Nagasaki. For Japanese urban entrepreneurs, however, the cost was a small price to pay for the peace and prosperity brought by the powerful shoguns. Educational reforms created a high level of literacy and a vigorous free enterprise economy was permitted to flourish in the growing towns. The growing prosperity of the towns was not matched in the countryside, where both the traditional lords and the peasants tended to become poorer.

The Opening of Japan

In 1854 the navy officer Matthew Perry was commissioned by the President of the USA to open up the Japanese market. His Treaty of Kanagawa brought the years of isolation to an end. The shogunate did not long survive it, and the Emperor resumed direct power in 1868. There was now a fierce debate within Japan as to whether the country should adopt western ways wholeheartedly, or follow the example of China and remain separate. The reformers were able to point to the disastrous results of conservative policies, as applied in China. The largest feudal families voluntarily surrendered their rights and the government systematically set about the modernization of their country. The changes were based on the solid structure, bequeathed by the Tokugawa shogunate, but there remains no example in history of a comparable change in social life within a single generation. By 1900 an advanced system of state education had been constructed western experts were imported to train the people in engineering, and young Japanese students were sent to study overseas. At first the new industries, like textiles and shipbuilding, were faithful copies of western prototypes, but they gained an increasing share in world markets. By the 1920s Japan was a formidable industrial competitor to the European nations.

Japanese Expansionism

The era of peace had left the samurai caste deprived of employment. They bequeathed an aggressive nationalism to the new state. The Japanese also recognized that European world domination had been based on the use of force. The now popular motto 'Asia for the Asians' was intended as a Monroe Doctrine for a Japanese sphere of influence.

Russian power was particularly menacing. The transcontinental railway had now reached Vladivostok, and the Russians were showing interest in the newly independent Korea. In 1902 Japan concluded a treaty with Britain, which provided security against intervention and two years later she attacked Russian shipping in the Manchurian Port Arthur. The city fell in January of the next year and the Russian Baltic fleet was destroyed in the Tsushima Straits in May.

This victory of an Asian over an essentially European power in the Russo-Japanese War marked the end of the European military domination of the world, which had survived since the fifteenth century. In the years that followed, Japan continued to build an empire, first by the annexation of Korea and then by the acquisition of wide Chinese lands. These conquests were accepted as a fait accompli by the European powers at the Treaty of Versailles in 1919.

The Pacific

The Aborigines of Australia

Over 50,000 years ago, great ice caps in the polar regions made the world's seas lower than they are today. The Indonesian islands formed a great peninsula, and Australia was joined to Tasmania and New Guinea in a single land mass. At this time the ancestors of the Australian aborigines arrived in their isolated home. Despite the lower waters, they had still crossed a wide stretch of ocean, making them possibly the world's first seafaring people. These early settlers brought their dogs, but the other animals would have provided a strange sight to people accustomed to the fauna of Asia. In their new home, they adopted a hunter-gatherer lifestyle, delicately in balance with the unique environment.

The Polynesians

Much later, some 3–4,000 years ago, a different race of people began to spread out across the islands of the Pacific Ocean. The methods by which they navigated their great canoes are little understood; they probably followed the paths of migrating birds, and it is suggested that they could feel the current off distant land masses on the surface of the water with their hands. Certainly they made successful voyages of up to 2000 miles to colonize unknown islands. It appears that they went via Fiji and Samoa to the remote Marquesas Islands, from where they fanned out, north to Hawaii, south east to Easter Island and southwest to New Zealand, which they called Ao-te-roa, or Long White Cloud. The earliest settlers were probably fleeing from war, but in time warfare followed them to their new homes.

The Arrival of the Europeans

Australian aborigines and Polynesian islanders alike were for long protected from European ships by unfavourable trade winds. In the seventeenth century several Dutch sailors, operating from the East Indes, made voyages in the area, but they were not attracted by what they saw as the region offered no prospect of profitable trade. In 1770 the English Captain James Cook sailed along the east coast of Australia and landed at Botany Bay. He later commanded two more voyages through the Pacific Islands. The sailors found the Pacific island societies to be living examples of the 'noble savage' existence, extolled by writers such as Rousseau – and bequeathed the devastations of syphilis to the islanders.

Australia

The Penal Colony

The war with the American colonies shut Britain off from the penal colonies of Georgia and the Carolinas, and so posed the British government with a problem of how to dispose of its surplus criminal population. As long as the war was in progress, convicts were kept in hulks moored in river estuaries.

One of those who had landed off Captain Cook's ship in Botany Bay was a geographer and scientist called Joseph Banks. In the years that followed he had become the driving force behind an exploration movement, intended to open new areas of the world to British trade. Banks argued the case for establishing a penal colony in Botany Bay. The land was good, he argued, the climate mild and the natives few in number.

The first convoy sailed in 1787, under the command of Captain Arthur Phillip, carrying 571 male and 159 female convicts, supervised by over 200 marines. Most of those transported were hard-core criminals, but there were also a significant number of political prisoners, particularly from rebellious Ireland. Large numbers of enforced immigrants suffered dreadfully on the long journey and in the penal settlements, and many continued to nurse resentment against the 'old country' and the forces of law and order.

Exploration

By the end of the century it was established that New South Wales in the east was linked to New Holland in the West in a single continent. In 1813 pioneers crossed the Great Dividing Range, which hemmed in the eastern coastal plain to discover the broad grasslands of the interior. By 1859 the landmass of the continent had been divided into six colonies.

It is said that, when these first white men appeared on the central plain, an aborigine scrambled into a tree and let out a long, high-pitched shriek. The establishment of European civilization in Australia was an immense achievement, but, yet again, the heaviest price would be paid by indigenous people in the age-old clash of interests between nomadic hunter-gatherers and settled agriculturalists.

Economic growth

The earliest settlers did not readily find cash crops to make the colony self-sufficient. Lieutenant John Macarthur is credited with recognizing the immense potential of the interior for sheep farming. He developed new breeds that would flourish in the New South Wales grasslands and was able to live in the style of an English country gentleman. His example was followed by emancipated convicts and a new generation of free settlers. The influx of cheap Australian wool to the home country stimulated the Yorkshire woollen industry at a time when woollen fabrics were gaining popularity in world markets. Towards the end of the nineteenth century the development of refrigerated ships boosted the meat trade. Then, in the early years of the twentieth century, strains of wheat were developed to suit the dry climate.

Early on, it was also established that the continent possessed great mineral wealth. Gold and copper mines were in operation by the middle of the nineteenth century, and the great Broken Hills complex was opened up in 1883. Despite such development in the interior, the cities proved to be the main beneficiaries. By 1901, 65 per cent of the population lived in the six capital cities.

Political Development

Progress with self-government in Canada encouraged the British government to devolve increasing political responsibility in its colonies of European settlement. In 1901 the six colonies became states to form the Commonwealth of Australia. Old links proved decisive when Australian soldiers fought with the British army in the wars of the twentieth century.

During World War Two, however, the nation's leaders, recognizing that Britain could contribute little against an expansionist Japan, turned to the United States for support. Since the war, extensive non-British immigration into Australia, and the increasing orientation of Britain towards Europe has further weakened traditional ties.

New Zealand

European Settlement

In 1814 a group of missionaries arrived in the land that had been described by Captain Cook. It is estimated that at that time there was a population of about a quarter of a million Maori people, who had lived in complete isolation for many centuries. In 1839 Edward Gibbon Wakefield established the New Zealand Association, with a view to buying land from the tribes and organizing settlements. The British government, hoping to control the movement, formally annexed the country in the following year.

The British proclaimed equality between Maori and European people, but practice never matched theory, and the colonists' land hunger provoked the Land War of 1845–48. After further settlers arrived, many from Scotland, war broke out again in the 1860s. By 1870 the Maori people had effectively lost control of their land.

Constitution and Economy

The country was granted a constitution in 1852 and in 1907 it became a self-governing dominion within the British Empire. Its dependence on agriculture, however, left it heavily dependent on the British economy. Early prosperity was based on wool and gold, but the introduction of refrigerated shipping in the last years of the nineteenth century favoured low cost New Zealand farmers, at the expense of their British competitors. This brought a period of prosperity, and ties with Britain were reinforced by disproportionate contribution made in two world wars. As with Australia, these have weakened in the second half of the twentieth century, during which time the country has suffered from its heavy dependence on primary products.

Japan and The United States

By 1914 Britain was withdrawing from direct involvement in the Pacific region but neither the emerging Australia or New Zealand were showing potential as a regional power. The Dutch still controlled the East Indies, modern Indonesia, but only at the cost of a series of major struggles against an emerging nationalism on Bali, Sumatra, and Java. Two powers now faced each other: the United States, with forward bases in Samoa, Guam and the Philippines and the emerging power of Japan. The foundations of a major regional conflict were already laid.

North Africa

Egypt

In classical times, North Africa had been an integral part of Mediterranean civilization. After the early flowering of Islamic civilization, however, it became increasingly cut off from the countries on the northern, Christian shore of the inland sea. Egypt was for centuries isolated under Mameluke rule. When Napoleon led an army into Egypt in 1798, he took with him not only fighting men, but also scholars, who would be able to interpret the remains of the country's fabled ancient civilization.

French interest in the area survived the fall of Napoleon, and, when Mehemet Ali broke the power of the mamelukes and established effective independence from Ottoman rule, French influence remained powerful. Under Mehemet Ali and his grandson Ishmael, Egyptian power was taken south into the Sudan and along the Red Sea. Ishmael contracted with France for the construction of the Suez Canal, which was opened in 1869. He staved off financial collapse, however, by selling a controlling interest in the canal to Britain, who now controlled this lifeline to India. In 1881 the Egyptian government was threatened by a nationalist rising in Egypt and by the Mahdi in the Sudan, and Britain responded by sending a force to protect the canal. It was not intended as an army of occupation, but Britain became involved in a protracted war in the Sudan and in administering a protectorate over Egypt.

Algeria

The coast of Algeria to the west had long been the home of Barbary pirates. In the 1830s, France began a major advance into the area. The pirates were driven from their harbours, and the French moved south to the Atlas mountains. Here they met fierce resistance, led by Abd el Kadir, but they won control of the mountain passes. Military success was followed by an influx of French settlers into the coastal region.

Sub-Saharan Africa

An Unknown Continent

For centuries the interior of Africa had been viewed by the outside world as little more than a source of human merchandise. European merchants had shipped slaves by the million out of the west coast. Bedu and Tuareg tribesmen had driven them across the Sahara to the markets of North Africa; they had been carried across the Red Sea in dhows by Arab traders; they had been beaten into submission by Dutch settlers in the south. The slave trade had had a profoundly brutalizing effect on African life, far beyond the boundaries of foreign exploration.

Yet in the early nineteenth century, Africa had its own political movements. In the grasslands of West Africa, an aggressive Islam was expanding in Hausaland under the Fulani Uthman dan Fodio and in Futa Jallon, under Al-hajj Umar. Far away, in the southwest, the Bantu people were experiencing a period of unrest. Shaka founded the Zulu kingdom in 1818, setting neighbouring people on the move.

European Explorers and Missionaries

In the early days of the industrial revolution, there was a general view, vigorously fostered by Joseph Banks, that Africa was a land of unbounded wealth, which offered untapped opportunities for trade. Since Britain had most to sell, British interests funded the earliest explorers. Early explorers, such as Mungo Park, acted as commercial travellers, carrying samples of Lancashire textiles and other manufactures. Results were disappointing but some solid business was established on the coast in products such as palm oil.

By the middle of the century European interest was increasingly focused on 'the dark continent', and explorers, such as David Livingstone and H. M. Stanley became major celebrities. Livingstone maintained an interest in 'legitimate trade', which he hoped would displace the continuing traffic in slaves in Central Africa, but he travelled as a missionary. European civilization had now achieved an unassailable self-confidence. Romantic concepts of the noble savage were forgotten and it was readily assumed that Africa was in need of Christianity, Western customs, and the post-industrial working practices that alone could provide the basis for economic advance.

Explorers, mainly following the routes of the great rivers, penetrated deep into the continent. They were followed by missionaries from a wide range of denominations from Europe and America, who were at times almost as much at competition with each other as they were with traditional practice. Expectation of life for explorers, traders and missionaries in malarial West Africa could be measured in months until quinine was introduced as a prophylactic in the 1840s and even afterwards the coast was still considered unfit for European settlement.

The Scramble for Africa

In 1880 active European political interest in Africa was limited to the French colony in Algeria in the north and the British Cape Colony in the south. The old Portuguese colonies, various ex-slaving trading outposts and settlements of freed slaves retained only tenuous links with Europe. By 1914 in the whole continent, only Ethiopia was a truly independent nation. In the intervening decades the continent was divided up between colonizing powers. Lines were drawn on maps in European capitals; boundaries sometimes followed rivers, often placing a village in one country and its farm land in another. The colonizing movement was in places the focus of national policy; elsewhere it was the product of adventurers or commercial companies working on their own initiative.

The British assumption of control in Egypt provoked the jealousy of other European countries. In particular, the French army was suffering from the bitter humiliation of the defeat at Sedan in 1870. Africa offered a forum for the recovery of a lost military prestige.

France and Britain were the main protagonists in the northern half of the continent. French colonization followed two thrusts. The first came south across the Sahara from Algeria into the grasslands of West Africa. The second went east from Senegal along the upper Niger to Lake Chad towards the Nile. The British also had a dual thrust, south from Egypt and north from South Africa. The imperialist Cecil Rhodes dreamed of establishing an unbroken chain of British possessions from the Cape to Cairo. French and British forces met where the thrusts intersected at Fashoda in the southern Sudan in 1898, when for a time it seemed likely that the two countries would be involved in a colonial war.

Meanwhile the British had also established West African colonies, based on their old slaving stations. The Germans were active in West, South West and in East Africa. King Leopold of the Belgians gained control of the Congo as a private venture. This was taken over by the Belgian state in 1908. Spain won control of much of the northwestern Sahara and shared influence in Morocco with France. Italy belatedly joined the scramble by invading Libya in 1911.

In the early years colonization was largely bloodless, but the process became increasingly violent. Britain faced African revolts as far apart as the Gold Coast and Rhodesia and France the Niger and Madagascar. The brutality of King Leopold's exploitation of the Congo was exposed in 1904. In the same year a major rebellion broke out against the Germans in South West Africa, which ended when they drove the Herero people to virtual extinction in the desert. The Italian invasion of Libya was also conducted with widespread brutality. By the beginning of 1914 the redrawn map of Africa could be seen as a symbol of a dangerously aggressive and expansionist mood within Europe.

South Africa

The Great Trek

During the Napoleonic Wars Britain occupied the Cape of Good Hope, and the territory was retained, as the Cape Colony, in 1814 for its strategic value in controlling the sea routes to the east. At that time, however, there were no British settlers, the land being shared between nomadic Bushmen and Hottentots and Afrikaans-speaking Boers of Dutch and French Huguenot origin. Soon the new government began to bring in thousands of British settlers. The Boers were angered when their black slaves were freed and laws were introduced that they considered to be unduly favourable to the previously subject black people. In 1835 some 10,000 Boers left their homes at the Cape and settled on land of the Vaal and Orange Rivers. More Boers followed when the British annexed their republic of Natal. The settlers set up the new republics of Transvaal and the Orange Free State where they could live free from British interference.

The movement of the Boers from the south coincided with migrations of Bantu people, displaced by the Zulu kingdom. The two people clashed, but the main losers were the native nomadic people, who were driven to a precarious existence in the desert.

The Boer War

Resentment between Boers and the British continued to grow. The British briefly annexed the Transvaal, and, although they withdrew, this left the Boers feeling that they would never be left in peace. Then, in 1886, gold was discovered in the Transvaal, and, within a few years, a new city of Johannesburg had grown to a population of 100,000. Most of the newcomers were British, but they were excluded from the running of the republic. Angry that the world's great empire, the modern Rome, could be frustrated by a small number of intransigent Boer farmers, Cecil Rhodes provoked a confrontation. President Kruger of the Transvaal, an implacable opponent of British rule, responded with an ultimatum, and war broke out in 1899.

Liberal opinion in Britain and Europe saw the Boers as an oppressed minority, and, when they were finally defeated in 1902, there was pressure for a generous settlement. A few voices were raised in the British parliament to defend the rights of the black peoples, but these found no support. In 1909 the four territories were brought together into the self-governing Union of South Africa, which lost little time in passing laws that discriminated against the non-white peoples. In 1948 the Afrikaans-speaking people won power within the country and put in place the formal structure of apartheid.

The Nation State in Crisis

The Eastern Question

The Decline of Ottoman Power

In 1683 armies of the Ottoman empire laid siege to the city of Vienna for the second time and Europe was threatened once more from the East. The armies withdrew, but the Emperor at Istanbul still controlled almost three quarters of the Mediterranean coastline – North Africa, the Arab lands of the Middle East, the homeland of Turkey, Greece and the Balkans.

By the eighteenth century, statesmen could recognize that the Ottoman Empire, like other empires before it, was in decline. Administration was clumsy, and the sultan had to rely on local rulers, whose loyalty was often in doubt. Also, the social military structure of the empire was becoming increasingly out of date.

Russian Objectives

Russian statesmen took the closest interest in the Ottoman decline. Peter the Great had won a warm water port, but, for both trade and strategic reasons, the country still badly needed an outlet into the Mediterranean. In 1768–74 Catherine the Great fought a successful war against the Turks and won the Crimea and other territory on the north bank of the Black Sea along with rights of navigation into the Mediterranean. She also established that Russia had the right to act as protector of eastern Christians within the Turkish dominions.

Russia continued to make advances after the defeat of Napoleon. She won control of the ancestral Ottoman homeland in the grasslands east of the Caspian Sea, taking her empire as far as the mountain passes of the Himalayas. Still further east, she won the Pacific port of Vladivostok from the Chinese. Russian territorial ambitions were backed by huge military forces, and other European powers perceived her as an aggressive imperial power.

Concern focused on the fate of the Turkish European territories. In a private conversation with the British ambassador, Tsar Nicholas I described Turkey as 'the sick man of Europe'. He implied that it would be better for the powers to consider how to share the sick man's possessions, rather than to wait and fight over them when he died. Other powers, however, preferred to support Turkey so that it could continue to act as a check on Russian ambitions in Eastern Europe.

In 1841 the European powers came together in the Convention of the Straits to guarantee Turkish independence. It was agreed then that the Bosphorus should be closed to all ships of war. This shut Russia out of the Mediterranean, and meant that she could not protect her merchant ships, now carrying increasing grain exports by the Black Sea.

The Crimean War

In 1851 Russia invaded Turkey's Danube lands, and in 1853 her navy sank the Turkish fleet, so winning back her outlet to the Mediterranean. Excitement ran high in Paris and London. Napoleon III was looking for a way of rebuilding the family's military prestige. Britain was concerned for her links with India, for, although the Suez Canal was not yet built, traffic was already following the Mediterranean route. In March 1854 the two powers declared war on Russia in support of Turkey. Combined forces were despatched to capture the Russian naval base at Sebastopol in the Crimea. The huge Russian army was unable to dislodge the invading force and in 1856 she was forced to accept peace on the terms that she would keep no fleet in the Black Sea and build no bases on its shores.

The battles of the Crimean War were made famous because the armies were followed by a journalist, who published detailed reports in the London *Times*. For the first time in history, the public was able to read first hand reports of the sufferings of the soldiers. The modern profession of nursing dates itself from the work done by Florence Nightingale and her staff in this campaign.

Disintegration

Victory over Russia in the Crimean War could not long delay the final disintegration of the Ottoman Empire. France and Britain, who had fought as allies of the Turks, were happy to help themselves to territory in North Africa. Britain also occupied Cyprus and extended her influence in the Middle East. Russia continued her forward movement in the less sensitive territory to the east of the Caspian Sea. In Eastern Europe, Greece was already independent and in the half century after the end of the Crimean War, Serbia, Romania and Bulgaria would also break free. Russia, always ready to stand as protector of the oppressed Slav peoples, went to war with Turkey again in 1877. For a time Europe stood on the brink of another war as the powers prepared to shore up the tottering empire once again. However, in 1878, Russia, faced by the combination of Prussia, Austria and Britain, was forced to accept terms at the Congress of Berlin.

In 1907 a rebellion broke out in Turkey itself. A group, who called themselves the Young Turks, demanded constitutional reforms, along European lines. In 1909 the long reigning Abdul-Hamid was deposed. The new rulers dressed their government as a constitutional monarchy, but it was effectively a dictatorship, dedicated to reviving Turkish power, at home and in the remaining Ottoman lands of the Middle East.

Nationalism

Western Europe

The Napoleonic conquests and the reactions against them had aroused fierce emotions of nationalism, which were to influence European politics. Germany and Italy began their discovery of a national identity, but the mood also affected smaller peoples, such as Belgians and Norwegians. Britain had her own problems in Ireland. The situation was complicated by the fact that Westminster politicians had to reconcile two vocal nationalist groups. The majority Catholics considered themselves to be under a foreign power, discriminated against in their religion and insecure in their land holding. The minority Protestants of the north, mostly of Scots descent, used their political connections with English conservatives to defend accustomed privileges. After 1848, however, concern on issues of nationality centred on eastern Europe.

Poland

Russia might stand as the liberator of oppressed Slav peoples in the Balkans, but, on her own western frontier, she was the oppressor. The decline of Poland began with long wars against Sweden, which ended in 1709. Depopulated and weakened, with no natural frontiers, she stood between aggressive powers to east and west. In the last decades of the eighteenth century, she was partitioned between Russia, Austria and Prussia. A supposedly free Poland, created in 1815, was effectively a Russian colony. A series of nationalist rebellions were a failure and Russian administrators tried to eliminate all traces of Polish nationalism, insisting that even primary school children should be taught in the Russian language.

The Austro-Hungarian Empire

Metternich recognized very clearly that the new nationalism could undermine the whole structure of the Austrian empire. The house of Hapsburg ruled over different nationalities, speaking a wide range of languages. Defeat by Prussia and then the loss of Italy had pushed the western boundaries of the once great empire back to the Austrian heartland. Alone of all the major European powers, landlocked Austria was not in a position to participate in the scramble for colonial possessions. Any expansion had to be towards the east, and foreign policy now focused on the Danube and the Balkans.

The new nationalists of the region, however, saw Austria, as much as Turkey as a threat to their aspirations. The Hungarians exploited the weakness of the Empire after the Prussian victory at Sadowa to negotiate a new Covenant with Vienna. The Hapsburgs now ruled a dual Austro-Hungarian empire, in which military and foreign policy was coordinated, but in other ways the eastern part had virtual self-government. The new Hungarian section of the Empire contained a number of national minorities, and trouble was never far from the surface.

In 1878, after the war between Russia and Turkey, Bosnia and Herzegovina were placed under Austrian administration, and in 1908 they were annexed by Austria. The independent Serbia, with Russian support, now stood as the focus of pan-Slavic aspirations, and so as protector of the nationalist movements in the two territories. The Austrian government, angry at this subversion, looked for an opportunity of crushing Serbia.

Russia

Despotism

In the decades before the Crimean War, Russia was ruled by the autocratic Tsar Nicholas I. He tried to keep all western ideas of liberalism and socialism at bay by a suffocating censorship. At the same time the administration became ever more corrupt and inefficient. The repression of this period was primarily directed against the intelligentsia, who were traditionally close to developments in the west. Nicholas did recognize, however, that the position of the serfs had become such an anomaly that it endangered the Russian state. As in France before the Revolution, these poorest people had to carry by far the bulk of the load of taxation. Nicholas declared a desire to make changes and he did make progress in codifying peasants' rights and bringing them within the legal system. He was unable, however, to tackle the medieval structure of serfdom, which tied the mass of the people to their villages, and left them as the virtual possessions of their masters.

Emancipation and Reform

Nicholas was succeeded by his son, Alexander II, during the Crimean War. The failure of the superior Russian armies and the humiliating nature of the peace, left no doubt that the state needed radical overhaul. Although conservative by nature, the new Tsar supervised a major overhaul of the army, the law and the administrative system.

Most difficult, he put in train the process of emancipation for the serfs. 'Better,' he said, 'to abolish serfdom from above, than to wait till it begins to abolish itself from below.' Emancipation was pronounced in 1861, but problems still remained to be solved. Landlords needed to be compensated and a system had established whereby the peasants could buy their own land. This took the form of a tax, which left many, in practice, worse off than they had been before emancipation.

The Prelude to Revolution

The first shot was fired at Alexander only five years after his emancipation decree; he was assassinated in 1881. The reforms of his reign were matched with a continued autocracy, which aroused profound frustration, particularly amongst the intelligentsia. The education system, in particular, was subject to the tightest control by a reactionary bureaucracy. Also during these years, individuals within government gave support to pogroms against the Jews. After the murder of Alexander II in 1881, government fell increasingly into the hands of the opponents of reform.

Opposition was divided between liberals, socialists and groups of nihilists, all of whose leaders were drawn from the intelligentsia. They appealed first to the suffering peasants, demanding a programme of land reform. Towards the end of the century, however, large numbers of peasants were leaving the land to make up the industrial proletariat of the long delayed industrial revolution. Revolutionary activists now found it productive to work in the growing slums of the cities, building up revolutionary cells of workers.

Success is the ultimate justification of autocratic government, and defeat by Japan in 1905 brought the imperial government to the brink of collapse. The battleship *Potemkin* mutinied and terrorized the Black Sea. Massive strikes, particularly by railway workers, crippled the economy. In October 1905 the Socialist groups organized themselves into the First Soviet, based on the principle of the cells that had been established in the factories. Nicholas II, like Louis XVI before him, was forced to attempt to rally national unity by calling a national parliament, or *duma*. Experiments in representative democracy were, however, half-hearted and failed. In the years that followed, the weak Tsar shut himself increasingly within his family circle, now increasingly dominated by the eccentric Rasputin. When the European war broke out in 1914, Russia was ill prepared for such a disaster.

The Armed Peace

The Alliances

In the years after 1871, there were two fixed points in European diplomacy. Austria and Russia faced each other over the control of the liberated Turkish lands in the Balkans. Fighting could break out at any time within the region, leading to the risk of 'superpower involvement'. France also, smarting from defeat at Sadowa and the occupation of Paris, was chronically hostile to Germany. She was, however, militarily weak and the autocratic powers of Austria and Russia looked on her as a threat, and so she remained isolated and impotent.

In previous centuries, alliances had been formed under the immediate threat of war, and they had disintegrated immediately after the threat was over. During these decades, however, the European powers began to form themselves into permanent alliances, committed to help each other in the event of war. By the beginning of the twentieth century, a new alignment of powers had become established. Germany allied with Austria, and they were later to be joined by Italy to form the Triple Alliance. To meet this threat, France and Russia joined to form the Dual Alliance. Britain was not a significant continental power, and as late as 1898 the two countries narrowly avoided a colonial war. In 1904, however, policy changed dramatically as Britain concluded a nonbinding *entente cordiale* with France, which was followed by a similar agreement with Russia. Hostility towards Germany increased as the German government set about a major naval construction programme, which was interpreted as a direct threat to Britain. The British government responded with its own programme, and a major arms race was under way.

Military Strategy

With Europe organized into armed camps, the generals considered strategy in the event of conflict. Failing to take account of the bloody attrition of the American Civil War, they assumed that events would be settled, as in Bismarck's wars, by one swift, decisive campaign. Germany was faced with the prospect of fighting on two fronts. Strategists decided that, while the Russian war machine was massive, the bureaucratic inefficiency would prevent rapid deployment of forces. They therefore developed a plan that, in the event of impending war, the German army would make a first strike to knock out France, so that it could then give its full attention to the eastern front.

In the early years of the century, there was a mood of militarism throughout Europe, fed by accounts of colonial wars and victories against non European people. It was most evident in Germany, where theorists declared that war was the natural state of man, but it spread much wider. In Britain, for instance, metaphors of war and sport were subtly mingled in the public school education of the nation's elite.

The Outbreak of War

Austria and Serbia

By the summer of 1914 Serbian support for rebels in Bosnia and Herzegovina had brought relationships with Austria to a low state. On 28 June 1914 the heir to the throne, the Archduke Franz Ferdinand, and his wife were murdered in the Bosnian capital of Sarajevo. Encouraged by her ally Germany, Austria used this as a pretext for invading Serbia on 28 July. On 30 July Tsar Nicholas II ordered mobilization, not only in the Balkans, but along the whole border.

First Strike

It appears that, at the last moment, Kaiser Wilhelm II of Germany may have had doubts about plunging Europe into war. The British foreign minister tried to gather support for a conference to localize the conflict, but the German war machine was now moving under its own impetus. On 3 August Germany attacked France through undefended neutral Belgium. Italy declared that the conflict was none of her concern, so the central powers of Germany and Austria faced France and Russia. Britain had no treaty obligation to enter the war on behalf of France, but did consider herself bound by the guarantee made to Belgium after the 1830 uprising. Her formal position for taking up arms was therefore as defender of the rights of small nations. Italy later entered the war on the side of the Allies, as they were now called, while Turkey and Bulgaria aligned themselves with the Central Powers. Military enthusiasts forecast a short war, to be decided by Christmas, but the British Foreign Secretary, Sir Edward Grey, warned, 'The lamps are going out all over Europe. We shall not see them lit again in our lifetime.'

War and Revolution

Stalemate

The German first strike strategy involved high risk. Russia mobilized more rapidly than anticipated and the German army was defeated at Grumbinnen on 20 August. In early September the western offensive became bogged down on the Marne. Germany was fighting the war on two fronts, which her generals had feared. On the western front, the opposing armies dug in for their long years of attrition. The new German navy remained in port as the British fleet set about sapping German resistance by blockade. Allied attempts to break the stalemate by offensives in the Dardanelles and Salonika, were unsuccessful.

The Russian Revolution

The huge open spaces of the eastern front kept war more mobile. Early Russian success was undermined by the failure of the political structure. In March 1917 a wave of unrest swept the Tsar from power. The opposition was divided between liberal politicians, who now set up a provisional government and the socialist Soviet – itself divided between the moderates and a radical Bolshevik wing. The moderate provisional government pledged itself to continue the war, but in April the Bolshevik, Vladimir Ilyich Lenin, returned from exile and announced the arrival of world revolution. Russian workers, he claimed, should not be dying in a bosses' war. The provisional government staked everything on a last great offensive, but this failed, and on 7 November, Lenin staged a Bolshevik coup d'état. In March 1918 he concluded peace between his newly born Soviet Union and the Central Powers at Brest Litovsk. In July of 1918 the Tsar and his family were shot at Yekaterinburg.

American Intervention

Germany now had to fight on only one front, but, during this period, another, even more formidable enemy had been drawn into the war. Desperate at the success of the British naval blockade, the German navy mounted its own submarine blockade of Britain. To be successful it had to attack American ships that were carrying supplies to Britain. This brought the United States into the conflict in April 1917. The German High Command recognized that the intervention of American troops would tilt the battle against the Central Powers, but it staked everything on defeating Britain and France before the Americans arrived. Throughout 1917 and 1918 there were huge and costly offensives from both sides on the western front. In the autumn of 1918 Germany's allies, Austria and Bulgaria began to crumble, the German fleet mutinied and there was increasing unrest in the German cities. Finally the Kaiser abdicated and the generals sued for peace.

The World of Versailles

The Cost of War

All the major continental nations emerged weakened from the First World War. Russia, involved in civil war, was no longer a factor in international politics. France, although victorious, had suffered grievously. Austria was now not a power of significance. Germany, although defeated, was no longer surrounded by serious rivals. Loss of life had been severe in all the combatant nations, but wealth had also drained away. The United States was the main beneficiary of the war at a cost of fewer casualties than had been suffered by the Dominion of Australia. In the past she had been a major debtor nation, but now she moved into a period of being the world's main creditor nation.

A New World

The war was also an emotional and intellectual landmark. It was as if the great optimism, which had buoyed up a successful and expansionist Europe was suddenly pierced. The belief in an inevitable tide of progress, prevalent since the time of Descartes, no longer seemed tenable in the face of sustained barbarity on European soil. Liberal thinkers, in disciplines such as theology as well as in politics, found themselves on the defensive. New absolutisms, of both left and right, emerged in confrontation, both threatening to overwhelm traditions of representative government.

The conflict had also brought permanent changes in the structure of society. Women, who had been mobilized to fill men's jobs, could no longer be denied political and a growing economic emancipation. The war brought technological advances in areas such as aeronautics and the development of motor vehicles. Output had increased to meet the demands of a technological war, and, in the process, labour unions had established a stronger position for themselves. Many felt threatened by the rapid social change, evident in almost every field of life.

In the years before the war, artists had already been working in strange and disturbing new forms. Stravinsky's *Rite of Spring* and Picasso's *Demoiselles d'Avignon* created scandal in their fields. In 1922, Joyce's *Ulysses* dispensed with the convention of the English novel. It seemed as though all recognizable values were now fractured as creative artists abandoned both classical and romantic forms to explore abstraction and an inner life, now provided with a whole new vocabulary by the works of Sigmund Freud. The arrival of jazz from America, exploiting the interaction between African and European popular music, only served to heighten the alarm of traditionalists.

The Treaties

The Treaty of Versailles, ratified by Germany in July 1919, was the first of a series of treaties imposed on the defeated Central Powers. The leading architects of the new order were President Woodrow Wilson of the United States, Georges Clemenceau, premier of France and David Lloyd George, prime minister of Britain. Clemenceau, recognizing the continuing potential of Germany, pressed for financial reparations, intended to retard industrial recovery, the return of Alsace-Lorraine to France, and the demilitarization of the Rhineland. The map of eastern Europe was redrawn, with Poland, Hungary, Czechoslovakia and Yugoslavia created as new nations. In the north, Finland, which had won independence from Russia in 1917, was joined by the three newly independent Baltic States, Estonia, Latvia and Lithuania. The pattern of nationalities was, however, more complex than could be accommodated within national boundaries, and all these nations had substantial minorities. Of greatest significance for the future, substantial numbers of German-speaking people found themselves within Czechoslovakia and Poland. The treaties attempted to protect minority rights, but there was considerable movement of peoples across national boundaries. The largest movement came at the end of the war between Greece and Turkey from 1920 to 1922. In particular, Greek people left the coast of Asia Minor, where they had lived since ancient times. The two communities continued in uneasy coexistence in Cyprus.

The treaties also changed the wider world. Germany's East and West African possessions were divided between Britain and France, while Southwest Africa, the future Namibia, was placed under the trusteeship of South Africa. The concept of trusteeship was also used to extend western influence over the old Ottoman territories of the Middle East.

The League of Nations

President Wilson hoped that his country, with its democratic tradition, could take the lead in creating a new atmosphere of goodwill. He therefore proposed a League of Nations, which would serve as guardian of world peace. Wilson was to be bitterly disappointed when his own Congress refused to let the United States join the new body. Unhappy about the way in which their country had been plunged into European affairs, the majority of Americans were anxious to return to a traditional isolationism. It became evident that the new body lacked credibility as early as 1920, when Poland successfully seized Vilna from Lithuania. Later incidents reinforced the fact that successful international collaboration to repel aggression could not be organized through the League. The Italian government took full advantage when, in Europe's final African venture, it launched an attack on Ethiopia (then called Abyssinia) in 1935.

Ireland

Attempts by prewar Liberal administrations to give home rule to Ireland had been frustrated by the collaboration of Ulster Protestants and conservative politicians. Prime Minister Lloyd George now faced destructive guerilla warfare from nationalists. In 1921 the moderate nationalists accepted partition of the island, which left a significant Catholic minority within the Protestant-dominated northern provinces. This led to civil war within the new Irish Free State, and laid the foundations of continuing strife in the north.

The World Economy

The Postwar Boom

During the 1920s world trade appeared to be returning to its prewar vigour, but, even during these boom years, there were signs of problems ahead. The war had created an increased potential for production, but demand was stagnant. The Soviet Union was in no position to import goods from abroad, and new nations raised tariff barriers to protect fledgling industries. The United States now produced over half of all the world's manufactures, but American consumers, like the Japanese 70 years later, showed little desire to buy goods from abroad and domestic industry was protected by import duties.

As industry boomed, so the price of raw materials, including agricultural products, decreased, creating problems for primary producers. At the same time, the fact that workers did not share the profits of their industries, brought outbursts of industrial unrest, such as the British General Strike of 1926.

The Great Depression

By 1928 world trade had become heavily dependent on American finance. In that year Wall Street experienced The Great Bull Market as the price of shares rose to unrealistic heights. Then, on 28 October 1929, the stock market crashed. American capital for investment dried up, leading to a rapid world-wide collapse of industrial confidence. Governments took what action they could to protect their own industries against imports, so further inhibiting world trade. It is estimated that at the depth of the recession, in 1932, industrial production in the United States and Germany was only half of what it had been three years earlier. Unemployment reached record levels in all the industrial countries, bringing times of great hardship.

The New Deal

In America, the parties divided over the political response to the problems. The Republicans, favouring a traditional *laissez-faire* approach, were defeated in the 1932 elections by a Democratic party, led by Franklin Roosevelt. He instituted a New Deal, based on substantial public investment. The showpiece was the publicly owned Tennessee Valley Authority. Designed to provide an industrial infrastructure for one of the country's poorest regions. Roosevelt won great popularity, going on to win an unprecedented four presidential elections, but the improvement brought by the New Deal was as much psychological as practical, and real recovery had to await the stimulus of a second world war.

The Rise of the Dictators

Italy

In the elections of 1921, a new party won just 36 seats in the Italian parliament. Its leader, Benito Mussolini had a background as a socialist, but he now proclaimed that he would save Italy from the menace of communism. The party appealed to ancient Rome in its extended arm salute and the symbol of the *fasces*, which gave the movement its name. The black-shirted fascists used intimidation, first to come to power and then to eliminate all political opposition. Mussolini's rule achieved some legitimacy when, in 1929, he negotiated a treaty with the highly conservative papacy.

Germany

The Austrian-born Adolf Hitler became leader of the German National Socialist, or Nazi, party in 1921. Having failed in an early attempt to take control of the Bavarian government, he set about reorganizing his party as a military movement, not hesitating to purge his own followers. He directed his appeal to a German people, who were frustrated by military defeat, humiliated by the loss of empire and European territory, and, in many cases, impoverished by hyper-inflation. Hitler's philosophy was laid out in his early book *Mein Kampf*. This described both his military ambitions for Germany, and his obsessive hatred of the Jewish people.

The struggle appeared to lie between Hitler's new right, and the parties of the left. But the left was divided. The communists, taking their orders from Moscow, attempted, and sometimes succeeded, in fo-

133

menting revolution. The social democrats were therefore forced into alliance with conservative military leaders. Capitalizing on these divisions and on the economic problems brought by the Depression, Hitler took his Nazi party to power in 1933. He then quickly set up a reign of terror. While the Jews were the prime target, political opponents, gypsies, the handicapped, and anybody not considered to be of true Aryan descent also suffered. Despite this, his popularity remained high among most Germans. His armaments and other public works programmes appeared to be bringing a return of prosperity, while military success retrieved national pride.

The Soviet Union

The Bolshevik revolution of 1917 was followed by three years of civil war, during which White Russian armies, supported by foreign troops, tried to overthrow the new communist state. Lenin and his followers emerged successful, but at huge cost. It is estimated that some 13 million died in the war and through the famine it caused; economic life was at a standstill. In 1921, as an emergency measure, Lenin largely freed the economy and recovery followed rapidly.

Lenin died in January 1924, leaving two men contending the succession. Trotsky proclaimed that the new society could only flourish within a communist world, and the prime task was therefore to export the revolution. His opponent, Stalin, argued that the priority was to rebuild the Soviet Union, by creating 'communism within one state'. When Stalin emerged victorious, it appeared as though the forces of moderation had prevailed.

Stalin assumed autocratic power and created a personality cult, not dissimilar to those constructed around the fascist dictators. He set himself the objective of changing the Soviet Union from a largely medieval economy, to a major modern state within a few decades. This involved the conversion of agriculture from its peasant structure by wholesale collectivization, and the rapid development of heavy industry. The programme was forced through at huge human cost. Industrially the results were dramatic. Production of coal, iron and steel and other basics increased many times over. The expansion of heavy industry was, however, bought at the expense of consumer goods, and the people, were constantly disappointed in the promised general improvement in living standards. Peasants on the collective farms, also resentful at being expected to produce low cost food for the growing cities for little return, remained obstinately unproductive.

Stalin's increasingly paranoiac behaviour was now demonstrated in a series of show trials and purges. Virtually all the old political leaders and a high proportion of military officers were executed to ensure that nobody would be able to challenge for power. Millions more suffered and died in labour camps. The new administrators of the country were tied to Stalin by a common guilt, and by an increasing web of petty corruption.

Spain

By the 1930s the days in which Spain had been a great European power were long past, and she had therefore avoided involvement in the First World War. In 1933 a right wing government came to power, which provoked rebellion by national minorities. In early 1936 a left wing government was elected with a large majority. General Franco, modelling himself on the fascist dictators, led a mutiny of the army in Morocco and invaded the mainland. The army, the political right and the Roman Catholic church aligned with Franco, while left wing groups and the national minorities aligned with the elected government. Franco received assistance from the fascist states, while the government was supported by the Soviet Union and a variety of international volunteers. The bitter war lasted until 1939, when Franco achieved the position of dictator, which he held until his death in 1975.

The Second World War in the West

German Expansion

From the beginning, Hitler followed a programme for the creation of a German empire in central Europe. His first objective was to win back land lost at Versailles; he then planned to conquer the whole of mainland Europe, including European Russia, and create an empire in which 'lower' races, such as the Slavs, would be reduced to a servile status. He exploited the weakness of the League of Nations, American isolationism, and lack of unity among other European powers in a series of successes – the recovery of the Saarland by plebiscite, the remilitarization of the Rhineland, unification with Austria, and finally the dismemberment of Czechoslovakia. When Britain and France acquiesced to the last of these at Munich, it appeared as though no other power had the will to frustrate his ambitions.

In 1939 Hitler and Stalin concluded the Nazi-Soviet Pact to preserve Russian neutrality. The Soviet Union was awarded eastern Poland and took the opportunity to advance further into the Baltic States and Finland, where Russian armies were halted by fierce national resistance. Unlike Czechoslovakia, Poland was protected by treaty links with Britain and France, and the German invasion provoked a joint ultimatum and war. Mussolini took the opportunity of entering the war in support of Germany and invading Greece.

German Successes

After defeating Poland, in 1940, the German army repeated the 1914 tactic of invading France across Belgium. This time Paris fell and a puppet government was installed in southern France. Successful campaigns to the north and south reduced Denmark, Norway, Yugoslavia and Greece. In early 1941 the Afrika Corps landed in Libya and within two months was threatening Cairo and the Suez Canal. Britain, now rallied by the charismatic leader, Winston Churchill, held off an air offensive, intended to prepare the way for invasion, in the Battle of Britain.

On 22 June 1941 Hitler launched Operation Barbarossa against an unprepared Soviet Union. The invasion followed the logic of Hitler's master plan, but it dangerously overstretched German resources. The imbalance was made greater when the Japanese attack on Pearl Harbour brought the United States into the war in December of the same year. Stalin demonstrated his character as a national leader in rallying his people for a massively costly defence. The war turned in November 1942, when the Russians broke the German front at Stalingrad and a British army defeated the Afrika Corps at El Alamein. Once the Allies had re-established a western front with the Normandy landings of June 1944, the final defeat in 1945 was inevitable.

The years from 1939–45 gave a new and terrible meaning to warfare. The Germans mobilized conquered people for slave labour, and perpetrated mass genocide on European Jewry; the Russians deported whole national populations for alleged collaboration; residential areas of cities were targeted in large-scale bombing by both sides. Among some 50 million dead were an estimated 27 million Russians, 6 million Jews and $4^{1}/_{2}$ million Poles.

Europe Divided

The Yalta Settlement

The future political shape of Europe was negotiated in February 1945 at a conference at Yalta in the Crimea, attended by Stalin, Roosevelt and Churchill. Germany was to be partitioned and the countries of Eastern Europe were to form a zone of Russian influence. In the event, Austria and Greece – the latter after civil war – remained within the western sphere.

The Recovery of Western Europe

At the end of the war, western Europe was in a state of serious economic collapse. Once again, there were large movements of displaced people, and food shortages continued for years after the war. In June 1947, the US Secretary of State, George Marshall, announced a major aid programme, directed, 'not against any country or doctrine, but against hunger, poverty, desperation and chaos'. The Soviet Union was offered the chance of participating but turned it down. The Marshall Plan provided much needed capital for reconstruction.

The United Nations

During the last years of the war, thought was given to the reasons why the League of Nations had failed to preserve world peace. In 1945 representatives of the nations met in San Francisco to set up the new United Nations. In its constitution, great influence was given to the Security Council, which had five 'great powers' as permanent members and representatives of other nations. The right of veto given to the great powers, but at least all the major powers were now involved in the organization and debates were subject to the scrutiny of the world media.

The European Community

Some European leaders now argued that the nation state was no longer capable of providing a secure structure for world peace. In particular, the long standing enmity between France and Germany was no longer tolerable. In 1952, the Federal Republic of Germany, France, Italy, Holland, Belgium and Luxembourg, formed the European Economic Community. This was designed to be both a trading group, capable of competing with the new superpowers, and also a stabilizing influence on the volatile European political scene.

The Cold War in Europe

It soon became clear that European nationalism had run its destructive course, and the danger to world peace now lay in the confrontation of the United States and the Soviet Union. In the words of Winston Churchill, an 'iron curtain' had descended across Europe.

The Soviet Union emerged from the Second World War in control of a vast empire. It had inherited imperial conquests, and had further added the Baltic Republics. It also now controlled puppet regimes in Eastern Europe, bound together in the Warsaw Pact, which maintained huge land forces on its western front. Stalin's policy was still primarily directed at preserving national security, which had been so devastatingly violated by Hitler's army. He and later Soviet leaders therefore felt threatened by American superiority in nuclear weapons. A crash nuclear programme was put in hand and advances in rocketry were clearly illustrated when, in April 1961, Yuri Gagarin became the first man to be launched into space.

America and her allies in the North Atlantic Treaty Organization (NATO) relied heavily on nuclear superiority. The Americans responded to the Russian space programme and, in July 1969, with a wondering world watching on television, men were placed on the moon.

Berlin, divided between the four occupying powers, lay exposed within the Russian area of influence and in 1948–49 conflict loomed as the Russians shut off western communications with the city. A later crisis ended with the building of the Berlin Wall in 1961. This stood for the next 28 years as a potent symbol of the Cold War and the division of Europe into two hostile camps.

After Empire

The Expansion of Japan

The Beginnings of Aggression

The 1914–18 war brought prosperity to the rising Japanese economy. European competition in Asian markets was reduced and Japanese factories were able to export to the combatants. During this period, heavy industries, such as shipbuilding, were able to build up a firm base. Competition returned in the postwar boom years, but Japan continued to export successfully. During the boom years, companies reinvested profits in preparation for more difficult times. Japanese industry, none the less, suffered badly in the Depression. With foreign markets closed and the home market as yet undeveloped, industry worked at only a fraction of capacity. The weakness was exacerbated by the country's lack of raw materials. Foreign policy therefore became directed at the winning control of the export markets and natural resources of East Asia. China was the first target for expansion.

China's Weakness

After the fall of the Manchu Empire in 1912, China plunged back into chaos. Sun Yat-sen's Nationalist (Kuomintang) party struggled for power with independent war lords. During this time communist cells were coming into existence. Following Marxist orthodoxy, they initially concentrated on the cities, but later, under the influence of the rising Mao Tse-tung, they worked increasingly among the mass of the peasants, who had suffered greatly during the upheavals. Under his influence, the communists built up communes in scattered and remote areas. Sun Yat-sen died in 1925, to be succeeded as Kuomintang leader by the more conservative Chiang Kai-shek. After a period of collaboration, Chiang attempted to exterminate the communist opposition. Driven from their southern bases, the communists only survived by coming together in the Long March of 1934–35 and establishing a new northern headquarters, based on Yenan.

The War in the East

The Attack on China

Japan exploited the weakness and growing corruption of the Kuomintang government by strengthening its control over Manchuria and areas of the north in the early 1930s. In 1936 the Kuomintang and the communists made common cause against the foreigners, but in the following year, Japan launched a major assault on China. In December 1937 the Japanese army captured the capital at Nanking and the Chinese government had to retreat to remote Szechwan, leaving the Japanese in control of the north, and most of the Pacific coast, including the major industrial cities.

Victory brought Japan into conflict with the Pacific colonial powers, and their concessionary ports were blockaded. The Americans and British responded by supplying Chiang Kai-shek along the Burma Road, and the United States renounced its commercial agreement with Japan.

Control of the Pacific

Japanese foreign policy was now set on winning control over the whole of the Pacific rim. With the outbreak of war in Europe, she allied herself with Germany. Then in 1941, as German troops were sweeping into Russia, she launched her first attack on French Indo-China. On 7 December 1941 her air force attacked the American navy in Pearl Harbour, Hawaii, and, at the same time, she launched assaults on the Dutch in Indonesia and the British in Malaysia and Burma. The campaigns were brilliantly successful and by mid-1942 both India and Australia were under threat.

Defeat and the Atom Bomb

The attack on Pearl Harbor put and end to isolationism and united Americans behind President Roosevelt. As the world's greatest industrial power became geared for war, the tide turned against Japan. In June 1942 the Japanese fleet suffered a reverse at the battle of Midway Island, and thereafter a relentless American offensive drove them from their Pacific conquests, while the British also fought back through Burma. From November 1944 the Japanese cities came under direct air attack. The war ended with the use of the new atomic weapon on the cities of Hiroshima and Nagasaki in August 1945.

Decolonialization

The Japanese victories, and, in particular, the fall of Singapore on 15 February 1942, involved a profound loss of face for the colonizing powers. The invading armies were seen by many Asians as liberators from western regimes. Many of those who had assumed control, under Japanese direction, now became prominent in independence movements. The United States handed over political control of the Philippines in 1946 after negotiating a continued military presence. The Dutch, themselves newly liberated, at first fought to preserve their possessions but in 1948 they accepted the independence of the Republic of Indonesia. The British fought a communist rebellion in Malaya before handing over to a more acceptable national government in 1957. The French became involved in a long war for Indo-China before being defeated in 1954.

China and her Neighbours

Communist China

The fall of Japan left the two forces of the Kuomintang and the communists vying for the control of China. China's miseries continued when civil war broke out in 1947. In one battle, half a million men were engaged on each side. By 1949 the communists were gaining the upper hand and in May 1950 Chiang Kai-shek retreated to Taiwan with his government.

The new communist government was faced by a huge task of reconstruction. According to Mao's estimate, some 800,000 'enemies of the people' were executed, largely from the old village landlord class. The communists had long experience with the collectivization of agriculture within their own territories, and they did not follow Stalin's example of imposing it from above. Peasants were organized to control their own operations and, despite setbacks, the conditions of life for the mass of people improved.

Mao Tse-tung capitalized on the age-old Chinese respect for authority to provide a strong central government, which had for so long been lacking. He adapted western Marxist ideology to traditional thought patterns, and showed a strong hostility to western culture, which was given full rein in the Cultural Revolution, which he launched in 1966.

To western eyes, China appeared now to be a part of a united Communist bloc, intent on achieving world dominance. In practice, however, Mao had largely rejected the Russian brand of communism. By the 1960s, acute strains were appearing in the relationship between the two countries. When China developed its own nuclear capability in 1964, it was primarily as a deterrent against potential Russian aggression. The Chinese reconquest of the old province of Tibet also led to a successful war with India in 1962.

The Korean War

In 1945 the Japanese colony of Korea was occupied by Russian troops from the north and Americans from the south. This led to partition, with both governments claiming the whole country. In 1950 the northern armies invaded the south. The United States and other western nations, with the backing of a United Nations resolution, responded by sending forces to support the south.

For a time it appeared as though the north would be defeated, but China, concerned at her own security, sent an army across the border. The American President Truman refused to become involved in a war on Chinese soil, and the war was concluded in 1953 by an armistice that perpetuated partition.

Conflict of Ideologies

American analysts saw the communist strategy in South East Asia and being a process of 'slicing the salami'. Territories were to fall to communism, not in one major conflict, but one by one. The communist uprisings, which faced almost every nation of South East Asia in the coming decades, were in fact little coordinated and variously owned allegiance to Moscow, Peking or neither. That in the new nation of Indonesia was put down with great violence.

American policy became dedicated to holding the line against communism in the region. This involved providing support to noncommunist regimes, including Chinese nationalist government in Taiwan. The United States was therefore deeply involved in the politics of the region.

The French defeat in Indo-China left the new country of Vietnam divided, with a communist regime under the old nationalist Ho Chi Minh established in the north. The United States became increasingly involved in the struggle, supporting unstable noncommunist administrations, based in the southern capital of Saigon. In 1965, faced with the possibility of the defeat of the client regime by the northern-backed Vietcong guerillas, President Johnson authorized massive involvement in the conflict. The weight of American fire-power proved ineffective against a highly motivated enemy. In 1973 the American government, confronted by a mounting antiwar campaign at home, withdrew from the conflict. In the next two years the three countries of Indo-China fell to the communists. The people of Cambodia, having experienced American bombing, now suffered from the worst aberrations of Marxism, as interpreted by the Pol Pot regime.

The Pacific Rim

Japanese Reconstruction

United States troops occupied Japan, in an enlightened manner, from 1945 until 1952. The first objective was to ensure that the expansionist phase was over. A new democratic constitution was established, the Emperor renounced his divinity, and expenditure on defence and armaments was radically curtailed. As with Germany, industrial reconstruction followed fast. After the humiliation of defeat, both nations needed to experience success. Also, the imposed limitation of defence expenditure proved a powerful boost to the civilian economy.

The Technological Revolution

Soon Japan was no longer a low cost economy and her heavy industries began to suffer some of the problems experienced in the West. By this time, however, the nation had developed skills that enabled it to take the lead in the third, technological phase of world industrialization. Automobile production boomed, winning markets in Europe and North America, and Japanese labour and management skills proved highly suitable to the detailed work involved in the production of hi-tech goods. Supported by a huge balance of payments surplus, she has established a position of dominance in world markets in a wide range of product areas.

An Area of Growth

In the last decade of the twentieth century it became clear that the region of the Pacific rim is established as a formidable competitor to the established industrialized regions of western Europe and North America. It remained, however, a region of wide diversity. South Korea, Taiwan, Singapore and – at least until reunification with China in 1997 – Hong Kong participated in the economic prosperity pioneered by Japan. At the other extreme, peoples of many of the nations of Southeast Asia continue to survive on low per capita incomes. China herself emerged from the isolation of the Cultural Revolution to rebuild international links, but, unlike communist regimes to the west, it has successfully repressed those who wished to liberalize the political structure of the nation.

The Indian Subcontinent

The Independence Movement

Indian troops made a significant contribution to the allied victory in the First World War, and in 1918, nationalist politicians looked to see their country start its progress towards the self-government that had already been given to the white dominions. In 1919, however, a British general ordered troops to fire on a demonstration in Amritsar, killing some four hundred people and injuring many more. Although the government disavowed the act, many British residents were loud in support, fuelling bitterness between the two communities. One of those radicalized by the Amritsar massacre was Mohandas Gandhi, known as Mahatma (Great Soul). During the next decades, he led a civil disobedience movement, based, if not always successfully, on nonviolent principles.

In the face of opposition at home, as well as from residents in India, the British government slowly moved towards accepting the principle of granting dominion status to India, and the Government of India Act of 1935 gave substantial power to elected representatives. The movement for complete independence, however, continued to grow. With the outbreak of the World War Two, some Indians sided with Japan in the hope of bringing down the colonial power.

Partition

The independence movement still faced the problem of reconciling the two major religious groupings of the subcontinent. Mohammed Ali Jinnah emerged as leader of the Muslim League, which now demanded that an independent state of Pakistan should be established at independence for the Islamic community. In 1945 a Labour government was returned in Britain and in March 1946 it made an offer of full independence. As disputes continued, it announced that Britain would withdraw not later than June 1948. Faced with this ultimatum, the Hindu leaders accepted partition – for which decision Gandhi was assassinated by an extremist Hindu.

The new state of Pakistan was established in two blocks in the north west and north east. The rulers of princely states on the boarder of the two nations were permitted to decide their allegiance, leaving Kashmir as disputed territory. Independence was marked by communal rioting, which left some half a million dead, and the mass movement of peoples in both directions across the frontier.

Independence

Jinnah died in 1948, and a decade later the army took control of Pakistan. Leadership of India fell to Jawaharlal Nehru and later passed to his daughter, Indira and grandson Rajiv Gandhi. The new country faced formidable problems. Independence was quickly followed by famine in 1951, and, with rising population it appeared as though Malthusian disaster was imminent. A combination of a reduction in the rate of population growth and an agricultural 'green' revolution has, however, improved the supply of food. The fragile ecology of eastern Pakistan, however, continued to bring disasters, and a cyclone in 1970 led to rebellion that, with Indian help, brought into being the separate Islamic state of Bangladesh.

Partition did not bring the end of India's communal problems. Indira Gandhi was assassinated by discontented Sikh nationalists, and her son Rajiv by Tamils of the south. Mahatma Gandhi allied himself with outcasts and hoped to see the end of the caste system, but this has been frustrated by a resurgence of Hindu fundamentalism. For all its problems, however, India remains the world's largest democracy.

Sub-Saharan Africa

Decolonialization

British governments of both parties continued the policy of giving independence to colonies, which had begun with India. The sheer size of the British Empire had meant that expatriate manpower was spread thinly. The second layer of administration was already staffed by African personnel and a machinery of local government was in place. Riots in the Gold Coast in 1948 gave notice of a growing nationalist movement. In 1957 the Gold Coast became the first independent country, within the British commonwealth, under its new name, Ghana. Three years later the much larger Nigeria became a sovereign state.

Across the continent, in Kenya and Rhodesia the problem was complicated by the presence of a white settler population, bitterly opposed to any move towards majority rule. The most serious challenge was posed by the Mau Mau disturbances in Kenya of 1952–56. Many of the white minority left the country when it received its independence in 1963. Two years later the white minority government of Southern Rhodesia declared unilateral independence and seceded from the British commonwealth. The British government failed to take effective action against this colonial rebellion and war continued between the white government and black nationalist groups, until the latter won to set up the state of Zimbabwe in 1976.

French governments, disillusioned by prolonged war in Indo-China and Algeria, gave independence at an even faster pace. In 1960 the Sub-Saharan colonies were offered either complete separation, in which case, they would receive no continued assistance, or association with France, within a French Community.

The two largest African empires were therefore dismantled within a few years with comparatively little strife. Independence for the remaining colonies proved a more painful process. In 1960, the Belgians withdrew from the Congo, which became the state of Zaire. Until that time, Africans held no positions of responsibility, and there was little preparation for the event. When the mineral-rich area of Katanga attempted to secede, the Cold War superpowers became involved in the ensuing civil war.

The last African empire was also the oldest. The Portuguese colonies of Guinea-Bissau, Mozambique and Angola achieved independence only after prolonged struggle.

After Independence

The emergent nations faced formidable problems. Some new nations spent unwisely on and military prestige projects, but, even where this was avoided, as, for instance, in Tanzania, falling world commodity prices led to a serious reduction in government revenue. Industrialization has proved unattainable, both through lack of capital, but also because it has proved hard for products from new nations to break into the controlled markets of the developed world.

Independent African nations found themselves caught in the Malthusian nutcracker of increasing population and falling revenue. This led to a decline in already low living standards and a failure by governments to deliver the public health and education programmes expected within a newly liberated nation. This exacerbated traditional communal rivalries, which in turn frequently erupted into civil war, like the Nigerian Biafran War of 1967–70 and later struggles in the Sudan, Ethiopia and the Horn of Africa. Political instability led to the emergence of authoritarian, often military, regimes. An already difficult situation has been made worse for nations immediately south of the Sahara by climatic change and desertification, which have destroyed large areas of productive land.

South Africa

The violently imposed apartheid system led to South Africa being increasingly ostracized from the world community. She withdrew from the British Commonwealth in 1961 and was later expelled from the United Nations. Economic sanctions imposed by the USA and a world sporting boycott had an effect, and in the early 1990s the legal apparatus of apartheid was dismantled. Following the country's first all-race elections, held in 1994 and won by the African National Congress (ANC), led by Nelson Mandela, South Africa re-entered the world fold.

Latin America

Capital and Industrialization

In the years before the First World War there was heavy European involvement in the economy of Latin America. The war then led to a drying up of European capital and the United States became the main investor in the region.

The world depression of the 1930s hit the region hard. The price of primary products, which were the mainstay of the economies, collapsed. After the war many of the larger nations instituted industrialization programmes, at times with a measure of success, but this was achieved only by borrowing the required capital, which left the nation with a heavy burden of debt and vulnerable to currency and interest rate fluctuations on the international market.

Economic problems created political instability. The rural poor had always lived in conditions of poverty, but they did not pose the same immediate problem to political stability as the growing and highly volatile urban populations.

Political Structures

The economic problems of the region meant that reforming governments did not have the revenue to deliver the social programmes needed to combat deprivation. When reforms were attempted they created inflation that weakened the economic base of society. Reforming democracies have therefore been under constant pressure from more authoritarian systems of government. These took three broad forms – popularist leaders, military regimes and revolutionary governments.

The archetype populist leader was Getulio Vargas, who came to power in Brazil in 1930, and the best-known Juan Peron, who ruled the Argentine from 1943–55 and then returned briefly in 1973. Both drew comparison with European dictators, but they had wide support among the urban poor, who believed that they alone could take on powerful vested interests on behalf of the people. They depended, however, on army support, and both were vulnerable when this was withdrawn.

Cuba and Revolution

The revolutionary movement had early roots in Mexico, but it became focused on Cuba with the success of Fidel Castro's revolution in 1959. An attempt by the United States to undermine the revolution came to disaster at the Bay of Pigs in April 1961 when they were overwhelmed by Cuban troops. In the following years Cuba, now aligned with Russia, exported revolution into Latin America. Che Guevara, a symbol to the new left across the world, was killed fighting with Bolivian guerillas in 1967. The United States became involved, supporting anti-communist regimes within the region, even when these had a poor human rights record. The democratic left wing government of Salvadore Allende in Chile, for instance, was overthrown by the military in 1973 with American support. Contra rebels against the Cuban-inspired government of Nicaragua were funded from Washington, and the government of the island of Grenada was overthrown by American invasion in 1983.

The Missile Crisis

In 1962 Cuba was the focus of the most dangerous crisis of the Cold War. In October, intelligence reports showed that sites were being built on Cuba from which missiles would be able to reach any city in the United States. President Kennedy demanded that all missiles in Cuba should be withdrawn and announced that ships bringing more would be intercepted. The superpowers stood poised for nuclear confrontation, but the Russian President Khrushchev broke the crisis by agreeing to withdraw the missiles. President Kennedy had successfully reasserted the Monroe Doctrine that the American continent would remain an area of United States influence, and the powers would not again come so close to open war.

The Middle East and North Africa

The New Turkey

In 1918, a proposal was put forward that Turkey itself should be divided into French, British and Italian spheres of influence. The successful general, Mustafa Kemal, led resistance against Greek and French forces, and established independence for the new, smaller nation. He set about a process of modernization of the nation, which went as far as westernizing its script and converting the country into a secular state. His people gave him the name of Ataturk – 'father of the Turks'.

The Mandates

The old Ottoman lands of the Islamic Middle East, now finally separated from the Ottoman Empire, had acquired new strategic importance with the early development of oil reserves – although the scale and future importance of these were not as yet recognized. National boundaries were drawn up and the region was divided between France and Britain under the mandate of the League of Nations. This implied that the newly defined countries were destined to move towards self-governing status. France was awarded Lebanon and Syria, although she had to take possession of the latter by force, and continued to rule it with considerable oppression. Britain received Palestine, Iraq, and Trans-Jordan, and she also controlled the emirates of the Persian Gulf. In 1932, Britain largely withdrew from Iraq, but the Palestinian mandate turned out to be something of a poisoned chalice.

The Founding of Israel

The objective of founding a Jewish national home in Palestine was first put forward in a Zionism Congress as early as 1897. It was to be a refuge for Jewish people who were persecuted in the pogroms of eastern Europe, and it also attracted many from minority Jewish communities within the Arab world. In 1917, the British government gave support to the project, with the contradictory provision that it should not interfere with the rights of the indigenous people. The movement was given further impetus by German persecution of the Jews under Hitler. In the post war years, large numbers of European Jews sought entry, and the British authorities had the impossible task of reconciling the opposing interests. In 1947 the United Nations voted for the partition of Palestine in the face of opposition from the Arab states and in 1948 the British withdrew. In the ensuing war, large numbers of Arabs left their homes for refugee camps in the neighbouring countries. The Arab states refused to accept the existence of a Jewish state in the Islamic heartland. The refugees remained, unsettled, waiting to return to their homeland as Israel and her neighbours continued in a state of war.

North African Independence

After the Second World War the British presence in Egypt was restricted to a defensive force in the canal zone and, by 1956, Libya, Tunisia and Morocco had shaken off foreign ties. Armed conflict centred on Algeria, where over one million French settlers resisted any move towards independence. The country was declared an integral part of metropolitan France and a bitterly fought dispute continued from 1954–62. When General de Gaulle finally decided to give independence, colonists allied with army generals and France itself was taken to the brink of civil war.

Nasser and Pan-Arabism

In 1952 a group of Egyptian army officers overthrew the monarchy. Two years later, Gamal Abdel Nasser became president of the country. His objective was to establish Egypt as the unquestioned leader of a new and more coherent Arab people. Lacking oil resources, however, Egypt remained a poor country and Nasser planned a development programme based on the construction of the Aswan High Dam on the Nile. When the Americans and British withdrew offers of funding, Nasser turned to the communist bloc for support, so introducing cold war politics into the Middle East.

In 1956 he nationalized the company that administered the Suez Canal. In October the Israelis invaded Egyptian territory, ostensibly to destroy guerilla bases and this was followed by a joint attack by the British and French on the Suez Canal zone. World opinion was outraged, and the American government applied pressure that forced the invaders to withdraw.

The Suez fiasco left Nasser as the leading figure within the Arab world, but his attempts to take this towards political union were unsuccessful. In 1967 he closed the Straits of Tiran to Israeli shipping and the Israeli army launched a 'first strike' in what has become known as the Six Day War. After a successful campaign, Israel controlled new territory, including, from Jordan, the whole West Bank of the River Jordan, and, from Syria, the tactically important Golan Heights. Jerusalem, a city of great symbolic importance to all three Semitic religions, now passed under full Israeli control. Successive Israeli governments, in time reinforced by the possession of nuclear weapons, have failed to comply with United Nations resolutions demanding withdrawal from the occupied territories. Indeed, increasing numbers of Jewish immigrants have been established in West Bank settlements. As Israel's neighbour, the Lebanon, collapsed into civil war, many Arabs resorted to international terrorism.

The Oil Crisis

In 1961 Britain withdrew from her interests 'east of Suez'. Much of the, now increasingly vital, oil production of the region, however, remained under the control of western companies. A further outbreak of hostilities between Israel and her neighbours in 1973 led the Arab countries to 'play the oil card' by taking more direct control over their own reserves and withholding supplies from Israel's allies in the developed world. This led to an increase in price, which had a sharp effect on the world economy. The Arab nations and other oil-producing nations, led by Saudi Arabia now organized themselves into OPEC (Organization of Petroleum-Exporting Countries) with a view to controlling world prices. This was less successful than had been anticipated because the depression caused by the price rise restricted world demand, and Britain and Norway, opening new North Sea reserves, stood outside the cartel.

In 1978 Nasser's successor, President Sadat, made peace with Israel under American sponsorship at Camp David. This did not end the conflict within the region, but rather took Egypt out of the mainstream of Arab politics.

Iran and Islamic Fundamentalism

With Egypt returned to the American sphere of influence after Camp David, the Soviet Union turned increasingly to the radical, though mutually hostile, governments of Syria and Iraq. The United States, looking for a buffer between the Soviet Union and the oil-rich Middle East, put heavy backing behind the conservative and corrupt administration of the Shah of Iran. In 1979 discontent erupted into revolution, and the Shah was replaced by a fundamentalist regime, dominated by the Ayatollah Khomeni. This sparked a wave of Islamic fundamentalism that gave expression to pent-up Arab anger at the imposition of alien values by aggressive western societies. Equally hostile to capitalist and to communist ideologies, Islamic fundamentalism has threatened governments of different complexions, from Afghanistan to Algeria. Indeed, the fail-